Writing the Truth

Writing the Truth

Authority and Desire in Rousseau

Thomas M. Kavanagh

University of California Press

Berkeley / Los Angeles / London

University of California Press
Berkeley and Los Angeles, California

University of California Press, Ltd.
London, England

© 1987 by
Thomas M. Kavanagh

Library of Congress Cataloging-in-Publication Data

Kavanagh, Thomas M.
  Writing the truth.
  Bibliography: p.
  Includes index.
    1. Rousseau, Jean-Jacques, 1712–1778—
Criticism and interpretation. 2. Authority in
literature. 3. Desire in literature. I. Title.
PQ 2053.K38   1987   848'.509   85-28935
ISBN 0-520-05677-9 (alk. paper)

Printed in the United States of America

1   2   3   4   5   6   7   8   9

The publisher gratefully acknowledges the
support of the Andrew W. Mellon Foundation in
the publication of this book.

To Monique

Contents

Preface

What is truth? Impossible as the question itself may be to answer, what we perceive as our *relation to truth* nonetheless affects profoundly everything we do, desire, say, and write. This paradox, and the dilemma it implies, is present everywhere in the works of Jean-Jacques Rousseau. In a recent essay, Jean Starobinski observes that Rousseau is so eloquent a spokesman for the eighteenth century because in his writings he confronts not only the concrete reality of that period but also what Starobinski calls its "ultimate affective consequences." Rousseau, by turns a citizen of, an outcast from, a supplicant in, and a preacher to Geneva, was acutely concerned not only with truth but also with the difficult question how truth might manifest itself and be recognized in an atmosphere of suspected guilt clearly related to his experience of that closed Calvinistic city. As someone who, feeling himself questioned, tried to imagine how other men might imagine him, Rousseau was eminently a man of his time and of our own.

The most important studies of Rousseau published during the last two decades have tended to obscure the urgency of this question of truth for Rousseau. As acts of allegiance to one of two antithetical approaches, these studies have concerned themselves instead with different questions. The works subsumed under Rousseau's common signature must be studied, some critics insist, as a pure textuality calling for the "deconstruction" of their rhetorical strategies but precluding all recourse to our knowledge of the man behind the works. Other critics contend that Rousseau's writings are so thoroughly embedded in the precise social and psychic circumstances of their author that no understanding of them can begin without an exhaustive evaluation of Rousseau and his times. These alternatives, so much a part of the rumbling salvos and strident battle cries of old, new, structuralist, and post-structuralist critics, enforce, ironically enough, precisely what Rousseau saw as the fallacious distinction with which his enemies had set out to destroy him. Beautiful thoughts, indeed; but written by a man whose life was so totally at odds with what he preached that they could finally be the work of only a hypocrite or a madman.

I have chosen the phrase "writing the truth" as the title for this study because I wish to emphasize the impossibility in Rousseau's case of separating textuality from existence. Rousseau's "life," as it interests us here, *is* itself an act of writing. And Rousseau's "writing" *is* the essential adventure of his life, an impossible attempt to state not only his own but a universal truth. Rather than approach Rousseau's works as reflections or results of influences in his biographical past, I present these attempts to "write the truth" as bridges to the future, acts carried out to determine what would come. To approach Rousseau's work from this perspective means accepting writing itself as the principal arena of a desire aimed at the future, a desire to make that future something different from both past and present.

The importance of this attempt to write the truth is also obfuscated by the consistent apportioning of the study of Rousseau's works among distinct academic disciplines. The majority of his critics have collaborated in producing the mirage of two separate and all-but-incommensurable Rousseaus: one for political scientists, another for students of literature and psychology. Inevitable though this distinction may appear, it has led to a compartmentalized critical inquiry whose liabilities go beyond the simple and, for the moment, fashionable rejection of any attempt to read the multiple works through their single author.

My approach to Rousseau centers on the question of the extent to which the meaning of his political vision depends on the literary and autobiographical writings. Likewise, I argue that any understanding of Rousseau's literary representations of the self demands a careful attention to the socialized dialectic of self and other always at work in the political writings.

The study of Rousseau must not, even before it begins, foreclose the possibility of our grasping in his works the complex paradoxes that crucially balance the literary against the political, the psychological against the anthropological. My hypothesis in this study is that a careful consideration of these paradoxes might help us understand the unified textual matrix that generates them. Only when we accept these paradoxes and apparent contradictions as such can we begin to see in Rousseau's writings the working out of a dialectic of allegiance and refusal, of submission to authority intended as a radical defense of individual autonomy. The dialectical tension between these elements generates a radically authentic voice that invites the reader to discover in Rousseau's work a profound meditation on that relation of the self to truth and of the self to the community that constitutes the essence of our modernity.

Mine will be an oblique path through Rousseau. Sometimes passing quickly over the major, best-known, and superbly read works, my analyses will focus instead on supposedly minor, neglected, and lesser-known texts that, as I hope to show, provide astonishing insights into the overall coherence of Rousseau's endeavor. At other times, I will approach a major work through a rarely read and often-suppressed sequel.

Beginning with a juxtaposition of key sequences from the *Confessions* and *Julie*, I attempt to show how their common concern with a unified metaphorics of the paternal reveals a pattern important throughout Rousseau's works. What presents itself as an abolition of authority and a resulting fulfillment of unmediated desire is in fact always dependent on the intervention of a hidden yet absolute principle of authority. My second chapter, centering on the *Letters to Malesherbes* and Rousseau's description of the premiere performance of *Le Devin du village*, examines Rousseau's consistent definition of himself as someone who could address his fellows only by "writing from afar." Calling on the entire community of mankind to recognize and judge his truth, he nonetheless insists that to state that truth he must hold himself safe from the violence of speech, from the presence of his fellows. My third chapter examines how *The Essay on the Origin of Languages*, Rousseau's most ambitious philosophical statement on the nature of language, delineates an impossible archetype of language that not only excludes the lie but also guarantees both the enunciation and communication of truth. My fourth chapter, a reading of *Emile* through its long-suppressed sequel *Les Solitaires*, argues that the pupil's unsettling equation of freedom with servitude must not be dismissed as the aberration of a deranged author but accepted as the one conclusion consonant with Rousseau's understanding of truth as a dialectical movement between authority and desire.

The next movement of my study brings these findings to bear on Rousseau's political writings. I begin by analyzing Rousseau's most neglected work: *The Levite of Ephraim*. The explicit portrayal of a sacrificial victim whose statement of truth and whose death reestablish justice in the threatened community, this work crystallizes in a single narrative a paradox encompassing all the problems that determine Rousseau's depiction of the individual in relation to the community. My sixth chapter considers Rousseau's major political works: the two *Discourses* and the *Social Contract*. Concentrating on the difficult figure of the Lawgiver, I argue that his presence at the center of Rousseau's politics must not be distorted into a proof that the author imagined himself exercising some totalitarian power over his fellows. On the contrary, the Lawgiver might be better understood as both the sustaining principle and the single elected reader of a political truth Rousseau felt he alone could enunciate. The Lawgiver, as an authority necessary to, yet always absent from, the community as Rousseau knew it, is the unique figure able both to recognize and to justify his decision to write the truth as the sacrificial act of a martyred paraclete. My final chapter attempts to close the gap between Rousseau's political and literary works. The unfinished *Reveries* represents Rousseau's last attempt to write the truth. Cut off from other men, alone with nature, Rousseau became a botanist of the self. This text, written for his eyes only, is an herb book of consciousness and memory. Each reverie attempts to recapture a privileged coincidence of consciousness and truth. Only in writing a truth intended for himself alone could Rousseau preserve what he experienced as an ecstasy of self-comprehension, an ecstasy of commiseration with a self finally palpable only as victim.

My reading of Rousseau is in large part inspired by the works of Jacques Lacan and René Girard. Although their works are seldom linked, their combined insights allow us to understand the central tensions governing Rousseau's works. I draw upon the elaboration of the "imaginary" and the "symbolic" in Lacan's reading of Freud as the poles of a conflict whose stake is nothing less than the very shape of the subject's desire. Girard's investigations of mimetic desire, its concomitant violence, and the designation of a victim as the only escape from that violence provide a conceptual framework that allows me to move from Rousseau's representations of individual consciousness to the larger question of his relation to the community of men in which and for which he must write. Lacan and Girard, moving in their distinct directions, help us understand the implications of Rousseau's decision to write the truth and address it to his fellows. They clarify the reasons why Rousseau, as he wrote, found himself forced to imagine the community of men as possible only at the cost of his own expulsion and sacrifice.

The reader should not expect to meet Lacan and Girard on every page of this study. Their inspiration is at work in the structure of this investigation, in the choice and arrangement of its topics, in the progressive movement of the whole toward a redefinition of its parts. It would be, I feel, a dubious homage to Lacan and Girard to imply that only a constant and self-conscious recourse to their thought might render Rousseau pertinent to the contemporary reader.

All quotations from the works of Rousseau included in the four published volumes of the *Oeuvres complètes,* edited by Bernard Gagnebin and Marcel Raymond (Paris: Gallimard, Bibliothèque de la Pléiade, 1959–1969), will be followed by a parenthetical citation of title, volume, and page. Editions used in discussions of Rousseau's other works will be indicated in a note, with subsequent citations given parenthetically in the text. References to Rousseau's correspondence will be followed by a parenthetical citation of R. A. Leigh's edition of the *Correspondance complète* (Geneva: Institut et Musée Voltaire; Oxford: The Voltaire Foundation, 1965–). All quotations in the body of my text are given in French, followed by the English translation. I have not tried to standardize the orthography of quotations from eighteenth-century writers. Sources of the English translations are indicated in the notes.

Acknowledgments

This book owes more debts than I could ever hope to acknowledge. It owes a debt of thanks to Pierre Pachet for pushing me to think through what I wanted to say about Jean-Jacques Rousseau. René Emery and, in more somber climes, Roy Roussel provided me with the genuine interest and prodding friendship I needed to get the book written. In its final stages, this book profited from the wise counsel of Len Tennenhaus, himself the happy legacy of a lost friend, Dennis Turner, who is not absent from these pages. I also thank the University of Colorado for its support of this project.

A preliminary version of chapter 5 appeared in *Eighteenth Century Studies* 16, no. 2 (Winter 1983), under the title "Rousseau's *The Levite of Ephraim:* Dream, Text, and Synthesis." I wish to thank the editors for their permission to use parts of it here.

1. Wolmar's Game

Book 1 of Rousseau's *Confessions* opens by proclaiming its absolute singularity. The text we are about to read exists as the unique member of a class closed to both past and future: "une entreprise qui n'eut jamais d'exemple, et dont l'exécution n'aura point d'imitateur" (an enterprise which has no precedent, and which, once complete, will have no imitator).[1] To justify this claim of singularity, the text does not look forward to its own enterprise but turns back to the past of its subject as a consciousness generated by a series of circumstances that defy replication: "Je ne suis fait comme aucun de ceux que j'ai vus. . . . Si la nature a bien ou mal fait de briser le moule dans lequel elle m'a jetté, c'est ce dont on ne peut juger qu'après m'avoir lu" (I am made unlike anyone I have ever met. . . . Whether Nature did well or ill in breaking the mould in which she formed me is a question which can only be resolved after the reading of my book) (*Confessions*, 1:5). The mold, the matrix, the mother: what has formed the subject and what, simultaneously and by a design attributable only to nature, was broken by the subject's very production. The autobiographical text, the representation of self, establishes its subject as not only the fruition but also the destruction of its origin.

Although the text looks for its origin to the feminine and the maternal, its goal, its purpose in relation to the reader, moves in a different direction. Rousseau, in writing this text, intended to provoke a confrontation with judgment, with law, with the paternal in its most absolute form: "Que la trompette du jugement dernier sonne quand elle voudra" (Let the trumpet of judgment sound when it will) (*Confessions*, 1:5). Anticipating and preparing this scene of judgment, the text being written and offered to all assumes for its author, the writing subject to be judged, a role corresponding to what Derrida has described as the paradoxical function of the supplement: adding something essential, it nonetheless neither changes

nor disfigures that to which it is added.[2] Thus with the written text
as a representation of truth, the reader's vision of the subject becomes clearer, less impeded, and more distinct.

Moving from the maternal to the paternal, from the matrix to the
sovereign judge, the text escapes redundancy before the Omniscient
by summoning to this scene of judgment "l'innombrable foule de
mes semblables" (the numberless legion of my fellowmen) (*Confessions*, 1 : 5). By calling all mankind to the author's final judgment by
an already all-knowing authority, the text begins to transform its
function from *confession* to *justification* and, finally, to *accusation:*
"Que chacun d'eux découvre à son tour son coeur aux pieds de ton
trône avec la même sincérité; et puis qu'un seul te dise, s'il ose: *je
fus meilleur que cet homme-là*" (Let each one of them reveal his
heart at the foot of Thy throne with equal sincerity, and may any
man who dares say "I was better than he") (*Confessions*, 1 : 5).

As though sensing that this foreshortened trajectory from origin
to judgment is an impossible beginning, a beginning that excludes
all possible continuation, Rousseau moves back from these abso-
lutes to a second, more limited, beginning: "Je suis né à Genève en
1712 d'Isaac Rousseau Citoyen et de Susanne Bernard Citoyenne"
(I was born at Geneva in 1712, the son of Isaac Rousseau, a citizen
of that town, and Suzanne Bernard, his wife) (*Confessions*, 1 : 6).
No sooner is this written, however, than it, too, is recognized as a
false start, an inadequate beginning—one that in spite of its temporal, genealogical, and social coordinates has left something out,
something that took place before the subject's life but is essential to
the reader's judgment of him. Yet another beginning, preceding and
giving meaning to the juridical facts of Rousseau's birth, must be
found in another, already enacted, story: the kind of story that
Serge Leclaire has aptly described as a *roman familial,*[3] and one
marked by all the conventions and manipulations of a *roman
d'amour* in miniature. Isaac Rousseau and Suzanne Bernard, Rousseau's father and mother, were themselves the protagonists of a love
story predestining them to each other even from the moment of
their childhood walks along the banks of the Treille. These two beings, intensely affectionate and sensitive, had only to meet to find
each other. But just as inevitably, Rousseau goes on, society con-
spired to thwart this union of a minister's daughter and a simple
clock maker. In a peripety worthy of Molière, the girl's class-
conscious parents were brought to accept their daughter's marriage
only when their son happened to fall in love with the clock maker's

sister—a woman who thoughtfully demanded as a condition of her own consent that Suzanne and Isaac be allowed to marry.

My use of the term *roman familial* to describe Rousseau's singularly romanesque explanation of his origin becomes particularly appropriate when we realize that Rousseau's mother was not the daughter but the niece of the famous minister Samuel Bernard and that Rousseau's father was better known in Geneva as a dancing teacher than as a clock maker. That other marriage between uncle and aunt, Gabriel Bernard and Theodora Rousseau, in fact took place five years before that of Rousseau's parents. The unseemly rapid birth of Gabriel and Theodora's first child led to their public censure and expulsion from religious services *pour avoir anticipé leurs noces*—an event hardly putting them in a strong position to deal with the minister's social prejudices.

Having drawn this imaginary portrait of his parents' lifelong devotion to each other, Rousseau proceeds to the second, sadly final, chapter of their love story. Suzanne implores her husband to abandon his duties as clock maker to the Sultan's harem in Constantinople and return to Geneva to rescue her from the concerted attentions of Monsieur de la Closure, the French Resident. Rousseau tells Isaac and Suzanne's story as the story of a love stronger than family, stronger than class, stronger than all the dictates and restrictions of an established social order. It is a story of the past, the relevant past, the past already speaking and defining the precise meaning of Rousseau's birth: "Je fus le triste fruit de ce retour. Dix mois après, je naquis infirme et malade; je coûtai la vie à ma mere, et ma naissance fut le premier de mes malheurs" (I was the unhappy fruit of his return. For ten months later I was born, a poor and sickly child, and cost my mother her life. So my birth was the first of my misfortunes) (*Confessions*, 1 : 7). By the simple fact of his birth, the Rousseauian *I* abolishes a union that all society could not forbid.

In retracing this prehistory of Rousseau's birth, in pointing out its "distortions" of historical fact, in referring to it as a *roman familial*, I am emphasizing its importance to Rousseau as one of what Lacan has called the "enveloping symbols" of his existence. It is, in the fullest sense of the word, a scenario already written, defining the subject's awareness of self through an array of forces and meanings at work both long before and long after the moment of his birth:

Les symboles enveloppent en effet la vie de l'homme d'un réseau si total qu'ils conjoignent avant qu'il vienne au monde ceux qui vont l'engendrer "par l'os et par la chair," qu'ils apportent à sa naissance avec les dons des astres, sinon avec les dons des fées, le dessin de sa destinée, qu'ils donnent les mots qui le feront fidèle ou renégat, la loi des actes qui le suivront jusqu-là même où il n'est pas encore et au-delà de sa mort même, et que par eux sa fin trouve son sens dans le jugement dernier où le verbe absout son être ou le condamne.[4]

These symbols envelop the life of man in a network so complete that even before he comes into the world, they have brought together those who will engender him "of flesh and bone." These symbols bring to man's birth, along with the gift of the stars, if not the gift of the fairies, the design of his destiny. They provide the words that will make him faithful or renegade, a law governing his acts that will follow him where he has not yet gone and even beyond his death. Through these symbols his end finds its meaning in that last judgment where words must absolve or condemn his being.

The *I* of the son is left to define itself through an ongoing dialogue with the *you* of the father. As the agent and sign of death, this *I* becomes, in the most literal sense, the presence of an absence. The son, alone with the bereaved father, can perceive himself as desirable only to the extent that a "bitter regret" for all that has been lost remains essential to the father's every caress: "Jamais il ne m'embrassa que je ne sentisse à ses soupirs, à ses convulsives étreintes, qu'un regret amer se mêloit à ses caresses; elles n'en étoient que plus tendres" (He never kissed me that I did not know by his sighs and convulsive embrace, that there was a bitter grief mingled with his affection, a grief which nevertheless intensified his feeling for me) (*Confessions*, 1:7). Born under the sign of death, Rousseau sees tenderness as the tearful commiseration of those left in solitude before the broken matrix of nature.

Rousseau presents his early childhood as the complicitous acting out of this dubious role assigned him by the father. Each time the subject of the dead mother arose, Rousseau, warning his father of the tears to come, would struggle with an impossible demand: "Rend-la moi, console-moi d'elle; rempli le vide qu'elle a laissé dans mon ame. T'aimerois-je ainsi si tu n'étois que mon fils?" (Give her back to me, console me for her, fill the void she has left in my heart! Should I love you so if you were not more to me than a son?) (*Confessions*, 1:7). Rousseau's earliest sense of self is elaborated as an impossible response to the father's plea that he restore as origin and as presence a state whose loss was the very condition of his existence. The son finds his sense of existence fashioned by a tenderness palpable only as it is redefined by the irreparable moment of difference that was simultaneously his own birth and his mother's death.[5] As though he has recounted everything of importance in this dialogue between father and son, Rousseau closes this sequence with a simple declaration projecting his story four decades into the future: "Quarante ans après l'avoir perdue, il est mort dans les bras d'une seconde femme, mais le nom de la premiére à la bouche, et son image au fond du coeur" (Forty years after he lost her he died in the arms of a second wife, but with the first wife's name on his lips, and her image imprinted upon his heart) (*Confessions*, 1:7).

Numerous critics have underlined the relevance to Rousseau's autobiographical works of what, since Freud, we call the Oedipal conflict. It is important, however, to understand how these opening pages of the *Confessions*, Rousseau's concerted attempt to set forth his earliest memories, present a highly idiosyncratic and foreshortened version of the Oedipal situation. The traditional understanding of the son's struggle for the mother's affection—the struggle to preserve, in the face of paternal authority, an imaginary symbiosis with the mother—is in Rousseau's case radically redefined. As though in response to her death, this struggle for the mother's affection is not only displaced to a time before the child's birth but is also vicariously projected onto a paternal figure whose worldly joy is abolished by the very existence of the son. The son's one remaining link to the lost mother is a tearful complicity with the father, a plea for the forgiveness of everything he is. The son, who gains access to the lost mother only as the ambiguously pardoned double of the bereaved father, can vicariously enter the contest only through his allegiance to a paternally imposed *roman familial* of which he is himself the fatal denouement.

The young Rousseau, then, does not choose between what Lacan would describe as an imaginary plenitude of his coincidence with the object of the mother's desire (*être le phallus*) and his submission to a paternally enforced integration in a symbolic mediation of desire (*avoir le phallus*). For him the essential question is not whether *to be* or *to have* the phallus, but whether the phallus itself might be anything other than an inexhaustible source of tears.[6]

□   □   □

As though struggling to understand the mysterious sway exercised over his life by a series of parental figures whose loss would determine everything that was to come, Rousseau assigns a particular importance to one moment in the period he consistently pointed to as the happiest of his life: the months spent, on his return from Italy, with Madame de Warens and her lover, Claude Anet. Rousseau's narration of his questionable actions during the day following Anet's death stands in stark contrast to the normal mode of self-imposed admissions that punctuate this text and give the *Confessions* their title. Unlike the avowals of past turpitude that were postponed until forty years after the fact—the pleasure taken during the *fessée voluptueuse* and the heinous lie incriminating the innocent Marion—Rousseau's confession of his shameful reaction to Anet's death is immediate and irrevocable.

> Le lendemain j'en parlois avec Maman dans l'affliction la plus vive et la plus sincére, et tout d'un coup au milieu de l'entretien j'eus la vile et indigne pensée que j'héritois de ses nippes et surtout d'un bel habit noir qui m'avoit donné dans la vue. Je le pensai, par consequent, je le dis; car près d'elle c'étoit pour moi la même chose. Rien ne lui fit mieux sentir la perte qu'elle avoit faite que ce lâche et odieux mot, le desinteressement et la noblesse d'ame étant des qualités que le défunt avoit éminemment possédées. La pauvre femme sans rien répondre se tourna de l'autre côté et se mit à pleurer. Chéres et precieuses larmes! Elles furent entendues, et coulérent toutes dans mon coeur; elles y lavérent jusqu'aux derniéres traces d'un sentiment bas et malhonnête; il n'y en est jamais entré depuis ce tems-là. (*Confessions*, 1 : 205 – 6)

> Next day I was speaking of him to Mamma in the deepest and sincerest of grief, when suddenly, in the middle of our conversation, the vile and unworthy thought occurred to me that I should inherit his clothes, and particularly a fine black coat which had caught my fancy. No sooner did it occur to me than I gave utterance to my thought: for in her presence thought and speech were to me as one. Nothing made her more conscious of her loss than those mean and odious words, for disinterestedness and nobility had been outstanding qualities in the dead man. The poor woman did not reply, but turned away from me and began to weep. Dear and precious tears! They were understood and flowed right into my heart, from which they washed away every trace of that low and contemptible thought. Never since has any similar thought entered there.

Anet, Madame de Warens, and the young Jean-Jacques formed what might seem to be a classic lovers' triangle. Anet's death comes well after Rousseau's *dépucelage philosophique* by Madame de Warens. The disposition of this triangle was ambiguous from its inception, however. After his almost clinical initiation to sexuality by Madame de Warens, Rousseau could only say "J'étois comme si j'avois commis un inceste" (I felt as though I had committed incest) (*Confessions*, 1 : 197). Similarly, Rousseau did not see himself competing with Anet for a common object of desire but respected and admired the man who was able to hold everything together around the erratic Madame de Warens: "Quoiqu'aussi jeune qu'elle, il étoit si mur et si grave, qu'il nous regardoit presque comme deux enfans dignes d'indulgence, et nous le regardions l'un et l'autre comme un homme respectable dont nous avions l'estime à ménager" (Although no older than she, Anet was so mature and grave that he almost looked on us as two children who deserved indulgence, and we both looked on him as a man worthy of respect, whose esteem we must cultivate) (*Confessions*, 1 : 201).

Rather than a rivalry between two men for a single woman, we find here the paternal Anet, someone Rousseau calls "Mama," and Rousseau himself in the role of *le petit*. As Rousseau represents Anet's ascendency, however, he implies that the relation between Mama and *le petit* was something other than that between mother and son.

In the context of this triangle, Rousseau's lapsus is ambiguous. In a way sure to evoke Madame de Warens's reproachful tears, Rousseau seeks to confirm the impossibility of the very desire that apparently motivated his enunciation: that he could inherit either the clothes or the role of the father. Although this triangle may appear to have been Oedipal, its unconditional premise was Rousseau's disavowal of any desire to occupy the place of the father. This same refusal manifests itself in Rousseau's obvious pleasure in detailing the many instances of his complicity with Warens's childlike incapacity to handle money matters—precisely the area of Anet's ascendency. Madame de Warens, the paid agent of a succession of Catholic princes underwriting her work for Rome in the cold-war atmosphere along Savoy's border with Protestant Switzerland, spent most of her adult life on the financial edge, always open to lucrative expedients, always vulnerable to passing swindlers.

The part of book 5 that follows Anet's death reads like the elaboration of a constantly displaced and constantly escalating series of symptomatic acts intended to underline and reinforce the message of the original lapsus: the impossibility of a sexuality that for Rousseau could only be incestuous. After a series of increasingly frequent short trips from Chambéry, Rousseau inscribes his plea in invisible ink; the chemicals he mixes for his *encre de sympathie* explode in his face, rendering him blind and, we might assume, otherwise incapacitated for several weeks. Shortly after, an episode occurs that might be read as emblematic of Rousseau's refusal to replace, or even confront, the rival as rival in an organized symbolic order. A certain Monsieur Bagueret of Geneva, a dubious speculator, is about to wrest control of the gullible Madame de Warens's finances. Sensing the young Rousseau's resentment, Bagueret sets out to cajole the boy by suggesting they play chess. Bagueret takes the first game but gives the second away. Hardly fooled, Rousseau buys a chess set and spends what he describes as months locked in his room studying the game and preparing his revenge. The moment of confrontation arrives: "Je vais au caffé, maigre, jaune, et presque hébêté. Je m'essaye, je rejoue avec M. Bagueret; il me bat une fois, deux fois, vingt fois; tant de combinaisons s'étoient brouillées dans ma tête, et mon imagination s'étoit si bien amortie que je ne voyois plus qu'un nuage devant moi" (I went to the café, thin, sallow, and almost stupefied. To try myself out, I played against Monsieur Bagueret again: he beat me once, twice, twenty times. So many combinations were mixed up in my head and my brain was so dull that I seemed to have nothing but a cloud before my eyes) (*Confessions*, 1:220).

This series of symptomatic acts, refusals refusing to recognize themselves as refusals, culminates as Rousseau succumbs to the "vapors": a debilitating languor in which his regret for a life he will never live is matched only by his horror at the dire straits in which he imagines himself leaving Madame de Warens. Only when he has established himself as not only unwell but dying will Rousseau accede to what he describes as the most perfect happiness he ever knew:

> Nous commençames, sans y songer, à ne plus nous séparer l'un de l'autre, à mettre en quelque sorte toute notre existence en commun, et sentant que reciproquement nous nous étions non seulement necessaires mais suffisans, nous nous accoutumames à ne plus penser à rien d'étranger à nous, à borner absolument notre bonheur et tous nos desirs à cette possession mutuelle et peutêtre unique parmi les humains, qui n'étoit point, comme je l'ai dit, celle de l'amour; mais une possession plus essencielle

qui, sans tenir aux sens, au sexe, à l'age, à la figure, tenoit à tout ce par quoi l'on est soi, et qu'on ne peut perdre qu'en cessant d'être. (*Confessions*, 1 : 222)

We began imperceptibly to become inseparable and, in a sense, to share our whole existence in common. Feeling that we were not only necessary but sufficient to one another, we grew accustomed to thinking of nothing outside ourselves, completely to confine our happiness and our desires to our possession of one another, which was perhaps unique among human kind. For it was not, as I have said, a love relationship, but a more real possession, dependent not on the senses, on sex, age, or personal beauty, but on everything by which one is oneself, and which one cannot lose except by ceasing to be.

In a way Rousseau qualifies as unique in human history, Mama and Jean-Jacques, on the brink of death, form a symbiotic union of self-contained and self-fulfilling desire. Their possession of each other is defined not in terms of their differences—in senses, sex, age, appearance—but rather in terms of "tout ce par quoi l'on est soi." *On:* neither "I" nor "she," but both fused together in an imaginary hypostasis beyond individuality.

Reacting to this passage, we might interpret the ideal as both the return and the reversal of the original signifier: the son dying before the mother expiates the fatal *Urszene* with which everything began. As the sequence of events following Anet's death has shown us, however, such a "return" can take place only if the participants in this apparently Oedipal triangle undergo a singular redefinition. The terms *father, mother,* and *son* are, as Benveniste has eloquently demonstrated in his examination of the linguistic bases of Freudian theory, conceptually interdependent and mutually implicative.[7] If sexualized desire, a product of the paternal prohibition against which it defines itself, is to be eliminated, the son and the mother, *le petit* and Mama, must establish themselves in a utopia founded on the denegation, the forced erasure, of all mediation by the father. A desire insistently excluding the sexual must refuse all mediation by a prohibition founded in the reciprocity between the father as possessor and the mother as possessed.

This erasure for Rousseau and Madame de Warens was accomplished when illness forcibly translated their entire relationship to a timeless abeyance on the brink of death. In the pure present of a deterioration penultimate to eternity, consciousness may reduce itself to the absolute *hic et nunc* of the couple's all-excluding duality.

That such an ideal could be held in place and remain palpable only with the implicit yet denegated mediation of a third, distinctly paternal, element (the still-lingering presence of the dead Anet on which Jean-Jacques's description of his original lapsus so eloquently insisted) becomes apparent when we compare the success of the Anet-Warens-Rousseau configuration with the failure of a similar triangular situation, again including Mama and *le petit,* in which Rousseau, however, is called on to occupy not the filial but the paternal position. After his stay in Montpellier under the care of Doctor Fizes for his vapors, having decided not to visit the inebriating Madame de Larnage in Bourg St. Andiol,[8] Rousseau arrives at Chambéry only to discover that, as he puts it, "his place had been taken" by Vintzenreid, another young Swiss whom Madame de Warens has accepted into her household.

Mama proposes a simple solution: the three of them can live together just as happily as before. This presupposes, however, that Rousseau accept precisely what his original lapsus had sought to prevent—his assuming the position left vacant by Anet. Faced with the choice of either leaving or agreeing to Madame de Warens's terms, Rousseau tries his best to play the role assigned him. His failure in this enterprise, whatever his good will, is immediate and complete. In sum, Rousseau could not assume the role of the husband-father in relation to mother and son. Both he himself and Vintzenreid were, as Rousseau saw it, fundamentally out of place in their respective roles. What Rousseau lacked in composure and paternal firmness was only exacerbated by Vintzenreid's total lack of docility and gratitude for the attention offered him. "Avec plus de douceur et de lumiéres je n'avois pas le sang froid et la fermeté d'Anet, ni cette force de caractére qui en imposoit, et dont j'aurois eu besoin pour reussir. Je trouvai encore moins dans le jeune homme les qualités qu'Anet avoit trouvées en moi; la docilité, l'attachement, la reconnoissance; surtout le sentiment du besoin que j'avois de ses soins et l'ardent desir de les rendre utiles" (Although gentler and better read than Anet, I had neither his coolness nor his firmness nor that strength of character which inspires respect and which I should have required if I were to succeed. Still less did I find in this young man the qualities that Anet had found in me: docility, affection, gratitude, and, above all, consciousness of my need for his help and the ardent desire to make good use of it) (*Confessions,*

1:265). Shortly after this failure, Rousseau left Madame de Warens's household for the last time.

Rousseau's revision of the Oedipal situation, we might suggest in a necessarily incomplete formulation, involved the denegation of any paternally mediated relation between mother and son. In place of such a relation we find the desire for a radically different, distinctly pre-Oedipal, symbiosis that would preserve the pair in an imaginary bliss beyond all mediation through the father. In contrasting the positions adopted by Rousseau in the Anet and Vintzenreid episodes, we see that the absolute fulfillment of the first depended on Rousseau's suspension with Madame de Warens in a relation he imagined resembling that of two children discovering themselves through their common but miraculously absent father. Rousseau's allusion to the shadow of "incest" hanging over his feelings toward Madame de Warens should be read not so much as a reference to mother-son incest as to that between a sister and brother standing before their mutually recognized yet always denegated father.[9]

□   □   □

My discussion patently begs the question of the change this "incest" implies in the status of the father as the foundation, always present but always denegated, of the symbolic order that sustains such desexualized bliss. The period of perfect happiness with Madame de Warens described toward the end of book 5 may well have resulted from a collapsing of the Oedipal triangle to the self's blissful capture in its imaginary double. As I have tried to show, however, this happiness presupposed the transformation and obfuscation of a third, distinctly paternal, term that, even as it is denegated, confirms its role in both circumscribing and sustaining the apparently self-sufficient diad. For Jean-Jacques and Madame de Warens, the solution was to declare this third position empty, to effect its evacuation by a metaphorics of illness pointing toward the anticipated incorporeality of death.

In an attempt to understand what is at stake here, I would like to look at another text, another solution, another version of the triangle, that suggests its importance as a structuring element in Rousseau's every attempt to write the truth—whether personal or political, whether applied only to himself or to the whole of the society around him. The importance of Rousseau's work to theoreticians of democracy on two continents does not, after all, rest on his ability to portray a state of perfect happiness achieved on a deathbed. We find a more fully enunciated version of this triangular configuration, one in which the sustaining importance of the paternal is made explicit, in Rousseau's most important novelistic work: *Julie.*

In shifting my attention to this text, I am, of course, referring to the triangle formed by Wolmar, Julie, and Saint-Preux described in parts 3 through 6 of the novel. Ernest Seillière, condemning what he sees as Rousseau's undermining of society's *imperialisme vital* in favor of a debilitating, mystical romanticism, chose the provocative phrase "*Le Mari sous le charme de l'amant*" to entitle the chapter containing his remarks on this particular triangle.[10] It is understandable that someone of Seillière's resolute conservatism be struck by the potential chaos implicit in Wolmar's open-armed reception of his wife's former lover. My point, however, in citing this chapter title from Seillière's analysis of *Julie,* on the whole unremarkable, is to call attention to the distortion it represents. The second half of this novel, the part following Saint-Preux's return to Clarens, is far more the story of "the lover charmed by the husband" than its obverse. It is Saint-Preux who rejoices in his transformation by the all-knowing Wolmar into someone at last worthy of the solicitude lavished on him: "O mon Bienfaiteur! ô mon Pere! En me donnant à vous tout entier, je ne puis vous offrir, comme à Dieu même, que les dons que je tiens de vous" (O, my Benefactor! O, my Father! In giving myself to you entirely, I am only offering to you, as to God himself, the gifts I have received from you).[11] Saint-Preux thinks of Wolmar far less as anyone's "husband" than as his own "father."

Wolmar's function in *Julie* is crucial. It is he, the apogee of incarnate reason, the older, wiser man to whom Julie has been entrusted by her father, who summons both wife and lover to a union that takes them beyond passion and beyond sexuality to the enduring happiness of purified virtue. What I refer to as "Wolmar's game" is a carefully orchestrated ascesis of desire in which Julie and Saint-Preux's progress depends on their inspired complicity in Wolmar's decision to play present against past as a dialectic promising to redefine the future: "Mes enfans, nous dit-il d'un ton d'autant plus touchant qu'il partoit d'un homme tranquille; soyez ce que vous êtes, et nous serons tous contens. Le danger n'est que dans l'opinion; n'ayez pas peur de vous et vous n'aurez rien à craindre; ne songez qu'au présent et je vous réponds de l'avenir. Je ne puis vous en dire aujourd'hui davantage; mais si mes projets s'accomplissent et que mon espoir ne m'abuse pas, nos destinées seront mieux remplies et vous serez tous deux plus heureux que si vous aviez été l'un à l'autre" ("My children," he said to us in a tone all the more touching for his being so placid a man, "be what you are and we shall all find happiness! Danger lies only in opinion; do not fear yourselves and you will have nothing to fear. Think only of the present and I will speak for the future. I can say no more of this today; but if my plans are successful, and if hope does not deceive me, our destinies will be better fulfilled and you will both be far happier than if you had belonged to each other") (*Julie*, 2:496).

Even though Wolmar's role in this transformation is crucial, nonetheless the ideal he designates for Julie and Saint-Preux is latent, as it were, even before his appearance in the novel. One of the strangest letters from the first section of this work, letter 50 of part 1, is Julie's expression of her "sadness" and "indignation" at the otherwise unnarrated (and, it might be added, scarcely imaginable) scene of Saint-Preux's postprandial *impudeur* toward her. This "indecency" must be understood as a vaunting, even if only to his beloved, of the intimacy and mutual possession Saint-Preux sees as a corollary to their now-consummated love. In this early letter Julie lays the foundations of what becomes, only much later and under Wolmar's guidance, a fully elaborated insistence on the separation of happiness from possession and, by implication, of love from sexuality: "Malheur à qui n'a plus rien à desirer! il perd pour ainsi dire tout ce qu'il possede. On jouït moins de ce qu'on obtient que de ce qu'on espere, et l'on n'est heureux qu'avant d'être heureux" (Woe to him who has nothing more to desire! He loses the very thing he possesses. There is less pleasure in what we have than in what we hope for, and we are happy only before being happy) (*Julie*, 2:693).

Likewise, Julie's letters following Saint-Preux's departure from Clarens consistently give evidence of a relation that is all but purged of the dynamics of desire. In letter 27 of part 2, after Saint-Preux apologetically confesses his Parisian escapade with the Swiss officers, Julie's reaction, untouched by sexual jealousy, remains one of stolid anxiety about his poor choice of companions and the grave risks to his health.

Just as Julie has transformed herself from mistress into concerned friend, Wolmar himself is immediately recognized by Saint-

Preux as a paternal presence: "Il me parla comme un père à son enfant" (He spoke to me as would a father to his son) (*Julie*, 2:423); and shortly afterwards: "M. de Wolmar commençoit à prendre une si grande autorité sur moi que j'y étois déja presque accoutumé" (Monsieur de Wolmar began to exercise so great an authority over me that I grew almost accustomed to it) (*Julie*, 2:425).

After his return to Clarens, thanks to Wolmar's careful mediation, this second, almost fraternal, dimension of Saint-Preux's relation to Julie is carefully developed. Taking Saint-Preux by one hand and his wife by the other, Wolmar admonishes them: "Embrassez votre soeur et votre amie; traittez-la toujours comme telle; plus vous serez familier avec elle, mieux je penserai de vous" (Embrace your sister and your friend; treat her always as such; the closer you are to her, the better I shall think of you) (*Julie*, 2:424). Later, in the bower scene, again taking each by the hand, Wolmar pronounces them "my children."

I underline these ambiguities to call attention to the way Wolmar, the successful rival, the husband imposed by the father's law, nonetheless functions as both the cause and the effect of Julie and Saint-Preux's transforming their love toward a new structure, one consonant with the implicit dilemma of desire at work throughout Rousseau's properly autobiographical texts. This parallelism helps us understand why, on the one hand, Julie began to function as Saint-Preux's sister long before she ceased to be his mistress and why, on the other, both Julie and Saint-Preux must, if their love is to endure, become like children before their common father.

Thus far I have approached the figure of Wolmar as he both mediates and is mediated by the couple whose story provides this novel's principal subject. As their guide to an affection beyond sexuality, he beckons them to erase passion so completely as to leave no trace of it. Only then may its absence exalt itself as an achieved plenitude of virtue and transparency. Wolmar's role, however, is crucial not only to the story of Julie and Saint-Preux, but also to a parallel, distinctly socialized metaphorics of the revered paternal presence as the sustaining principle of an organized community, of an ideal social order. Around him, and in response to his careful interventions, the entire society of Clarens has become what Saint-Preux describes in his letters to Milord Edouard: an economically self-sufficient microcosm of equality, freedom, and happiness guaranteed by the mutual affection of all for all.

The public celebration of Wolmar's beneficent reign occurs each year with the wine harvest, the *vendanges* described in letter 7 of part 5. Narrating the happy concord of master and servants, Saint-Preux notes that "tout le monde est égal, et personne ne s'oublie" (everyone is equal, and no one forgets himself) (*Julie*, 2:607). Each day's labor in the vineyards culminates in a dinner attended by one and all. In the description of the respective attitudes of those present at this meal, the implications of the surprising "et personne ne s'oublie" become clear. The equality Saint-Preux refers to in his letter to Milord Edouard tacitly presupposes that neither master nor servants "forget" their respective superiority and inferiority. The workers' sentimentalized gratitude toward the Wolmars for their kindhearted encouragement of this shared illusion only reinforces the fact of difference, the reality of rank. In his acute analysis of the meaning of this equality in *Julie*, Starobinski points to the essential condition of its functioning, its limitation to the annual feast of the wine harvest: "L'égalité nous y est offerte comme un moment très intense: mais cette intensité passagère n'a pas le pouvoir de se perpétuer sous la forme d'une véritable institution. Il faut en jouir dans l'instant même, sachant d'avance que seuls en demeureront le souvenir et le regret" (Equality is offered to us as a particularly intense moment: but this fleeting intensity lacks the power to perpetuate itself as a real institution. It must be enjoyed at the moment it occurs, with everyone well aware that it will live on only as memory and regret).[12]

An analysis of the daily, year-round reality of life at Clarens would show that this bucolic idyll depends on a careful exercise of authority by the master. This authority is, in fact, so complete that Rousseau's more fastidious critics have not hesitated to refer to it as Machiavellian. Earlier, in his general description of Clarens, Saint-Preux expresses his admiration for Wolmar's governing of his household by comparing it to the *other* option of the republic: "Dans la République on retient les citoyens par des moeurs, des principes, de la vertu: mais comment contenir des domestiques, des mercenaires, autrement que par la contrainte et la gêne? Tout l'art du maitre est de cacher cette gêne sous le voile du plaisir ou de l'intérêt, en sorte qu'ils pensent vouloir tout ce qu'on les oblige de faire" (In a Republic the citizens are governed by custom, principle, and virtue. But how can servants and hirelings be governed other than by force and punishment? The master's entire art consists in hiding his force under the veil of pleasure and self-interest in such a way that his people believe they have chosen everything they are obliged to do) (*Julie*, 2 : 453).

At the heart of the social ideal represented by Clarens lies its enlightened master's exercise of justice and virtue, which penetrate and regenerate even the murky depths of the servant class. Because the absolute authority of this patriarchal principle has been accepted, it can generate all the appearances of a universal liberty and equality.[13] In this sense Wolmar's social engineering, his effect on the entire community at whose center he stands, might be read as a praxis of intervention marked by the same power to efface all traces of itself as coercion that we saw at work in his redefinition of Julie and Saint-Preux's experience of their lingering love.

The New Clarens, the Wolmarian Clarens discovered by Saint-Preux on his return, is marked by elements that mirror and extend the paradoxical movement of an intervention erasing its traces. Julie's garden, the Elysée, is especially important because it brings together around the problematic of the redefined Oedipal triangle I have described two themes that become essential to Rousseau's specifically political vision: the delineation of a perfectible social order and the simultaneous celebration of nature as both a lost ideal and a potentially regenerative moral force. Letter 11 of part 4 is devoted almost entirely to a description of the Elysée, the hidden, enclosed garden that Julie has constructed at Clarens since Saint-Preux's departure. The Elysée functions in the novel as a supersignificant microcosm. Marked by its own space and time, it is separate from its surroundings and impenetrable to the alien eye. Seen from within, however, it presents itself as a self-sufficient whole capable of abstracting its visitor from the world outside at the same time that it summarizes in miniature all that is best in that world.

Entering this garden for the first time, Saint-Preux is struck by its wild, uncultivated appearance. His impression is that he has chanced upon some solitary corner never touched by human hand. Julie quickly points out, however, that this apparently virginal nature is in fact the creation of her own meticulous planning: "Il n'y a rien là que je n'aye ordonné" (There is nothing here that I have not ordained) (*Julie*, 2 : 472).

In the Elysée, a privileged space separate from the rest of Clarens, an internal hierarchy nonetheless exists, a gradation of values generating a second, even more cherished, part within the marvelous whole. After Saint-Preux has reviewed all the various plants, grasses, and trees making up this other world, Julie points out that he has seen so far only vegetable and inanimate nature: a nature always tinged with solitude and sadness. She then leads him to what, judging from the bird song he hears in the distance, he assumes is a *volière*, an enclosed aviary. But once again he is mistaken. In this garden no cages, nets, or barriers restrict the flight of the birds. They are the free wild creatures of nature. They choose not to leave the spot traced out for them but to warble there in circumscribed joy because their every need has been carefully anticipated and attended to. Protected from all outside disturbances, the birds are surrounded by a luxuriant growth of every plant and seed they might enjoy. Each year at the proper moment, Julie explains, quantities of twine, straw, and cotton are laid out for them so that they find immediately available all the nesting material they need to prepare for their fledglings. While they remain wild birds in a natural state, the nature they depend on has been so arranged that they themselves are effectively transformed from *wild* into *domestic* animals. They are, as Saint-Preux's metaphor tells us, Wolmar's chickens: "Alors M. de Wolmar faisant le tour du basin sema sur l'allée deux ou trois poignées de grains mélangés qu'il avoit dans sa poche, et quand il se fut retiré, les oiseaux accoururent et se mirent à manger comme des poules, d'un air si familier que je vis bien qu'ils étoient faits à ce manege" (Walking round the basin, Monsieur de Wolmar scattered over the path two or three handfuls of mixed seed that he had brought in his pocket. As he walked away, the birds flew over and began to feed like chickens in such a familiar way that I knew they were well accustomed to this practice) (*Julie*, 2:476).

Only on the basis of so universal an intervention can the aviary function as a metaphor for the human society at whose center it stands. Thanks to the Wolmars' enlightened management, all distinctions between domestic and wild, guest and prisoner, and master and servant have been reversed. We, Julie insists to Saint-Preux, are far more their guests here than they are ours.

Wolmar's remarks on the aviary end with a statement in which his status as naturalist gives way to his other, implicit, status as an astute social planner who in this microcosm has happily resolved the political problem most often debated in the eighteenth century—depopulation: "Voila comment la patrie des peres est encore celle des enfans, et comment la peuplade se soutient et se multiplie" (And thus it is that the country of the fathers remains that of the children, and the clan multiplies even as it continues) (*Julie*, 2:477).

In relation to the world outside, Clarens is a unique refuge of equality and peace; within Clarens, the microcosm of the Elysée is the part most privileged. Within the Elysée, the birds are privileged above the plants and trees; and the birds themselves are, in the scale of values, most admirable in their vernal apex of parental solicitude for their newly hatched young. When Julie alludes to this pinnacle of relative value, Saint-Preux finds himself left behind and declares himself incapable of understanding the joys of parenthood: "Madame, repris-je assés tristement, vous êtes épouse et mere; ce sont des plaisirs qu'il vous appartient de connoitre" ("Madame," I replied sadly, "you are a wife and mother. Those are pleasures you are able to understand") (*Julie*, 2:477).

What first appears as a dialectical development of parallel themes, nature's regenerative force and the elaboration of an ideal society, thus returns us to the very question of the parent-child relationship through which we first approached Rousseau's work. It is the voice of Wolmar, the voice of the father, the voice of a law articulating itself as a reinscription of both nature and society, that responds to Saint-Preux's doubts concerning his own position in this world of fathers and children: "Aussi-tôt M. de Wolmar me prenant par la main me dit en la serrant: vous avez des amis, et ces amis ont des enfans; comment l'affection paternelle vous seroit-elle étrangere?" (Immediately afterwards, taking me by the hand and squeezing it, Monsieur de Wolmar said to me: "You are with friends, and these friends have children. How can paternal affection be unknown to you?") (*Julie*, 2:477).

The effect of Wolmar's statement is immediate and devastating. Not only Saint-Preux but all three parties to this visit now find themselves locked in a communion of *regards*, culminating in Saint-Preux's repeated and convulsive embracing of his hosts: "Je le regardai, je regardai Julie, tous deux se regardèrent et me rendirent un regard si touchant que les embrassant l'un après l'autre je leur dis avec attendrissement: ils me sont aussi chers qu'à vous" (I looked at him, I looked at Julie; both looked at each other and returned to me a look so touching that, as I embraced each of them, I said with emotion: "They are as dear to me as they are to you") (*Julie*, 2:477). Wolmar's statement, his offer of yet another level of participation in the couple he forms with Julie, redefines both Saint-

Preux's sense of himself and his perception of Wolmar. No longer
bearing even the slightest trace of the rival, Wolmar becomes instead
the father of two children for whom Saint-Preux would gladly lay
down his life: "Je ne sais par quel bizarre effet un mot peut ainsi
changer une ame, mais depuis ce moment, M. de Wolmar me paroit
un autre homme, et je vois moins en lui le mari de celle que j'ai tant
aimée que le pere de deux enfans pour lesquels je donnerois ma vie"
(I do not understand in what strange way a single word can change
one's soul, but from that moment Monsieur de Wolmar seemed to
me to be a different man. I see far less in him the husband of the
woman I once loved than the father of two children for whom I
would give my life) (*Julie*, 2 : 477). The two children referred to here
are those of Julie and Wolmar's marriage. It is significant, however,
that the particular formulation of Saint-Preux's statement allows, at
least implicitly, another reading that both coincides with and confirms the hypothesis I developed from my analysis of the *Confessions*. During Saint-Preux's carefully described discovery of the
Elysée, the Oedipal triangle is redefined so that the self-effacing re-
structuring of past and present by a beneficent father results in his
adoration by a couple who themselves assume the status of desexualized brother and sister.

□   □   □

As a way of bringing together those aspects of the novel I have examined in this chapter, I offer in the accompanying chart a sche-
matic representation of a common three-stage movement of the diverse textual constellations. The first stage represents the set of
conventional expectations that Saint-Preux, returning to Clarens
after a long absence, brings with him. The second stage summarizes
the later judgments, still partial and ultimately incorrect, that he
makes on the basis of immediate appearances. The third and final
stage represents those conclusions the reader, with his knowledge of
all the letters exchanged, might arrive at regarding the reality underlying those appearances.

In this chart it is clear that the last category, what I have labeled
"The Wolmar Couple," is different from the other three. It is different in one sense because the first three categories are limited, discrete elements in the text. Each of them is marked by developments
with a defined beginning and ending. The story of the Wolmar
couple, on the other hand, ends only with the novel itself. This

	Conventional Expectation	*Immediate Appearance*	*Underlying Reality*
Social Organization of Clarens	Rule of Masters over Servants	Joyous Liberty and Equality of All	Unchallenged Patriarchal Authority
The Elysée	Cultivated Garden	Untouched Nature	Omnipresent Intervention Erasing Its Traces
The Aviary	Caged Birds	Birds in Complete Freedom	Birds Restrained by Unlimited Largesse
The Wolmar Couple	Julie as Wolmar's Lawful Wife and Possession	Saint-Preux Sharing the Couple's Happiness beyond Sexuality and Rivalry	An Absolutism of the Paternal Order Precluding Sexualized Desire

fourth category also differs from the others in that its final term, the reality underlying appearances, is not, unlike patriarchy, the simulacrum of nature, or the domesticated birds, an enduring, describable state. The absolutism of paternal authority, a law precluding desire, functions in this text as an ideal, only partially stated yet constantly exercising its effects. It is, as it were, a continually sought after but ultimately impossible solution to the novel's central conflict. Julie's death, the event effectively ending the novel, signals not the accomplishment of this ideal but the displacement of its quest to another world.

I have arrayed these four sequences in a common pattern to emphasize how Rousseau's description of an ideal society (Clarens) and his reflections on nature (the Elysée and the aviary) can be read both as variations on and partial resolutions of a contradiction, an impossibility, whose basic terms and structure are grounded in an essentially Oedipal situation. In each of the first three categories an exercise of authority that elaborates a universe governed by law is so constructed that the action of the lawgiver, the name of the father reigning in full supremacy, never inscribes itself on the elements it organizes as a legible, durable reference to the action of the law as law. Both patriarchy and recreated nature represent a displaced, extended metaphorics of the symbolic, of the father-husband's uncontested power to act in such a way that result might designate itself as origin and, in so doing, denegate its reliance on difference. The symbolic, the law, and the father are everywhere able to modulate their voices to a silence so complete that they seem never to have spoken.

2. Writing from Afar

C'est l'art qui les inspire
Et non le sentiment:
Moi, j'ose à peine dire
Que j'aime tendrement.
    —Rousseau, *Les Consolations*
        des misères de ma vie

Il faudroit pour ce que j'ai à dire inventer un langage
aussi nouveau que mon projet.
    —Rousseau, *Confessions*

In January 1762, at the age of forty-nine, Rousseau sent from
Montmorency to Paris, in the space of three and a half weeks, a
series of four letters to Malesherbes, the *Directeur de la librairie,*
the man charged with ultimate responsibility for royal censorship in
France. In his haste to get these letters—"the only thing I wrote
with facility in all my life"—into the hands of the forty-year-old
Malesherbes, Rousseau broke with his usual practice of keeping either a draft or résumé of his important correspondence. Ten months
later, in October 1762, already sensing the importance of what he
had tried to say in those four letters, Rousseau asked Malesherbes
to return them to him. Upon receiving them, he tied them together
with a paper band on which he wrote the intriguing title *le vrai
tableau de mon caractére et les vrais motifs de toute ma conduite.*

These letters signal a major shift in the form and intention of
Rousseau's writing. Although they came soon after the composition
of *Emile* and the *Social Contract* and a year after the publication of
Julie, their concerns are neither didactic nor romanesque. Their
unique intent is to trace a portrait of the self, to state the truth
about their author. These four letters to Malesherbes initiated the
long, never-finished series of autobiographical works that Rousseau
continued to write and rewrite until his death sixteen years later, in
1778. In that winter of 1762, however, Rousseau was convinced
that fate would never allow him the time to undertake a work approaching the dimensions of the *Confessions* or the *Dialogues.* The
catheter that had broken off in his urethral canal that fall had
caused him such intense pain that he was certain as he wrote these

letters that he was living his last days. If he were ever to state his truth, he had to do it quickly.

The decision to choose Malesherbes as the recipient of these first autobiographical writings begins, significantly enough, with Rousseau's acute embarrassment at having overreacted to delays in the arrival of the proofs for *Emile*. Rousseau saw these delays as tangible proof that his worst fears were justified: the Jesuits had infiltrated the enterprise and were confecting a falsified version of the "profession de foi" that, once he was dead and unable to disavow it, would be published under his name. Malesherbes, because of his official position, received one of Rousseau's overwrought pleas for help in undoing that plot. After the charge had been investigated and proven groundless, Rousseau wrote a letter of apology to Malesherbes, severely castigating himself for having surrendered to a tendency that, he now assured Malesherbes, was forever extirpated from his character.

On Christmas day of 1761 Malesherbes sent the reply that triggered Rousseau's sequence of four letters. Unlike the Citizen's ebullient tone, Malesherbes's is a monument to coolheaded common sense. He has taken no offense, he reassures Rousseau, for he has long understood that Rousseau's hypersensitivity results from his physical constitution, his recent illness, and the reclusive life he has chosen to lead. Enemies, Malesherbes observes with placid wisdom, are a fact of public life, an inevitable accoutrement of celebrity that anyone in Rousseau's position must accept without undue drama: "Le genre de vie que vous avés embrassé est trop singulier et vous estes trop celebre pour que le public ne s'en occupe pas. Vous n'ignorés pas que vous avés des ennemis et il seroit humiliant pour vous de n'en pas avoir. Vous ne pouvés pas douter que bien des gens n'imputent les partis extremes que vous avés pris à cette vanité qu'on a tant reproché aux anciens philosophes. Pour moy il me semble que je vous en estime d'avantage depuis que j'en ay vu le principe dans la constitution de vos organes et dans cette bile noire qui vous consume" (The kind of life you have embraced is too singular, and you are too famous, for the public not to be concerned with you. You have enemies and it would be humiliating for you not to have them. You cannot help suspecting that many people impute the extreme positions you have taken to nothing more than that vanity for which the ancient philosophers were so often reproached. As for myself, I only esteem you more since I understood that the real cause lies in the constitution of your organs and in that dark bile that consumes you).[1]

More than anything else, it was the unacceptability of this well-intentioned, but for Rousseau grossly disfiguring, judgment of himself that dictated his first attempt at serious autobiography. The danger of letting such a verdict stand seemed greater because it had come in this case from someone whose opinion carried considerable political weight, someone even Rousseau believed to be benevolently disposed toward him. Rousseau was sure to read nothing flattering in Malesherbes's carefully chosen words, which left him a choice between appearing a vain anachronism to those who knew only his writings or a physical freak to those who happened to know his person. In a more fundamental sense, however, Malesherbes, with his reference to what "many people" happened to think, implicitly invited Rousseau to assume the interpretive posture in which he would compose all his autobiographical writings: that of a consciousness struggling to achieve the impossible exteriority to itself that would allow the subject to imagine how others might imagine him.

These four letters to Malesherbes are texts of denial and denegation. Determined by judgments already made of his person and his works, Rousseau struggles to overturn them by refuting what has been said. This first attempt on Rousseau's part to state his truth is marked by his sense of the impossibility of completing the task before him. The last lines of the last letter point not to a goal that has been achieved but to a defeat: an exhaustion, a depletion of the energy necessary to redo them from the start: "Quoi qu'il en soit me voila tel que je me sens affecté, jugez-moi sur tout ce fatras si j'en vaux la peine, car je n'y saurois mettre plus d'ordre, et je n'ai pas le courage de recommencer" (Whatever might be the case, this is the way I feel myself affected by this affair. Judge me on the basis of these confused letters if you think I am worth the effort since I neither know how to put them in any better order nor have the courage to begin again).[2] At the end of each of the first three letters Rousseau declares his intention to write yet another, evidencing the same need that, once the physical crisis of the winter of 1762 has passed, dictates his decisions to refute the same negative judgments of his person in the *Confessions,* the *Dialogues,* and the *Reveries.* In these later texts, addressed not to a single recipient but to the whole of mankind, the enterprise of disproving what has already been said intensifies until it reaches the shrill pitch of the *Billet circulaire* addressed to "tout François aimant encor la justice et la vérité" (every Frenchman still cherishing Justice and Truth).[3]

Rousseau's constant concern in these four letters to Malesherbes was to explain what others incorrectly saw as a contradiction in his relation to other men. On the one hand, Rousseau was a writer: someone who, as Malesherbes recognized, has successfully and with distinction addressed himself to his fellows on questions of grave importance for society as a whole. On the other hand, Rousseau was a recluse: a man whose ultimate and most tangible message to the society around him was his rejection of and separation from it. First at l'Ermitage with Madame d'Epinay and later at Montmorency with the Duc de Luxembourg, Rousseau continued to choose a life outside the city, outside Paris, away from other men, in a countryside that allowed him to identify with a beneficent nature uncorrupted by any human presence.

The four letters to Malesherbes are, in the fullest sense of the word, a metatext. They self-consciously portray not only the conditions surrounding their composition but also Rousseau's continued insistence that any valid judgment of his person and his writings depends on a reader's first understanding his abiding desire *both* to write for the whole of mankind *and* to safeguard his truth through a concerted withdrawal from society. As irreconcilable as these desires might appear, they must never, Rousseau insists, be seen as a contradiction, an unmastered inconsistency, a transmutation of the love of mankind that he so often proclaimed into its opposite—the hatred and misanthropy his enemies have so resolutely asked all to see in its place.

My goal in this chapter is to examine these four letters—Rousseau's first direct attempt to defend his writings both as an expression of truth and as a communication with the other—as documents based in the same desire to achieve a relation to authority that allowed him to initiate and preserve a resolutely imaginary fulfillment: the self's unmediated congruence with its elected ideal. In the previous chapter we saw how, in the representation of self in the *Confessions* and in the parallel thematics of Rousseau's most successful novel, a drive emerges to rearrange the shape of desire and the dictates of authority so that apparent insurgencies against the arbitrary rule of law ultimately ensure an impossible reconciliation of the symbolic with the imaginary, of authority with desire. To what extent does Rousseau's reinscription of the relative positions of father, mother, and son help us understand the forces at play in his reflections on the nature and function of writing?

□   □   □

The letters to Malesherbes are a concerted attempt to explain, to establish as something other than contradiction, a love of mankind that demands the lover's separation from the very object he purports to love. The first letter, written on January 4, 1762, opens by addressing Malesherbes's view of the cause of Rousseau's recent agitation: that his seclusion has intensified "l'amertume de cette bile noire" (the bitterness of that dark bile) ("Malesherbes," 1:1131). On the contrary, Rousseau insists, any natural tendency toward melancholy on his part was infinitely more acute when he lived in society. If he had wrung his hands over *Emile,* he had done so only because the thought of that work's being falsified struck at his only link, after his imminent death, to future generations, to the whole of posterity. If while living in Paris, Rousseau adds, he had had to undergo the same ordeal, it would surely have cost him his life.

After this preliminary *mise au point,* Rousseau confronts the major accusation in Malesherbes's analysis of his situation: how could anyone hope to justify "cet invincible degout que j'ai toujours eprouvé dans le commerce des hommes" (that invincible disgust I have always experienced in my dealings with men) ("Malesherbes," 1:1132)? Perhaps, Rousseau suggests, by understanding that it results from his "indomptable esprit de liberté." This devotion to liberty, he quickly adds, is not some glorious virtue for which he congratulates himself. His need for liberty results instead from his inveterate indolence, his *paresse,* his innate aversion to finding himself burdened by even the slightest social obligation.

No sooner does Rousseau offer this explanation than he finds himself forced to anticipate yet another level of contradiction he feels his reader is sure to remark in his rationale. Isn't *indolence* a surprising term to apply to a man who, in the last ten years, has written and published, to mention only the major works, the two *Discourses, Julie,* the *Social Contract,* and now *Emile?* Recognizing an objection that prevents closure, Rousseau ends his first letter in promising to begin it anew: "Voila une objection à resoudre qui m'oblige à prolonger ma lettre et qui par consequent me force à la finir" (This objection obliges me to prolong my letter and, consequently, forces me to end it) ("Malesherbes," 1:1133).

In the second letter, a *retour en arrière* attempting to overcome the inconsistency he himself had denounced in his initial argument, Rousseau offers Malesherbes what might be described as a genetic history of his character. Rousseau begins with his childhood reading of Plutarch. That experience represented for him, he insists, the discovery of a universe of virtue and heroism that shaped his entire personality. Plutarch's vision of the individual and his place in society was so complete and so satisfying that it initiated in Rousseau, from the age of six, a continuing contempt for all imperfect imitations of Plutarch's ideal in the real world. Rousseau describes his readings of Plutarch and of his mother's novels, his intense joy upon entering their fictive, imaginary worlds, as experiences punctuated by tears. These readings represented, as the opening pages of the *Confessions* tell us, a contact with what the father had already designated an ideal radically separated from the real. The initial discovery of these texts, in other words, was characterized by the same affective valences associated with the lost mother. In her absence, father and son collaborated to evoke an imaginary ideal society that continued their contact with a world whose maternal stamp marked all that was best and all that had been lost.

Critics have long concurred with Rousseau on the importance of his early reading of Plutarch and its influence on his later works.[4] By way of Fabricius, Plutarch played an important role in Rousseau's original discovery of his vocation on the road to Vincennes; moreover, axial allusions to the *Parallel Lives* and the *Moralia* can be found in *Julie,* the *Confessions,* the *Dialogues* and the *Reveries.* Despite Rousseau's emphasis each time he considered the subject, the various studies of Plutarch as a literary source tend to neglect the way this childhood reading determined what might be called the abiding form of his desire: his immediate and total identification with a long series of persons, texts, and situations that assured his contact with an ideal of lost happiness. What is most important and most singular about the form of Rousseau's various enthusiasms can best be understood through the abiding primacy of this Plutarchian and romanesque model. Early in the *Confessions,* Rousseau explicitly recognizes how everything he believed to be best about himself was related to his identification with elements drawn from Plutarch's heroic universe: "De ces interessantes lectures, des entretiens qu'elles occasionnoient entre mon pere et moi, se forma cet esprit libre et républicain, ce caractére indomptable et fier, impatient de joug et de servitude qui m'a tourmenté tout le tems de ma vie dans les situations les moins propres à lui donner l'essor" (It was this enthralling reading, and the discussions it gave rise to between my father and myself, that created in me that proud and intractable spirit, that impatience with the yoke of servitude, which has afflicted me throughout my life, in those situations least fitted to afford it scope).[5] The discovery of Plutarch's works initiated, in other words, a radical discontinuity, a psychic break marked by the sudden eruption of an idealized model with which the young Rousseau identified completely, a model that also allowed him the experience of discovering himself as someone utterly renewed and redefined. Reading Plutarch brought with it the projection of a properly imaginary double in which the self came to anchor the experience of its essential identity: "Je me croyois Grec ou Romain; je devenois le personnage dont je lisois la vie: le recit des traits de constance et d'intrépidité qui m'avoient frappé me rendoit les yeux étincellans et la voix forte" (I pictured myself a Greek or a Roman. I became indeed that character whose life I was reading: the recital of his constancy or his daring deeds so carrying me away that my eyes sparkled and my voice rang) (*Confessions*, 1 : 9).

Reading Plutarch at age six generated a form of experience—the identification with an exalted ideal and the parallel rejection of a debased reality—that remains a constant throughout Rousseau's works. The cause-and-effect relation between these two movements is eminently reversible. What is here presented as the discovery of an ideal that renders the real insipid can also occur in reverse: the fundamental inadequacy of the real time and again initiates for Rousseau a flight to the imaginary. In book 9 of the *Confessions*, for instance, Rousseau reiterates precisely the argument he used in his letter to Malesherbes to justify his departure from Paris: "L'impossibilité d'atteindre aux êtres réels me jetta dans le pays des chiméres, et ne voyant rien d'existant qui fut digne de mon délire, je le nourris dans un monde idéal que mon imagination créatrice eut bientot peuplé d'êtres selon mon coeur" (The impossibility of attaining the real persons precipitated me into the land of chimeras; and seeing nothing that existed worthy of my exalted feelings, I fostered them in an ideal world which my creative imagination soon peopled with beings after my own heart) (*Confessions*, 1 : 427).

□   □   □

Rousseau structures his recollection of his childhood readings of Plutarch and his descriptions of their continuing effect on him as an immediate discovery of the self in an imaginary ideal from which that self draws an answer to the question of its own identity. In so doing, the self simultaneously closes itself off from, refuses, and brands as compromise and degradation all attraction to those other objects designated by what would have been a mediated, progressive, and always partial integration of the subject in a symbolic order that presupposes the self's recognition of its inability to coincide totally with its ideal.

This allegiance to the imaginary manifests itself not only in Rousseau's statements on his childhood reading of Plutarch but also in his continuing appeal to an idealized form of interpersonal relationship marked by the same refusal of all mediation through the symbolic. Rousseau explains his choice of solitude, his leaving the capital, and his seclusion in nature by making the surprising claim that he acted in the name of friendship, of *amitié*. The paradox of his position is obvious: if friendship is a paramount value, solitude must be experienced as privation. Conversely, if friendship is an illusion, solitude is little more than a pejorative misnomer for self-sufficiency. In Rousseau's case, however, the term *friendship* undergoes a singular redefinition that allows it to justify his renunciation of life in society.

In his first letter to Malesherbes, Rousseau, as we have seen, points to the genesis of his indomitable "spirit of liberty" not in any aggrandized sense of his own worth but in his inveterate laziness. Contrary to what we might expect, Rousseau proclaims his profound devotion to true friendship precisely at this point in his argument, directly following his admission of an absolute distaste for even the most minor social obligations: "Voila pourquoi, quoique le commerce ordinaire des hommes me soit odieux, l'intime amitié m'est si chere, parce qu'il n'y a plus de devoirs pour elle. On suit son coeur et tout est fait" (This is why, even though I find everyday exchanges with men to be odious, intimate friendship is so dear to me. With it, there is no such thing as duty. One follows one's heart and everything is taken care of) ("Malesherbes," 1:1132). True friendship for Rousseau, *l'intime amitié,* is not only totally unlike ordinary social intercourse, totally outside any sense of mutual obligation, but it is also characterized by a near symbiosis of the two parties so that "one [I? he? we?] follows one's heart and everything is taken care of." Rousseau continues: "Voila encore pourquoy j'ai toujours tant redouté les bienfaits. Car tout bienfait exige reconnoissance; et je me sens le coeur ingrat par cela seul que la reconnoissance est un devoir" (That is why I have always been so leery of favors. Every favor received demands recognition; and I feel my heart growing ungrateful for the simple reason that such recognition is now a duty) ("Malesherbes," 1:1132). True friendship can maintain its associations with both "laziness" and the "spirit of liberty" because, like them, it exists outside any law of reciprocity, any even implicit *do ut des* dictating that each party remain either a creditor or a debtor in his relation to the other. Even the slightest intrusion of such notions into consciousness, Rousseau insists, immediately unmasks the relation as something else. All models of exchange are radically inapplicable to true friendship. Rousseau is not, in other words, asking simply that the friend refrain from making demands on him. The true friend, he insists, always knows that he has already and forever bestowed on him the utterly priceless gift of his friendship. This gift, once its incommensurable value has been appreciated, necessarily initiates the other's friendship for him as a dual hypostasis lifting both parties into a realm beyond all quantitative considerations of reciprocity, obligation, and exchange.

Rousseau's reconciliation of seclusion and friendship is founded on the premise that the discovery of the true friend is the election of an imaginary double in whom the self encounters the most profound sense of its own identity. Rousseau's fascination with such persons as Bâcle, Venture, Altuna, and Sauttersheim, his abrupt yet total redefinition of his sense of self through his relation to them, are examples of the concomitant joys and risks of that blessed state. To Diderot, at the height of the quarrel that ended what was perhaps Rousseau's single most important friendship, he wrote: "Je ne veux que de l'amitié, et c'est la seule chose qu'on me refuse. Ingrat, je ne t'ai point rendu de Service, mais je t'ai aimé" (All I want is friendship; and it is the one thing everyone refuses me. Ingrate, I did you no favors, but I loved you) (*Correspondance*, 4:195).

True friendship, for Rousseau, had to be nothing less than a beatific transfixion of mutually elected doubles. The intensity of satisfaction Rousseau demanded of friendship clearly evokes the one relationship psychoanalysis consistently points to as the model for understanding such imaginary identifications: that between mother and child prior to the mediation of their relation by the symbolic, prior, that is, to their redefinition by paternal authority. Speaking of the intense friendships that regularly and disappointingly punctuated Rousseau's life, Alain Grosrichard astutely evokes as most appropriate to the situation the Lacanian metaphor of the mirror: "Sa jeunesse, cascade d'identifications imaginaires aussi totales que passagères, est comme la traversée d'une galerie de glaces" (His youth, a cascade of imaginary identifications as total as they were fleeting, was like a walk through a gallery of mirrors).[6] As an extraordinarily condensed self-portrait, an attempt to speak the truth as completely as possible in the relatively short space of four letters, this correspondence with Malesherbes reveals with exceptional clarity the underlying armature and organizing structure of Rousseau's most fundamental thematics of the self. Unlike the *Confessions,* an autobiographical enterprise spread out over an entire decade, these letters string together with a minimum of transitional elaboration a series of affective equivalences, a concatenation of desired ideals, all marked by their common insistence on an imaginary doubling held safe from all mediation by the symbolic, by the laws of exchange and reciprocity.

□ □ □

I call attention to Rousseau's ideal of true friendship because its refusal of all mediation by a third party makes it central to his attitude toward the act of writing. His discussion of friendship provides the implicit underpinning for Rousseau's essential point in these four letters to Malesherbes: the justification of himself as a writer, as the harbinger of a truth whose relevance to all mankind depends on the absoluteness of his separation from the very audience he must address.

To write from afar is, for Rousseau, the only possible way to speak from within. What Rousseau says of friendship is ultimately orchestrated to explain his position as the person who has written *Emile,* who would have it published in Paris, but who must, from Montmorency, appeal by letter to the *Directeur de la librairie* in his efforts to thwart the conspiracy he sees poised against it.

The reasons Rousseau gives for the impossibility of friendship may be read as delineating a dilemma similar to the one he faced in writing from afar. Rereading Rousseau's statements on friendship, attentive to their possible transposition to this other key, we note that the ideal to which no one has long been able to correspond is a state of absolute understanding shared exclusively by two friends. The essential effect of such friendship is to abolish any need for its manifestation through signs visible to a third party. Frustrating

Rousseau's longing for true friendship, each would-be friend has inevitably demanded that what was intended for him alone manifest itelf in the realm of appearances, through signs visible to an always-intrusive third party: "Mais ils ont toujours voulu mettre à la place du sentiment, des soins et des services que le public voyoit et dont je n'avois que faire. Quand je les aimois, ils ont voulu paroitre m'aimer. Pour moi qui dedaigne en tout les apparences je ne m'en suis pas contenté, et ne trouvant que cela, je me le suis tenu pour dit" (But instead of feeling, they always asked for favors that the public might see and that I eschewed. I loved them, but they wanted only to appear to love me. For someone like myself who disdains appearances, that was not enough; but finding only that, I understood) ("Malesherbes," 1 : 1145). Friendship for Rousseau is a dialogue carried out in an ideolect comprehensible only to the two friends. Its substance and vehicle are a language in which only pronouns of the first and second person exist: an *I* and a *you* who discover in each other an intimacy and comprehension whose intensity effectively closes off any third party who might pass judgment on their self-sufficient diad. A state without manifestation, a sign without a semiology, friendship is the regime of a law sufficient unto itself, a law abolishing all law. The *he* and the *they*—the third person, the seeing public—can exist only as discordant voices speaking from outside. Their presence, solicited or accepted, signals a fall from grace, a transposing of the absolute into the realm of appearance, obligation, and comparison. Friendship, a privileged relation to the unique other, represents an ideal aimed against the social, against the diad's perception through the mediating and necessarily degrading context of the society around them.

What is it about life in the society of other men that forces this choice? What is it about the alternative of speaking from within that establishes writing in solitude as the only possible solution to Rousseau's dilemma? To consider Rousseau's status as writer, the main subject of these four letters, we must understand his rejection of speech, of *socialized* speech.

On the most obvious level—not only as a theme repeatedly developed in the *Confessions* but as the major motivating force for the very *writing* of the *Confessions*—speaking in the presence of others means for Rousseau certain humiliation and self-parody. Paralyzed by timidity, Rousseau knows he will disgrace himself beyond the hopes of even his most implacable detractors: "J'aimerois la societé comme un autre, si je n'étois sur de m'y montrer non seulement à mon desavantage, mais tout autre que je ne suis. Le parti que j'ai pris d'écrire et de me cacher est précisement celui qui me convenoit. Moi présent on n'auroit jamais su ce que je valois, on ne l'auroit pas soupçonné même" (I should enjoy society as much as anyone, if I were not certain to display myself not only at a disadvantage, but in a character entirely foreign to me. The role I have chosen of writing and remaining in the background is precisely the one that suits me. If I were present, people would never know my value—they would not even suspect it) (*Confessions,* 1:116). Significantly, Rousseau reports this often-quoted judgment not as a conclusion he had spontaneously arrived at but, as he immediately points out, as an acquiescence to the repeated judgment of one of his feminine protectors, Madame Dupin—a judgment to which, in fact, Rousseau insists on citing important exceptions.

The exceptions he cites were not, of course, moments of extemporaneous brilliance, occasions when Rousseau excelled as a conversationalist meeting or surpassing the highest standards of Parisian repartee. On the contrary, the exception occurs only when Rousseau can transform his speech act into the recitation of a text already written. The exception depends on his being able, while speaking with others, to offer them what has already been written in solitude. In book 7 of the *Confessions,* Rousseau describes a dinner with Madame de Beuzenval, the Polish-born mother of Madame de Broglie. He was acutely conscious of his obligation to prove his value to the assembled guests. After all, when it had seemed to him he would be expected to eat with the servants, he had refused the invitation to stay on for dinner. Only after Madame de Broglie had discreetly informed her mother of their guest's sensibilities and after Madame de Beuzenval had in turn made it clear that he was to eat with the other guests did Rousseau decide he could postpone his previous engagement. Realizing he would never hold his own on the terrain of "ce petit jargon de Paris, tout en petits mots, tout en petites allusions fines" (that fashionable Paris jargon full of diminutives and subtle little allusions) (*Confessions,* 1:290), Rousseau decided to read before the group the verse letter to Parisot, written in Lyon, which he just "happened" to have in his pocket. The effect, Rousseau points out, surpassed even his own expectations. All three of the women present were moved to tears of admiration: "Ce morceau ne manquoit pas de chaleur; j'en mis

dans la façon de le réciter, et je les fis pleurer tous trois" (That piece
was not lacking in fire, which I exaggerated by my manner of reading it, and I moved all three to tears) (*Confessions,* 1 : 290). Speaking the written text provides a definitive answer to any lingering
question of his true value: "Je crus voir que les regards de Madame
de Broglie disoient à sa mére: hé bien, Maman! avois-je tort de vous
dire que cet homme étoit plus fait pour diner avec vous qu'avec vos
femmes?" (I seemed to read in Madame de Broglie's glance: Well,
Mama, was I wrong when I said that this man was fitter to dine
with you than with your servant women?) (*Confessions,* 1 : 290).

□   □   □

The letters to Malesherbes show how Rousseau, in explaining why
he writes, in painstakingly justifying the dual project "to write and
to hide," defines his writing as an act determined by the trajectory
of a specific desire. This desire, like the one at work in both the
Confessions and *Julie,* seeks nothing less than the impossible accommodation of the symbolic to the imaginary.

    In preferring what is written, in substituting it for the extempo-
raneously spoken, Rousseau both demands distance between writer
and audience and aims to provoke its opposite: a beatific identification with that audience, an imaginary union beyond the play of differences, beyond hierarchies, beyond the symbolic order against
whose operation he chose that distance in the first place. I would
like to consider here one particularly important example from the
vast field of Rousseau's experience governed by this structure, an example that reveals the precise dictates and strategies of this desire to
write from afar: his recounting of the premiere performance of his
most successful musical work, the *Devin du village.*[7]

    At first glance it seems paradoxical that to understand the struc-
ture and implications of this desire we should look to an event in his
life that might be described as the moment of his closest proximity
to power, the apogee of his career as a writer-musician struggling to
establish himself in Paris. The premiere of the *Devin* took place in
Fontainebleau on October 18, 1752, in the presence of "le Roi, la
Reine, la famille royale et toute la Cour" (*Confessions,* 1 : 377). Its
success was complete. Rumor had it that the King would offer Rousseau a royal pension at the next day's audience.

    We are, as the date indicates, in one of Rousseau's transitional
periods. Within three years of the illumination of Vincennes and the

composition of the *First Discourse,* he had already proclaimed his vocation as the castigator of Parisian society—a society in which, as the presentation of the *Devin* indicates, he was nonetheless still attempting to establish his reputation. Only two years after this event, in June 1754, he made the first of his "complete breaks" with Paris— this time by the brief return to Switzerland and the reconversion to Calvinism that allowed him to recover his legal status as a citizen of Geneva.

In the same way, however, that the premiere of the *Devin* takes us to a period that precedes the letters to Malesherbes by ten years, its actual narration, the way Rousseau chooses to describe it, leads us to a period seven years after this correspondence: to 1769, when Rousseau stayed at Monquin, where he composed books 7–11 of the *Confessions.* While, then, the event itself preceded his break with Parisian society, its narration reflects a later, far more exacerbated, stage of Rousseau's alienation from a world he had by then discovered to be quite ready to return in kind the full force of his anathemas.

Rousseau continued to see this event, even at the end of his life, as a high point of his accomplishments: "C'est ce que j'aime le mieux avoir fait. Mes ennemis ont beau dire, il ne feront jamais un *Devin du village*" (It is what I am happiest about having written. My enemies can say whatever they wish; they will never write a *Devin du village*).[8] In another sense, however, more psychological than historical, it can be argued that Rousseau's narration of this event was bound to be marked by a diction more ambiguous than that in his description of later events, which were shaped by the more defensive, overdetermined reactions following the order for his arrest in June 1762, when the period of his exile began.

In fact the same opposition between the personal and the social that Rousseau develops in his letters to Malesherbes determined his attitude toward the *Devin,* even from the time of its composition. As an opera, its performance implied both the collaboration of a professional company and its presentation to the general public. Nonetheless, Rousseau's fondest wish was that this work, like Lully's *Armide,* might be performed in a closed theatre with himself alone as audience. Since this was a whim clearly beyond his means and since the previous failure of *Les Muses gallantes* augured ill for any work presented under his name, Charles Duclos arranged the original audition by the Paris Opera so that Rousseau's authorship of the *Devin* remained unknown even to the musicians performing it. Once this first presentation of the work had given every indication of huge public success, Rousseau experienced the preparations for its performance as a loss of all control over what was rightfully his. He and Duclos, as Rousseau describes it, were forced by Monsieur de Cury, the king's *Intendant des Menus Plaisirs,* to stage the premiere not at the Paris Opera but before the court in Fontainebleau. The royal performance took place, then, as the ascension of Rousseau's work to the highest sphere of established authority, but as the ascension of something he would have preferred to keep entirely to himself and over which he felt he had lost all control.

In describing the premiere, Rousseau constantly contrasts his feelings as the author of the opera with his feelings as a member of the audience in Monsieur de Cury's box at the Fontainebleau theater. Placed directly across from the king, Rousseau struggles to overcome feelings of exposure and insecurity by concentrating on his status as author. This struggle depends for its success on the same transformation of his halting and confused person through a carefully refined representation of the self in the written work, his opera, that marked the opposition between conversation and writing developed in the letters to Malesherbes: "Quand on eut allumé, me voyant dans cet équipage au milieu de gens tous excessivement parés, je commençai d'être mal-à-mon aise: je me demandai si j'étois à ma place, si j'y étois mis convenablement. . . . Dès la prémiére scene, qui véritablement est d'une naïveté touchante j'entendis s'élever dans les loges un murmure de surprise et d'applaudissement jusqu'alors inouï dans ce genre de piéces. La fermentation croissante alla bientot au point d'être sensible dans toute l'assemblée, et, pour parler à la Montesquieu, d'augmenter son effet par son effet même" (When the theatre was lighted up, and I saw myself dressed like that in the middle of such an overdressed crowd, I began to feel ill at ease. I asked myself whether I was in my right place, and whether I was suitably attired. . . . From the first scene, which is really touching in its simplicity, I heard a murmur of surprise and applause, hitherto unknown at plays of this sort, rising from the boxes. The mounting excitement soon reached such a pitch that it was noticeable right through the house and, to use an expression of Montesquieu's, it began to increase its effect by its effect) (*Confessions,* 1:377–78).

Having provided his reader with the background of the *Devin's* presentation before the court, Rousseau steps back from his circumstantial narration and, as though sensing the importance of what will follow, affirms his intention to offer a purely factual, uncolored description of his actions during that performance. "Me voici dans un de ces momens critiques de ma vie où il est difficile de ne faire que narrer, parce qu'il est presque impossible que la narration même ne porte empreinte de censure ou d'apologie. J'essayerai toutefois de rapporter comment et sur quels motifs je me conduisis, sans y ajouter ni louange ni blâme" (Here I am once more at one of those critical moments of my life in which it is difficult to confine myself to a narrative because it is almost impossible that even the narration will not carry some hint of censure or apology. I will try, however, to convey how and with what motives I acted, without adding any praise or blame) (*Confessions*, 1:377). Immediately after this declaration of objectivity, Rousseau explains how he had dressed. With exquisite understatement, the simple use of the word *usual* (and this in a context already defined as in every way unusual), Rousseau insists that appearing at Fontainebleau was for him, contrary to what one might expect, a refusal of the seeming honor accorded his work: "J'étois ce jour-la dans le même équipage négligé qui m'étoit ordinaire; grande barbe et perruque assez mal peignée" (On that day I was dressed in my usual careless style with a rough beard and an ill-combed wig) (*Confessions*, 1:377). In the way he had dressed, in his grooming, in everything that marked his physical appearance as a series of readable signs, Rousseau sought to establish himself as someone acting outside social conventions, as someone undetermined by recognized hierarchies, as someone capable of refusing all dictates devolving from the presence of king and court.

Rousseau's status as someone beyond convention, however, is redefined by a second movement, a movement originating in his comparison of himself with those seated around him in the soft shadows of the house lights. Finding himself in the midst of that "overdressed crowd," he cannot help wondering if he is in his proper place.

Responding to this growing anxiety, Rousseau justifies himself and his actions and opinions as based not on appearances but on the solid contours of fact. As though totally out of control, however, his justifications take off in every direction at once. Of course he has every right to be there: he wrote the opera so that he could one day see it performed. It was Monsieur de Cury who instigated the premiere at Fontainebleau and insisted that he be present. No one has a more just claim to the fruits of his labor than the laborer himself. As for anyone who might claim otherwise, anyone who might see his presence there as implying some complicity with social conventions, the very "ordinariness" of his appearance is proof positive of his greater fidelity to *nature:* "Mon extérieur est simple et négligé, mais non crasseux ni mal propre; la barbe ne l'est point en elle-même puisque c'est la nature qui nous la donne et que selon les tems et les modes elle est quelquefois un ornement. On me trouvera ridicule, impertinent; eh que m'importe" (My outward appearance is simple and careless, but not dirty nor slovenly. Nor is a beard so in itself, since it is a gift of Nature and, depending on the times and the fashion, is sometimes considered an ornament. I shall be considered ridiculous, offensive. Well, what is that to me!) (*Confessions,* 1:378). Rousseau, it is worth pointing out, is not talking here about a beard, since he never wore one. He simply chose not to shave on the day he attended the royal premiere of his opera at Fontainebleau.

Between the justifications of himself before men and before nature, Rousseau, in the space of three short sentences, redefines and expands the whole sense of his relation to the audience around him. Through a deft manipulation of perspective, he reinterprets all the previously noted proofs of his independence so that they now signal a crucial moment in his own personal history: "Je suis mis à mon ordinaire ni mieux ni pis. Si je recommence à m'asservir à l'opinion dans quelque chose, m'y voila bientôt asservi derechef en tout. Pour être toujours moi-même je ne dois rougir en quelque lieu que ce soit d'être mis selon l'état que j'ai choisi" (I am dressed in my ordinary way, neither better nor worse. If I begin to pander to opinion over one matter, I shall pretty soon be doing so in everything. To be consistent with myself, I must not blush, wherever I may be, at being dressed according to the position in life I have chosen) (*Confessions,* 1:378). The premiere itself and Rousseau's reaction to it are thus redefined in relation to a personal sequence of past, present, and future: the past of a consciously chosen fidelity to self, the present of his contact with a servile society asking him to be otherwise, and the dangerous future of his total enslavement to that society should he ever allow himself to respond to the slightest of its demands.

If Jean-Jacques Rousseau, on October 18, 1752, happened to

find himself in Fontainebleau as the author of an opera whose premiere was to be attended by the entire court, the cause was a series of events entirely beyond his control, with absolutely no accommodation on his part to either convention or appearance. The entire panoply of a royal command performance had, as it were, erected itself around the innocent fruit of his labor. The laborer himself remained steadfast in refusing all solicitation by the symbolic order issuing such demands.

Rather than ridicule and blame, however, the actual performance of the *Devin* brought the exact opposite, success. The entire audience, so far as Rousseau could judge, was caught up in a common movement of surprise and admiration for both the opera and its author. Precisely at this point in his narration, Rousseau's points of reference in relation to the audience around him begin to undergo a profound change. The king, no longer a center whose effulgence obscures all around him into a vague, fawning group of courtiers, becomes instead a principle of limit and order. His presence, instead of threatening the author's sense of self, safeguards it against a disruption that might otherwise have jeopardized the very continuation of the performance: "A la Scene des deux petites bonnes gens cet effet fut à son comble. On ne claque point devant le Roi; cela fit qu'on entendit tout; la piéce et l'auteur y gagnérent" (By the scene of the two good women the effect was at its height. There is no clapping when the King is present; for that reason every note was heard, to the great advantage of the piece and its author) (*Confessions*, 1 : 378).

In this ebullient universe now held in order only by the presence of the king, a feminine element emerges in the foreground of Rousseau's perception, a group of women who, as though caught up in a collective trance induced by the intensity of their pleasure, cannot stop themselves from voicing their admiration: "J'entendois autour de moi un chuchotement de femmes qui me sembloient belles comme des anges, et qui s'entredisoient à demi-voix: cela est charmant, cela est ravissant; il n'y a pas un son là qui ne parle au coeur" (Around me I heard a whispering of women who seemed to me as lovely as angels, and who said to one another under their breath: "That is charming. That is delightful. There is not a note that does not speak straight to the heart") (*Confessions*, 1 : 378–79). As Rousseau begins to recognize himself, through his opera, as the cause of this pleasure shared by so many women in the darkened room, he, too, is moved to participate in what becomes a collective ejaculation of tears: "Le plaisir de donner de l'émotion à tant d'aimables personnes m'émut moi-même jusqu'aux larmes, et je ne les pus contenir au prémier duo, en remarquant que je n'étois pas seul à pleurer" (The pleasure of affecting so many pleasant persons moved even me to tears, which I could not restrain during the first duet, when I noticed that I was not the only one who wept) (*Confessions*, 1:379).

The terms of the paradox are clear: once his desired position has become accessible, Rousseau redefines the symbolic order of king and court, from which he had first declared his radical exteriority, as the locus of his most intense recognition. This desired position is not, it must be noted, one that the king might offer him directly. The monarch, like all authority, only embodies an order that both generates and preserves the tension of Rousseau's separation from the whispering women. They, because he now knows what intense pleasure his written work provides them, offer him in return a momentary but total identification with the most profound fantasy of his own personal imaginary: "Surement s'il n'y eut eu là que des hommes, je n'aurois pas été dévoré, comme je l'étois sans cesse du plaisir de recueillir de mes levres les delicieuses larmes que je faisois couler" (If there had been only men present I am positive that I should not have been devoured, as I constantly was, by the desire to catch with my lips the delicious tears I had evoked) (*Confessions*, 1:379). Culminating in the figure of a child nursing on the tears of joy shed by the ravished mother, the plenitude Rousseau experiences here is clearly marked as the return of an axial scene in his most profound imaginary, an imaginary generated by the loss of the real mother, who herself had likewise become a source of inexhaustible tears. Rousseau becomes the child trembling in delicious subjugation at his total yet inexplicable coincidence with the object of desire chosen by the crying women: "J'étois armé contre leur raillerie; mais leur air caressant auquel je ne m'étois pas attendu me subjuga si bien que je tremblois comme un enfant" (I was armed against jeering; but their unexpected attitude of kindness so overwhelmed me that I trembled like a child) (1:378).

Rousseau's narration of the *Devin*'s premiere is important because it reveals, with particular concision and clarity, two distinct yet related levels of paradox at work in his relation to authority and desire. On a first level, as we saw in Rousseau's description of his arrival at the theater, he presents himself as a noble savage: a purely natural, self-determining presence independent of all conventions by which society might judge him. At this first level, the paradox is that his everyday outfit, his unshaven face, and his badly combed wig are not, as he would claim, the natural, apodictic, and unmarked traits of an individuality that exists beyond social coding. They are themselves a carefully elaborated message, whose meaning depends, as much as that of the different accoutrements of the overdressed courtiers, on the symbolic order through which these elements signify. Rousseau's *nature,* to express the paradox in other terms, is everywhere derived from and dependent on the signifying systems of a preexisting culture. Rousseau's fidelity to a self defined as outside the social is his fidelity to a purely imaginary self. Another version of this same project manifests itself throughout the political works as Rousseau places himself outside the codes and conventions of established society yet finds he must speak within those very codes and conventions.

Because Rousseau's account of the *Devin*'s premiere is one of his rare narrations of something he considered a success, it allows us to see a second, more complicated, level in his relation to authority and desire. The position as noble savage described above is essential to Rousseau's project because it allows the disavowal, the saving denegation, of what is in fact a profound and abiding fascination with authority and the symbolic order. In this sense the stance as noble savage is Rousseau's most frequent and safest strategy for declaring himself impervious to all judgments of an authority he expects only to condemn him. In instances where he found himself exalted rather than condemned, Rousseau felt an overwhelming desire that his truth be recognized by an authority that both presented to him and held him from a feminine, maternal element whose ecstasy ensured his coincidence with his most profound imaginary. Authority must simultaneously approve and prohibit because only in the distant joy thus generated can desire escape its annihilation through fulfillment.

□   □   □

To speak without the pre-text of an already written statement, to allow what is said to float in and take its meaning from the ever-shifting eddies of conversation, for Rousseau makes speech the index of a susceptibility to victimage and aggression multiplied by the number of people taking part in the exchange: "Je ne comprends pas même comment on ose parler dans un cercle; car à chaque mot il faudroit passer en revue tous les gens qui sont là: il faudroit connoitre tous leurs caractéres, savoir leurs histoires pour être sur de ne rien dire qui puisse offenser quelqu'un" (I cannot understand how a man can have the confidence to speak in company. For not a word should be uttered without taking everyone present into account, without knowing their characters and histories, in order to be sure of not offending someone) (*Confessions,* 1 : 115). The danger Rousseau describes here results not only from his own particular susceptibilities, his own acute sense of how others might victimize him, but from his awareness of the unintended violence he himself has inflicted on some innocent party whose only sin was to be present at the exchange. In the one example "entre mille que j'en pourrois citer" (*Confessions,* 1 : 115) Rousseau offers to illustrate this law, he witlessly implies that the medication Madame de Luxembourg often took in front of her friends as a stomach remedy was in fact a quack cure for syphilis. Although his own timidity is certainly a factor in his argument, its essential element is his more generalized fear of the potential violence of any social gathering where all are by definition equally vulnerable. The choice to write in solitude, then, "the decision I have made to write and to hide," is dictated by the inevitability in social situations of a violence in which Rousseau, like all others, is both victim and aggressor.

When Rousseau describes his experience of society, he condemns himself as well as others. As someone forced to discover there what was worst about himself, he must always be counted among those responsible: "J'etois rarement content des autres, et jamais de moi" (I was rarely happy with the others, and never with myself) ("Malesherbes," 1 : 1141). Rousseau has chosen to write from afar, finally, because that option represents the only possible escape from a violence that he and all others are constantly forced to initiate and suffer. To leave society, he tells Malesherbes, is not only to "me rendre bon à moi-même" but also "nullement mechant aux autres" ("Malesherbes," 1 : 1142).

Because it allows no final designation of agent and object, the violence of the social represents a force whose grammatical equivalent obliterates all distinction between the active and passive voice. When Rousseau did violence to another, when he found himself obliged to "harm others," he insists that a prior motivating moment always existed when, before becoming the active subject, he was the passive and innocent object of violence. This reversibility of active and passive, the attenuation of their differences to the point where they become indistinguishable, reveals itself most clearly in the curious turn of phrase that concludes Rousseau's analysis for Malesherbes of why friendship, the obverse of social violence, was impossible in the world as he knew it: "Ils n'ont pas precisément cessé de m'aimer; j'ai seulement decouvert qu'ils ne m'aimoient pas" (They did not exactly stop loving me; I simply discovered that they did not love me) ("Malesherbes," 1 : 1145). Can *they*, the others, be pointed to as the active subject of the verb? No; because, precisely, they did not *stop* loving me. Can the *I*, then, be pointed to as the subject of an active verb? No; because the sense of the verb *discover* as Rousseau uses it here establishes him as the passive recipient of a realization only gradually imposing itself on his consciousness. Beyond active and passive, life in the presence of others inevitably becomes an encounter with a violence that leaves the would-be innocent the unique alternative of separation and seclusion.

This violence inherent in the social represents a threat whose virulence cannot be checked by the act of writing alone. The decision to write does not in itself guarantee an escape from violence. When carried out in a context other than that of resolute seclusion, writing, like speech, risks being transformed into an instrument of conflict and self-aggrandizement. The writers of Paris, *les gens de lettres,* as opposed to the writer of Montmorency, also write. But they do so, Rousseau insists, in an inferno of violence and petty intrigues. For them writing is no more than a service rendered so that it might be returned. Their writing is a maneuver to maximize their position in the public eye. Far from accomplishing any greater good than the recluse of Montmorency, these writers in fact do less than even the simple peasant laboring in his field: "Vos gens de lettres ont beau crier qu'un homme seul est inutile à tout le monde et ne remplit pas ses devoirs dans la societé. J'estime moi les paysans de Montmorenci des membres plus utiles de la societé que tous ces tas de desoeuvrés payés de la graisse du peuple pour aller six fois la semaine bavarder dans une academie, et je suis plus content de pouvoir dans l'occasion faire quelque plaisir à mes pauvres voisins que d'aider à parvenir à ces foules de petits intrigans dont Paris est plein, qui tous aspirent à l'honneur d'être des fripons en place" (Your men of letters can cry as loudly as they wish that a man living in solitude is useless to everyone and does not fulfill his duties to society. I judge the peasants of Montmorency to be far more useful members of society than that pack of idlers paid from the people's sweat to gab six times a week in some academy. I am far happier in being able occasionally to provide some service to my poor neighbors than I would be in adding my voice to the maneuvers of those petty plotters Paris is so full of, all of whom aspire only to be on top of the pile) ("Malesherbes," 1:1143).

This comparison begins to show how the two axial themes developed in the letters to Malesherbes—the desire for true friendship and the decision to write from afar—work together as mutually sustaining strategies for a success that can be achieved only as a confluence of failures. At the intersection of friendship's impossibility and writing's perversion, Rousseau finds the one abiding contact with the ideal still available to him.

True friendship is impossible because all those to whom Rousseau has offered it have insisted that it manifest itself before the public eye. Writing has become a degraded parody of itself because it is everywhere employed in the most egotistical self-aggrandizement. Rousseau's own ideal of friendship, then, will escape this dilemma by addressing itself not to any one individual who might proclaim his preference over the many, but to all mankind: "J'ai un coeur tres aimant, mais qui peut se suffire à lui meme. J'aime trop les hommes pour avoir besoin de choix parmi eux; je les aime tous, et c'est parce que je les aime que je hais l'injustice; c'est parce que je les aime que je les fuis, je souffre moins de leurs maux quand je ne les vois pas. Cet interêt pour l'espece suffit pour nourrir mon coeur; je n'ai pas besoin d'amis particuliers" (I have a very loving heart, but one that is sufficient unto itself. I love men too much to make choices among them. I love them all, and it is because I love them that I hate injustice. It is because I love them that I flee them. I suffer less from their evils when I do not see them. This interest for man as a species is enough to nourish my heart. I have no need of individual friends) ("Malesherbes," 1:1144). True friendship, having limited its expression to the form of the written text, will in turn redefine the very nature of writing. As the representation of a love extended to all men, writing will renounce its link to self-interest and become instead the daring enunciation of an exclusively altruistic truth, a truth capable of freeing men from the misery they everywhere inflict on each other: "C'est quelque chose que de donner l'exemple aux hommes de la vie qu'ils devroient tous mener. C'est quelque chose quand on n'a plus ni force ni santé pour travailler de ses bras, d'oser de sa retraite faire entendre la voix de la verité. C'est quelque chose d'avertir les hommes de la folie des opinions qui les rendent miserables" (It counts for something to have provided men with an example of the life they all should lead. It counts for something that, with neither the strength nor the health to work with my hands, I have dared from my retreat to give voice to the truth. It counts for something that I have warned men of the madness of those beliefs that make them miserable) ("Malesherbes," 1 : 1143).

True friendship, an ideal first defined as the plenitude of an imaginary communion beyond all mediation by forces outside the self-sufficient diad, finally justifies a vocation of service to the whole of mankind, attainable only in that most mediated and most symbolic register of the text written in seclusion.

□ □ □

One of my intentions in analyzing Rousseau's attitude toward speech and writing and their relation to violence and friendship is to suggest an understanding of these configurations that is not overwhelmed by—forced to the repetition of—Derrida's treatment of them in *De la grammatologie.* Any discussion of Rousseau's attitude toward writing must take into account Derrida's seminal treatment of that subject. Basing his analysis on a close reading of the *Essay on the Origin of Languages,* Derrida directs his comments toward the larger goal of deconstructing what he sees as a "metaphysics of presence" that sustains the assumptions of Western philosophy from Plato to Hegel. In so doing, Derrida presents his reader with a Rousseau who numbers among the most eloquent spokesmen for valorizing the *spoken* over the *written.* Rousseau's goal in the *Essay,* as Derrida reads it, is to elaborate a coherent rationale for condemning the sclerotic, lifeless, and perverse absence always lurking at the heart of what is written. Human society, redefined by its addiction to the written, has lost contact with a vital, transparent, and immediate presence that is possible only in the spoken. This reading of the *Essay* makes Rousseau an ideal test case for Derrida's argument that *différance,* the diacritical stamp of the written, is in fact always already at work in any ideology of unmediated presence that sustains the idealization of speech.

As cogent as this reading may be, the very brilliance of Derrida's treatment of Rousseau according to an ideology of presence coterminous with our philosophical tradition necessarily lessens our sensitivity to aspects of his work that move in a different direction. The essential absence marking the act of writing might also, I have tried to argue, be seen as sustaining a valorization of that form. To the charge that as a recluse he has chosen an unnatural refusal of friendship and affection for others, Rousseau replies in these letters to Malesherbes that, quite to the contrary, his intense devotion to true friendship and genuine affection has forced him to reject all the tawdry imitations of those sentiments his fellows have presented to him. To the charge that as a recluse he makes no positive contribution to the common good, Rousseau replies that his writings seek to express a truth so salutary that he must not risk its corruption by any contact with the degenerate society around him.

From another point of view, Derrida's portrayal of writing as a supplement, an always-flawed substitute meant to delay the inevitable disappearance of the speaking voice, is clearly oblique to certain motivations Rousseau offers for his own decision "to write and to hide." Writing, for Rousseau, as we saw, aims not so much against his *disappearance* as against his *appearance*—his reduction to self-parodying incoherence each time he must speak in the presence of others.

Presence rather than absence, one might argue, his finding himself caught up in the violence of the social, dictates Rousseau's choice of writing over speech, of writing that only disguises itself as speech. Speech and presence, he seems to say, always carry with them the grave threat that his enunciation, rather than representing him, will look instead to the context of the others around him, and, in so doing, lose all contact with, and all adequacy to, the truth he must express. Paralyzed by the potential violence always implicit in the presence of the other, Rousseau finds that speech can lead only to catastrophe. Writing and absence, on the other hand, the withdrawal to a space inaccessible to the other, the retreat into a temporality no longer governed by the necessity to respond immediately, bring with them the possibility that his truth and his value can, in the safety of this absence, elaborate an adequate representation of themselves.

Certainly absence is essential to writing. Far from vitiating it as a form, however, absence becomes for Rousseau the basis of his achieving a saving distance from the other. What is absent from writing is the certainty that his words will be misunderstood, misinterpreted—that the other as judge will be gulled by his presence and render his verdict in error. The written text alone allows the emergence of truth in discourse. For Rousseau, the decision to write from afar is a way of prolonging his all-important option of anticipating and, by anticipating, refuting those objections sure to come from the other to whom his message is directed. To force that objecting other into the position of reader rather than listener allows Rousseau as writer the time to project himself into the position of that other and, as in the letters to Malesherbes, to undertake the impossible task of responding to the objection even before it is made.

The importance of preserving the possibility of responding to the reader's objections is so great for Rousseau that the writing of his autobiography, a project begun in these four letters to Malesherbes and continued throughout the rest of his life, will remain his one essential endeavor. Although a particular work may be "finished," its very closure dictates that, as it begins anew under another title, Rousseau's ability to refute his readers' objections must be preserved.

□   □   □

This premium of writing, its ability to defer the closure of judgment by the other, carries with it an awesome liability. The written text, to the extent that it is inscribed as Rousseau's effort to project himself into, to occupy, and to prepare the space available to the reader's judgment, presupposes the author's alienation from the very self whose immediacy and integrity he sets out to communicate. There is, as it were, a double bind concomitant with every attempt to speak of the self to the other. Rousseau asks his reader to recognize him in his individuality, to judge him of and by himself. This recognition and this judgment, however, can be achieved only as the reader's response to the textualized, proleptic, and literally other-inhabited representation of the self in discourse. Having opted for his representation in language, Rousseau the writer, his goal defined as a concerted attempt to *convince* the reader, inevitably confronts the fact that language, the only vehicle available to him, is itself a preexisting, codified, and symbolic system. The reader can be persuaded, his judgment anticipated and directed, only through an exercise of *rhetoric*. The decision to justify the self necessarily implies attention to, and manipulation of, the semiotic processes through which the writer will inscribe his brief in the resolutely impersonal system of the language he shares with his audience.

The problem of rhetoric, everything it implies about the writer's relation to his reader, was central to Rousseau's definition of his task. Because rhetoric relies on a code, because it presupposes a way of using language that is unrelated to the specific individuality of the writer, Rousseau condemns its figures, feints, and syllogisms as a nefarious order, a sustained exercise in deception. Rhetoric, for Rousseau, is always a manipulative skill that perverts language into the representation of belief regardless of the writer's personal conviction. It is the evil trait Rousseau designates in one of his autobiographical fragments as distinguishing all modern literature: "Ce qui rend la pluspart des livres modernes si froids avec tant d'esprit, c'est que les auteurs ne croyent rien de ce qu'ils disent. . . . Ils n'ont qu'un objet qui est la réputation et s'ils croyoient qu'un sentiment contraire au leur les y menât plus surement aucun d'eux n'hésiteroit d'en changer" (What makes most modern works so frigidly brilliant is that their authors don't believe a word they are saying. . . . Their only goal is to consolidate their reputations, and if they thought feelings contrary to their real ones would more surely accomplish that end, not one of them would hesitate to change them).[9]

This threat of rhetoric, the art of persuasion, turns any attempt at autobiography into a dilemma. On the one hand, the goal of rhetoric, convincing the reader, is an essential part of Rousseau's project. On the other, the implications in rhetoric of authorial distance, control, and manipulation represent the antithesis of everything Rousseau wished to say about himself. In the second preface to *Julie,* the dialogue between R[ousseau] and N, the terms of this dilemma are most clearly expressed. In a movement that suggests the central concerns of the letters to Malesherbes, life in society, the opposite of Rousseau's cherished solitude, is defined as a condition that forces us to say what we do not believe. In so doing, it creates the prototypical situation in which we must resort to the devices of rhetoric: "Ce n'est que dans le monde qu'on apprend à parler avec énergie. Premiérement, parce qu'il faut toujours dire autrement et mieux que les autres, et puis, que forcé d'affirmer à chaque instant ce qu'on ne croit pas, d'exprimer des sentiments qu'on n'a point, on cherche à donner à ce qu'on dit un tour persuasif qui supplée à la persuasion intérieure" (It is in society that you learn to speak energetically. First, because you must always speak differently and better than the others. Then, because you are constantly forced to say things you don't believe, and to express feelings you don't have, you learn to give what you say a persuasive turn of phrase that makes up for real persuasion).[10] This "persuasive turn of phrase," the substance of rhetoric, has the paradoxical status of a sign that signifies the opposite of its explicit meaning. As a trait of socialized discourse, persuasiveness finally proves the speaker's lack of any real adhesion to what he is saying, his lack of all true sincerity. Rhetoric generates a semiology in which denegation becomes the hallmark of signification. The persuasive sign ultimately proves the very opposite of what it seems to say. As N ironically remarks, "C'est-à-dire, que la foiblesse du langage prouve la force du sentiment" (That is to say, the weakness of one's language would prove the force of one's feelings) (*Julie*, 2:15).

Given this dilemma, what alternative remains for Rousseau as a writer who, refusing to employ rhetoric, must nonetheless persuade his readers to accept his truth? In both the texts I have quoted here (the autobiographical fragment, usually dated 1756, and the Second Preface to *Julie*) the solution is the same. Immediately after rejecting rhetoric, Rousseau valorizes the author's *intention*, his state of mind at the moment he writes: "Croyez-vous que les gens vraiment passionnés ayent ces manieres de parler vives, fortes, coloriées que vous admirez dans vos Drames et dans vos Romans? Non; la passion pleine d'elle-même, s'exprime avec plus d'abondance que de force; elle ne songe pas même à persuader; elle ne soupçonne pas qu'on puisse douter d'elle" (Do you think that people who really feel passion have those vivid, forceful, and colorful ways of speaking you so much admire in your novels and dramas? No, a real passion expresses itself more with richness than with force. It doesn't even think about persuading. It never suspects that anyone could doubt it) (*Julie*, 2:14–15). This "elle ne songe pas même à persuader" does not imply that the text in question will not persuade its reader. It certainly does. Its persuasiveness, however, is assumed to have established itself independently of any conscious authorial attention to represent it in language. Writing in inspired oblivion to everything but the statement of his truth, the author does not even suspect that his sincerity could be questioned. The fragment from 1756 likewise celebrates this ideal of authorial self-containment in its claim that the inner conviction of good faith and honesty will free the author from all concern with persuading the other: "C'est un grand avantage pour bien parler que de dire toujours ce qu'on pense, la bonne foi sert de rhétorique, l'honnêteté de talent et rien n'est plus semblable à l'éloquence que le ton d'un homme fortement persuadé" (As far as speaking well is concerned, the greatest advantage is always to say what you think. Conviction takes the place of rhetoric, honesty of talent; nothing is closer to eloquence than the tone of a man who is convinced) ("Fragments," 1 : 1113).

Resolved to avoid a rhetoric that converts discourse into the counterproof of everything it proclaims, insisting that the prescriptural plenitude of sincerity is the only message he offers his reader, Rousseau undertakes an impossible project. He must forge for himself a language outside all mediation by the other, an ideolect capable of generating a representation of the self in its uniqueness. As an unimpeded flow of inspired words, the writing self must, to achieve the recognition he seeks, refuse the most fundamental corollaries of linguistic expression. The discursive representation of truth presupposes the impossible rejection of language as an always other-oriented and other-determined expression founded on the writer's necessary alienation from the resolute singularity of his unmediated experience.

Left to its own implicit trajectory, the written representation of sincerity ultimately becomes an unreadable message, a text whose motivation in sentiment obliterates whatever statement it might seek to make. Speaking of the notes he left for Sophie d'Houdetot at a spot midway between the Hermitage and Eaubonne, Rousseau describes what might be seen as the ideal text: "Pour me distraire j'essayois d'écrire avec mon crayon des billets que j'aurois pu tracer du plus pur de mon sang: je n'en ai pu jamais achever un qui fut lisible. Quand elle en trouvoit quelqu'un dans la niche dont nous étions convenus, elle n'y pouvoit voir autre chose que l'état vraiment deplorable où j'étois en l'écrivant" (To calm myself I tried to write with a pencil notes which should have been written with the finest drops of my blood. But I never succeeded in finishing one that was legible. When she discovered one in the niche which we had agreed upon, all that she could see on it was the pitiable state of mind in which I had written it) (*Confessions*, 1 : 445–46). The message in words is rendered unreadable by the sentiment motivating it; yet that unreadability becomes the most eloquent proof of the sentiment inspiring it. Positing sincerity as the only escape from rhetoric, Rousseau finds himself committed to the impossible project of elaborating for himself a language perfectly adequate to the truth and desire of the writing subject.

3. Speech Beyond Language

Les définitions pourroient être bonnes si l'on
n'employoit pas des mots pour les faire.
—Rousseau, *Emile*

In the opening paragraph of chapter 14 in the *Essay on the Origin of Languages,* Rousseau, speaking of melody and its role in music, makes a surprising claim: "Tous les hommes de l'univers prendront plaisir à écouter de beaux sons; mais si ce plaisir n'est animé par des inflexions mélodieuses qui leur soient familières, il ne sera point délicieux, il ne se changera point en volupté. Les plus beaux chants, à notre gré, toucheront toujours médiocrement une oreille qui n'y sera point accoutumée; *c'est une langue dont il faut avoir le dictionnaire*" (Everyone in the world takes pleasure in hearing beautiful sounds. But if this pleasure is not enlivened by melodious inflections that are familiar to them, it will not be at all delightful, it will not become voluptuous. The songs most beautiful to us will only moderately move those to whom they are quite unfamiliar. *It is a language for which one needs a dictionary*).[1] It is striking that the author of the *First* and *Second Discourses,* the apologist for a direct and unmediated contact with nature, should here claim that our passage from the simply pleasurable to the delicious and the voluptuous depends on initiation, apprenticeship, a learned response that he goes so far as to compare to our using a dictionary to understand a language. This metaphor of the dictionary implies that before he understands, the subject must interiorize a code, learn the equivalences dictated by a system of arbitrary connections between word and meaning. A dictionary we must acquire is, by definition, a dictionary we did not originally possess. To learn such a code, therefore, is to step beyond nature into culture. The transformation of our pleasure into our *volupté* necessitates, if we take Rousseau's metaphor seriously, a recourse to something outside of us, to a learned code we use as an interpretive instrument to open up new and previously unperceived dimensions of our otherwise direct experience of sound and music. Such a code may well give us something more; but it does so at a price—that of a learned response that mediates between reality and our unmediated experience of it.

Put this way, the conclusion, on its face, seems antithetical to Rousseau's most tenaciously held positions. In fact there can be little doubt Rousseau would deny that he is arguing here for a superiority of culture over nature. His call for the dictionary, he would insist, must be understood in its specific context: an analysis, as the *Essay*'s subtitle indicates, of melody and musical imitation. As anyone reading Rousseau's texts on music quickly discovers, the meaning of *melody*, like the meaning of most of the terms he uses in discussing music, depends on its opposition to a second, negatively marked, term with which it is contrasted. Melody for Rousseau is that aspect of musical composition that allows the listener to move beyond *harmony*, beyond a perception of musical sound limited to the internal structuring of its elements. Melody takes its meaning from its opposition to harmony. Harmony, with its obsessive attention to the laws of intervals and consonances, can be thought of as an internal algebra, a purely imminent accord of sound with sound. To emphasize harmonics, something Rousseau identifies with everything he sees as misguided about Rameau's work, is to truncate the listener's experience, to limit music to a necessarily insipid immanence, to sever its connections with everything beyond the experience of sound as sound. Harmony is the death of music.

Attempting to describe the saving *beyond* to which only melody can lead, Rousseau draws an extensive comparison between music and painting. The way a painting affects its viewer becomes a model for understanding the more abstract question how the relative emphasis of melody or harmony determines the listener's experience of music. Music, Rousseau argues, uses sound as painting uses color. And it is self-evident, at least in a period making no allowance for what we would call abstract or nonrepresentational art, that paintings must never simply harmonize color with color according to laws derived, for instance, from experiments with the prism. The status of painting as an art depends instead on what Rousseau calls "design" or "line" (*dessin*): the organization of chromatic contrasts so that some recognizable figure—a face, a countryside, a still life— emerges from their interplay. Like music, a painting interests us only to the extent that it leads *beyond* its chromatic surface, to the extent that it represents a pattern we perceive as the real in miniature. A truly artistic painting guides its viewer to its represented meaning instead of throwing him back upon a pure play of chromatic signifiers operating only in relation to themselves.

Once this opposition is established, Rousseau uses the same primacy of the represented *beyond* to justify his preference for melody over harmony: "Qu'est-ce qui fait de la peinture un art d'imitation? C'est le dessin. Qu'est-ce qui de la musique en fait un autre? C'est la mélodie" (What makes painting an art of imitation? It is design. And what makes music the same kind of art? It is melody) (*Essai*, p. 532). In looking at a painting or in listening to music, our attention must never be limited to a pure surface. It must be called beyond color and beyond sound to a signified meaning for which the surface has served as a transitive representation.

At this point in his argument the paradox of Rousseau's appeal to the metaphor of the dictionary becomes apparent. Recourse to a learned code may well provide *volupté*, but only on the condition that such an intensity of feeling be designated, thanks to the magic of line and melody, as our response not to the processes of representation themselves but to the signified meaning they produce. Both music and painting, in other words, may use codes, but only as the transitive means to a moment when the code disappears and we perceive a reality beyond all mediation by the code. Confronted with a process of artistic representation that points to its product as pure simulacrum, viewer and listener must perceive them as they would the immediacy of nature. Culture may lead us, but only back to nature.

□ □ □

This paradox of a code that serves to intensify our experience of a reality defined as prior to all codification is, in a sense, emblematic of the position Rousseau takes throughout the *Essay on the Origin of Languages*. On the most obvious level, there is clearly something of the "disappearing code" behind Rousseau's use of a language he roundly condemns as that of the slave to trace the form and sing the praises of *another* language, a lost idiom of truth from which the whole of man's history has irremediably separated him.

Faced with this paradox and the intriguing impossibility of its resolution, we might ask ourselves why Rousseau was so fascinated with the problem of the origin of language, why the attempt to resolve this enigma runs like a leitmotif throughout his works. One tradition tells us that the forty or so pages of the *Essay* should be seen as an expanded footnote to the more summary treatment of the origin of language in the *Second Discourse*. The most convincing historical evidence suggests that the *Essay* was begun as a separate piece roughly at the same time as the *Second Discourse* (1754), that it was revised for separate publication as a response to Rameau in 1761, and that Rousseau reworked it a final time and divided it into chapters in 1763. It can be argued, in other words, that throughout the most productive decade of his life, Rousseau grew more and more concerned with a problem that, first appearing as a minor point in his historical synthesis of man's relation to his various forms of social organization, became the subject of a much-expanded independent work.

The neatness of this answer tempts us to overlook the radical change in tone between the treatment of language in the *Second Discourse* and in the *Essay* itself. What Rousseau says about the origins of language in the *Second Discourse* reads like a scholarly quibble with Condillac's *Essai sur l'origine des connaissances humaines* (1746). The *Essay,* on the other hand, represents a far more fully developed and distinctly personal theory of human communication—a theory so ambitious as to argue for a dialectical relation between man's semiological systems and the forms of his social organization. This shift seems to indicate that in the decade following his first approach to the problem, Rousseau grew increasingly concerned to answer the question how languages, and systems of communication in general, originate from and interact with the major forces of human history.

To understand Rousseau's growing concern with this problem, I propose to approach the *Essay* as intimately related to the preoccupations I have examined in my earlier chapters. As Rousseau wrote and rewrote this work, he was, on some level, searching for an answer to the one question he came to pose ever more intensely: how could it be that he found himself in the midst of a society where two inexplicable but clearly related things were constantly happening? He had spoken and written the truth, yet it went unrecognized; others lied egregiously about him and his works, yet everyone believed them. In other words, during the decade of his continued attention to the problem of the origin of language, Rousseau came to formulate his vision of himself as a victim, as the target of a conspiracy to stifle his truth and to substitute for it grotesque lies. What is it about language itself, Rousseau asks, that allows it to serve such nefarious enterprises?

The truth refused, the lie acclaimed. As anyone reading the *Con-*

fessions and the *Dialogues* knows, these problems would long pre-occupy Rousseau. It is only reasonable to assume that he thought of them as he organized his reflections on the genesis and nature of human language. Unlike his approach in those texts that examine the particular motivations of various "liars," his approach to the problem here is more abstract and properly metacritical: if the lie is so astoundingly frequent a *parole,* what in the nature of our *langue* makes it so?

The answer Rousseau offers to this question takes us back to the problem of the code, of the "dictionary." For Rousseau, the history of man's languages (and "language" here must be taken as including gesture, cries, and song as well as spoken and written language) occurs as a series of responses to the demands placed on these systems by parallel changes taking place in man's social organization. These changes dictate the gradual yet inexorable replacement of directly meaningful and unmediated utterances (the child's cry for food, the lover's swoon) by more elaborate messages that depend on stabilized, coded, and communally mediated systems of speech and writing. They are, as Rousseau calls them, *conventional languages:* unless we have first learned the convention, no message articulated according to its rules will have meaning for us.

Our present form of syllabic writing, coming after hieroglyphic and ideogrammatic writing, represents the final stage of this progression. Syllabic writing is the coded, visual representation of a spoken language that is itself already and differently coded. Syllabic writing is a second encoding of what is already coded.

The one sure result of this proliferating reliance on codes is the dawning of an age of liars—an age Rousseau would define as coterminous with civilized society. As signs, the cry and swoon are marked by direct, unmediated links to the hunger and longing they signify. They are, to borrow Peirce's term, indexical signs. There is an unbreakable, existential relation between the form of their enunciation and the meaning they convey. By their very nature they are poorly suited to misrepresentation. At the other end of the spectrum, syllabic writing, the medium privileged by all advanced societies, lacks any necessary connection between the form of its expression and the represented meaning. Writing is the perfect tool of prevarication.

Rousseau so adamantly insists on a properly dialectical relation between the forms of man's expression (how, for instance, the development of syllabic writing in turn redefined the nature of the spoken language to which it was applied) because he was acutely aware that even as men speak face-to-face with each other, their accommodation to the greater opacity and secretiveness of writing encourages their erasing all visible signs of the deeper personal significance that might otherwise accompany what they say. As a detailed analysis of the *Essay* would show, Rousseau's particular history of man's languages is perfectly coherent with the hypothesis that his vision of their progressive degeneration depended on his first projecting backwards, as the ideal state from which everything began, a communicational mode in which both the *secret* and the *lie* are impossible. All subsequent forms of speech and writing are then ordered as they are ill-suited or well suited to the task of lying, of keeping one's secret.

Coded representational systems for Rousseau are the essential handmaidens of deception. What a man writes on a piece of paper, even what he says in the polite language of social intercourse, offers no guarantee that his statements correspond to his true feelings. A correct and convincing manipulation of the code ultimately proves nothing more than one's knowledge of that code. "J'ai cherché la Vérité dans les livres; je n'y ai trouvé que le mensonge" (I looked for truth in books, but all I found were lies) and "Chacun feint de vouloir sacrifier ses intérêts à ceux du public, et tous mentent" (Everyone pretends to be ready to sacrifice his interests to those of the public, and they are all lying) are sentences repeated in variants throughout Rousseau's works. The code, with its insistence on a superficial harmonizing of its constituent elements, not only facilitates but actively encourages a separation between inner feeling and outward expression. To the extent I am under the sway of a strong emotion, I lose my ability to articulate it. To the extent I articulate an emotion eloquently, I prove my effective distance from it. All convincing manipulations of a code are governed by rhetoric. And, as we saw in the previous chapter, all rhetoricians are, for Rousseau, liars.

□   □   □

Man's reliance on language represents the most important of his relations to the symbolic. As the most pervasive of those preexisting systems through which the subject must enunciate, define, and reiterate the only truth he may know, language is the primordial register of the symbolic.

As a symbolic system, as a form of authority concomitant with a given social order, language always operates through an encoding. By its very nature language is an open system of arbitrary yet socially predetermined equivalences of sign with meaning, of signifier with signified. Man is free to speak, but the interpretation of his utterances by the other is always mediated by a code over which neither he nor the other exercises complete control.

What, we must ask, do Rousseau's considerable misgivings about coded representational systems and his elaboration of an entire history of language to justify those misgivings tell us about his relation to the symbolic? Rousseau's case against the code rests on the charge that it inevitably opens up a chasm between feeling and representation, between subjectivity and language. Significantly enough, in considering the relation between subjectivity and language, Emile Benveniste, like Rousseau, insists that this problem can be resolved only through a more general consideration of the function and origin of language.[2] Although never mentioned by name in Benveniste's seminal article, Rousseau and his *Essay* clearly figure among the principal intertexts to which he is replying.

Rousseau begins his *Essay* with a discussion of gesture. This return to visible, as opposed to audible, signs is intended as a stepping back from what seems too obvious. It is meant to force the reader to place the analysis of speech and writing, the forms of language with which we are most familiar, in the context of the most basic function of language. Gesture for Rousseau, like speech and writing, is an instrument for communicating thought. The whole of the *Essay,* the sequential history of the various developments of our languages, continues to privilege this notion of instrumentality as the motivating force behind the evolution of our communicational systems. Change in language always occurs as an adaptation of man's semiotic systems to the task of expressing his passions and needs, ever more pressing and ever more complex. In all its forms, from the simplest to the most complex, language remains, for Rousseau, an instrument.

In his article "De la subjectivité dans le langage," Benveniste begins his analysis by pointing to the problem inherent in this position: every instrumentalist view of language belies a subtle confusion between language as a *form* and the various direct applications of that form to the needs of a specific situation: "Le comportement du langage admet une description behavioriste, en termes de stimulus et de réponse, d'où l'on conclut au caractère médiat et instru-

mental du langage. Mais est-ce bien du langage que l'on parle ici?
Ne le confond-on pas avec le discours? Si nous posons que le discours est le langage mis en action, et nécessairement entre par-
tenaires, nous faisons apparaître, sous la confusion, une pétition de
principe, puisque la nature de cet 'instrument' est expliquée par sa
situation comme 'instrument'" (The behavior of language admits of
a behaviorist description, in terms of stimulus and response, from
which one might draw conclusions as to the intermediary and in-
strumental nature of language. But is it really language of which we
are speaking here? Are we not confusing it with discourse? If we
posit that discourse is language put into action, and necessarily between partners, we uncover, within the confusion, a begging of the
question, since the nature of this "instrument" is explained by its
situation as an "instrument") (Benveniste, *Problèmes,* p. 258). Benveniste sees the danger of this instrumentalist view of language in its
assumption that there must be a break, a radical disjunction, between *natural man* and *man the communicator:* "Parler d'instrument, c'est mettre en opposition l'homme et la nature. La pioche, la
flèche, la roue ne sont pas dans la nature. Ce sont des fabrications"
(To speak of an instrument is to put man and nature in opposition.
The pick, the arrow, and the wheel are not in nature; they are fabrications) (p. 259).

There is little doubt that for Rousseau men had no innate proclivity to communicate with each other. Even primitive man's decision to attempt such communication presupposed his first arriving
at the conclusion, by no means obvious, that the other whom he
had encountered might in fact share a nature like his own. Written
and spoken languages as we know them are accidents that might
well never have happened, and their absence would in no way have
jeopardized the development of social structures capable of leading
man beyond his original, savage state: "Ceci me fait penser que si
nous n'avions jamais eu que des besoins physiques, nous aurions
fort bien pu ne parler jamais, et nous entendre parfaitement par la
seule langue du geste. Nous aurions pu établir des sociétés peu différentes de ce qu'elles sont aujourd'hui, ou qui même auraient
marché mieux à leur but. Nous aurions pu instituer des lois, choisir
des chefs, inventer des arts, établir le commerce, et faire, en un mot,
presque autant de choses que nous en faisons par le secours de la
parole" (This leads me to think that if the only needs we ever experienced were physical, we should most likely never have been able to

speak; we would fully express our meanings by the language of gesture alone. We would have been able to establish societies little different from those we have, or such as would have been better able to achieve their goals. We would have been able to institute laws, to choose leaders, to invent arts, to establish commerce, and to do, in a word, almost as many things as we do with the help of speech) (*Essai*, p. 503). Such a purely gestural language did not long hold sway over man's development—this history founded only on physical need never actually occurred—because man is subject to moral as well as physical needs, to what Rousseau calls passions. These passions are for Rousseau a potential inherent in human nature. As such, they are both prelinguistic and extralinguistic. They are forces that could have exercised themselves without drawing mankind into the whole history of degradation that the *Essay* recounts. Passions, as opposed to needs, drew man closer to his fellows and greatly intensified contact with the other, a closeness from which sprang the desire to communicate: "Toutes les passions rapprochent les hommes que la necessité de chercher à vivre force à se fuir. Ce n'est ni la faim, ni la soif, mais l'amour, la haine, la pitié, la colère, qui leur ont arraché les premières voix" (All the passions bring together those very men whom the necessity to subsist first forced to flee each other. It is neither hunger nor thirst but love, hatred, pity, anger, which drew from men the first words) (*Essai*, p. 505). Passions represent, in other words, a susceptibility to disaster. Although they are themselves natural, as forces they nonetheless exacerbate desires that, once acted out in a socialized context, open the way to all that is worst.

In distinct contrast to Rousseau, Benveniste insists that every attempt to explain the origin of language necessitates recourse to a fiction that reinforces the separation between *natural man* and *man the communicator*. For Benveniste every vision of what man might have been prior to his communication with the other is an exercise in pure myth: "Le langage est dans la nature de l'homme, qui ne l'a pas fabriqué. Nous sommes toujours enclins à cette imagination naïve d'une période originelle où un homme complet se découvrirait un semblable, également complet, et entre eux, peu à peu, le langage s'élaborerait. C'est là pure fiction. Nous n'atteignons jamais l'homme séparé du langage et nous ne le voyons jamais l'inventer. Nous n'atteignons jamais l'homme réduit à lui-même et s'ingéniant à concevoir l'existence de l'autre. C'est un homme par-

lant que nous trouvons dans le monde, un homme parlant à un autre homme, et le langage enseigne la définition même de l'homme"
(Language is in the nature of man, and he did not fabricate it. We
are always inclined to that naive concept of a primordial period in
which a complete man discovered another one, equally complete,
and between the two of them language was worked out little by
little. This is pure fiction. We can never get back to man separated
from language and we shall never see him inventing it. We shall
never get back to man reduced to himself and exercising his wits to
conceive of the existence of another. It is a speaking man whom we
find in the world, a man speaking to another man, and language
provides the very definition of man) (Benveniste, *Problèmes*, p. 259).

I am approaching Rousseau's *Essay* through Benveniste's antithetical treatment of the same subject because his critique brings
into focus the paramount importance of Rousseau's recourse to this
eminently mythic moment. Rousseau in fact devotes the entire third
chapter of his *Essay*, "Que le premier langage dut être figuré," to
the hypothetical staging of precisely this fiction: that of solitary, prelinguistic man struggling with the discovery of his fellows. What
Rousseau says there about man's passions and their mediation
through language is essential to understanding his fundamental relation to the operation of socialized codes, to those *langues de convention* that function both as the driving forces of his history and as
the foundation of the symbolic.

□   □   □

Rousseau's scenario of this discovery illustrates his contention that,
as his chapter title indicates, man's first language was figurative.
Stated this way, it is clear that Rousseau voluntarily adopted a position of paradox toward the relation between literal and figurative
language as this relation is traditionally understood. In the *Encyclopédie*, for instance, Diderot's definition of the figure leaves
little doubt that it represents a stage after the literal, that it deviates
from the preexisting literal: "FIGURE, *terme de rhétorique, de lo-
gique, de grammaire. . . .* Scalinger dit que la *figure* n'est autre
chose qu'une disposition particulière et relative à l'état primitif et
pour ainsi dire fondamental des mots et des phrases. Les différents
écarts que l'on fait dans cet état primitif, et les différentes altéra-
tions qu'on y apporte, font les différentes *figures* de mots et de pen-
sées" (FIGURE, *a term of rhetoric, logic, and grammar. . . .* Scal-

inger says that the *figure* is nothing other than an arrangement that is relative to the primitive and, so to speak, fundamental state of words and phrases. The different deviations from that primitive state, as well as its various alterations, make up the different *figures* of words and thoughts).[3] For Rousseau, the error of this position lay in its obliteration of an earlier and more profound figurative state of language prior to the literal. The normal and normative meaning that Scalinger accepted as the starting point, as the *primitive state,* must always, Rousseau insists, be seen as coming after a non-normative and properly figurative use of language occurring "lorsque la passion nous fascine les yeux, et que la première idée qu'elle nous offre n'est pas celle de la vérité" (when passion deceives our eyes, and when the first idea it offers us is not the true one) (*Essai,* p. 506). The forgotten figure is the passionate error, the misjudgment provoked by passion.

As Rousseau elaborates his argument for the primacy of figurative language, offering an illustration intended to make this abstract point more concrete, he effectively stages the crucial moment of man's concurrent discovery both of other men and of language: "Un homme sauvage en rencontrant d'autres se sera d'abord effrayé. Sa frayeur lui aura fait voir ces hommes plus grands et plus forts que lui-même; il leur aura donné nom de *géans.* Après beaucoup d'expériences, il aura reconnu que ces prétendus géans n'étant ni plus grands ni plus forts que lui, leur stature ne convenait point à l'idée qu'il avait d'abord attachée au mot de géant. Il inventera donc un autre nom commun à eux et à lui, tel par exemple que le nom d'*homme,* et laissera celui de *géant* à l'objet faux qui l'avait frappé durant son illusion" (Upon meeting others, a savage man will initially be frightened. Because of his fear he sees the others as bigger and stronger than himself. He calls them *giants.* After many experiences, he recognizes that these so-called giants are neither bigger nor stronger than he. Their stature does not approach the idea he had initially attached to the word giant. So he invents another name common to them and to him, such as the name *man,* for example, and leaves *giant* to the fictitious object that had impressed him during his illusion) (*Essai,* p. 506).[4] The word *giant,* then, as first uttered by the frightened primitive, represents man's original figurative language. When this utterance is examined in the fable's context, it becomes clear that, during what Rousseau calls its figurative phase, *giant* refers to two different things: it designates an exterior reality, the other person the primitive has unexpectedly encountered; simultaneously, it designates the speaker's passion, the fear that has led him to choose this particular term. Passionate error born of fear led the speaker to use a word whose signification, as he will discover only later, does not in fact correspond to the reality of the other men he has used it to designate. The original figurative phase of language lasts, in other words, only so long as the speaker remains unable to distinguish between these two referents. Furthermore, of the two meanings, the one that justifies Rousseau's hypothesis of the priority of figurative language is the one in which *giant* is an index of the fear motivating his error.

During the period of passionate error, *giant* refers both to the misinterpreted object and to the passion that inspires the misinterpretation. Experience, the slow discovery that these other men are in fact neither larger nor stronger than the speaker, progressively eliminates all justification for his using the word *giant* to refer to anything other than his memory of an image he now recognizes to be false. As a word, however, *giant* will nonetheless survive this shrinking of its referent. It will remain a part of the primitive's vocabulary, thanks to its other status as the index of a passion that he might again feel and express in relation to other objects. As the primitive passes from a figurative to a literal use of this word, coming to use the term *man* to designate those others to whom he has now convinced himself he is the equal, the word *giant*, the trace of an error recognized as error, becomes available to him as an entirely different kind of figure. Now able to speak figuratively *at a second degree,* he will use the word's indexical reference to passion without any illusion that it has grounding beyond his own subjectivity. This second degree of the figurative is, for Rousseau, the metaphor: "L'image illusoire offerte par la passion se montrant la première, le langage qui lui répondait fut aussi le premier inventé; il devint ensuite métaphorique, quand l'esprit éclairé, reconnaissant sa première erreur, n'en employa les expressions que dans les mêmes passions qui l'avaient produite" (The illusory image presented by passion being the first to appear, the language that corresponded to it was also the first to be invented. It subsequently became metaphorical when the enlightened spirit, recognizing its first error, used the expressions only with those passions that had produced them) (*Essai,* p. 506).

Something strange is happening here. In one of his letters to Christophe de Beaumont, the archbishop of Paris who signed the condemnation of *Emile,* Rousseau makes the point that "rien n'est moins rare que des mots dont le sens change par trait de temps" (nothing is less rare than words whose meanings change over time).[5] I quote this hardly astounding observation because it underlines what is perhaps the most unsettling aspect of the argument Rousseau develops here. Words, as Rousseau points out to the archbishop, constantly change in meaning. A greater knowledge of a given referent or a variation in the speaker's affective attitude toward it regularly influences a word's meaning without, for that, compromising that word's status as a sign that designates the referent in question. When, however, we examine Rousseau's argument about the transition from *giant* to *man,* we see that his position is different. Instead of gradually accommodating itself to the reassuring discoveries made about the objects it designates, the meaning of the word *giant* instead undergoes a more and more complete evacuation of the objects it designates until, physical freaks aside, it becomes the sign of an empty set.

How, we are justified in asking, can this be possible? We have already seen part of the answer, the part Rousseau explicitly insists on: "Pour m'entendre il faut substituer l'idée que la passion nous présente au mot que nous transposons; car on ne transpose les mots que parce qu'on transpose aussi les idées" (To understand me you must, since we transpose words only because we transpose ideas, substitute the idea with which passion presents us for the word we transpose) (*Essai,* p. 506). Rather than see *giant* as a word subject to the vicissitudes of the verbal, then, we must see it as the immutable token of its subjective referent, as an "idea" born in passion whose very substance is shot through with fear. As the indexical sign of that passion, it is semantically fixed and unchanged despite its tenuous and changing associations with exterior reality.

Such a reduction of the word *giant* to its passional nucleus is possible, however, only when another term "happens" to exist, another word, here *man,* that waits, as it were, to receive and designate all those dwarfed giants the primitive now discovers in his fellows. *Man,* Rousseau tells us, is "the true name." It represents a state of language unperturbed by passion's errors.

It should be clear in the argument Rousseau offers that he could have chosen *gnu* or any other term as the second word adopted by the primitive to designate his peers and still have made his point about that term's difference from the figure contained in the word *giant.* If Rousseau chooses *man* rather than *gnu,* he does so because

his argument depends for its cogency on the word *man*'s coincidence with an actual yet arbitrary state of language that apparently
has halted all semantic change; he offers instead a term his readers
might recognize as a "literal" state of language unmarked by passion's warp.

The contention that the shift from *giant* to *man* parallels the
shift from a passionate error to an absence of passion is acceptable
only when the reader goes along with Rousseau's own wordplay
that makes the calm of discovered equality a mental state somehow
less affectively charged than the primitive's earlier feelings of fear.
Why, we might ask, should the "joy," or "reassurance," or what
have you that might accompany the primitive's discovery that he is a
man before men rather than a dwarf before giants be posited as a
moment outside of passion, outside the indexical fixity of figurative
language? Is it not, in fact, well within the boundaries of Rousseau's
thought to imagine still other subsequent shifts, so that the primitive might go on to discover that this "equality" of his fellows is itself a passionate error, a figurative state of language that ultimately
must yield to the studied conclusion that their moral character is in
fact far inferior to his own?

Rousseau's privileging of passional tropes as prior to and different from the literal language to which they lead is possible only
when language as a *form,* a diacritical tracing out of oppositional
categories, is already present and has already done its work of setting up the very oppositions ("greater" is to "equal" as "giant" is
to "man") through which the literal distinguishes itself from the
figurative.

When Rousseau draws from his fable the conclusion that "le mot
figuré naît avant le mot propre, lorsque la passion nous fascine les
yeux, et que la première idée qu'elle nous offre n'est pas celle de la
vérité" (p. 506), the "truth" he alludes to can only be that of a language already at work. Based on the word *giant*'s incapacity to correctly designate others perceived in their equality to the speaker, it
is a "truth" only because that seme of equality has already been at-
tributed to the word *man.* It is the "truth" of a language waiting to
be discovered.

□   □   □

Rousseau based his argument about this axial moment in man's history on the surprising assumption that linguistic change results

from the thought processes and decisions of the individual speaker: "Il inventera donc un autre nom commun à eux et à lui, tel par exemple que le nom d'*homme,* et laissera celui de *géant* à l'objet faux qui l'avait frappé durant son illusion" (*Essai,* p. 506). The *he* in question here, the third-person singular pronoun functioning as the sentence's subject, refers to the lone primitive whose hypothetical mental states have provided the substance of Rousseau's analysis.

Language, it would seem, is a private affair. Even so important a shift as that from the figurative to the literal takes place entirely in the independent subjectivity of the isolated speaker. The primitive first used the word *giant* because to him his fellows seemed gigantic. As he discovered that impression to be false, however, he invented another word to express their similarity to him. At no point in this process, however, is the primitive described as effectively communicating with these other men. Without the means to do so, and afraid to do so, he remains a careful watcher from afar. Behind the monolithic *he* of this third-person narration, then, Rousseau asks his reader to imagine an *I* no less monolithic that is identified with the subjectivity of the primitive actually carrying out this linguistic shift.

Rousseau's reliance on this inventive *he* as a self-sufficient subject allowed him to avoid considering how subjectivity itself, the continuity of consciousness implicit in the consecutive judgments of a term's appropriateness, is related to the experience of language as a form, as a *langue* rather than as isolated modifications of a particular *parole.*

Returning to Benveniste's essay, we can begin to place Rousseau's history of language in his overall attitude toward the symbolic. Unlike the preexisting and self-sufficient subjectivity Rousseau points to as the seat of this shift from *giant* to *man,* Benveniste insists that "c'est dans et par le langage que l'homme se constitue comme *sujet*" (it is in and through language that man constitutes himself as a *subject*) (Benveniste, *Problèmes,* p. 259). Benveniste presents language as *preceding* subjectivity because for him all consciousness of the self as subject depends on the individual's communication with and mediation through a second consciousness, a *you* presupposed by his use of *I*: "La conscience de soi n'est possible que si elle s'éprouve par contraste. Je n'emploie *je* qu'en m'addressant à quelqu'un qui sera dans mon allocution un *tu*. C'est cette condition de dialogue qui est constitutive de la *personne,* car elle implique en ré-

ciprocité que je deviens *tu* dans l'allocution de celui qui à son tour
se désigne par *je*." (Consciousness of self is only possible if it is experienced by contrast. I use *I* only when I am speaking to someone
who will be a *you* in my address. It is this condition of dialogue
which is constitutive of *person*, for it implies that *I* reciprocally become *you* in the address of the one who in his turn designates himself as *I*) (Benveniste, *Problèmes*, p. 260).

Benveniste's argument helps us understand how Rousseau's approach to the question of the origin of language can legitimately be
read as one tactic in an overall strategy to preserve the monolithic
self-sufficiency of the individual consciousness, of an *I* discovering,
rather than being discovered in, language. For Benveniste, man
prior to language cannot be man. For Rousseau, man not only
exists before language but is endowed with a subjectivity so complete in itself that even the passage from figurative to literal takes
place as the single subject's isolated rectification of an ideolect.

As a way of clarifying the implications of this position, I would
like to examine another key scene in the *Essay*, one that Rousseau
places much later in man's evolution and through which he explicitly questions the role of language in expressing sentiments born in
the intersubjective relation of two individuals.

Toward the end of chapter 9, the longest in the *Essay*, Rousseau
carries his history forward. Men are no longer solitary hunters but
have grouped together to form family clans engaged in agriculture
and animal raising. Illustrating his general law that language evolves
in response to the need for a greater coordination of individual
efforts in accomplishing communal tasks, Rousseau sets this scene
in land whose aridity has led men to collaborate in irrigation projects. Rousseau here considers not Persia and China, where rivers
and mountains have led men to construct dams, canals, and dikes,
but those flat, riverless expanses where water can be found only by
digging wells. Particularly important to Rousseau's history is the
well because, more than any other solution to the problem of sup-
plying water, it necessitates concentrating many individuals around
a single fixed point. It represents the prototypical cause of advanced
social organization and linguistic change in warm climates.

Setting aside the abstract tone and generalized parallels between
social and communicational forms that characterize his text, Rousseau describes a particularly fervid scene that highlights significant
changes taking place around the communal well. It is a long, bu-

colic passage marked by a diction unlike that used elsewhere in the *Essay:*

> Là se formèrent les premiers liens des familles, là furent les premiers rendez-vous des deux sexes. Les jeunes filles venaient chercher de l'eau pour le ménage, les jeunes hommes venaient abreuver leurs troupeaux. Là, des yeux accoutumés aux mêmes objets dès l'enfance commencèrent d'en voir de plus doux. Le coeur s'émeut à ces nouveaux objets, un attrait inconnu le rendit moins sauvage, il sentit le plaisir de n'être pas seul. L'eau devint insensiblement plus nécessaire, le bétail eut soif plus souvent: on arrivait en hâte, et l'on partait à regret. Dans cet âge heureux où rien ne marquait les heures, rien n'obligeait à les compter: le temps n'avait d'autre mesure que l'amusement et l'ennui. Sous de vieux chênes vainqueurs des ans, une ardente jeunesse oubliait par degrés sa férocité: on s'apprivoisait peu à peu les uns avec les autres; en s'efforçant de se faire entendre, on apprit à s'expliquer. Là se firent les premières fêtes: les pieds bondissaient de joie, le geste empressé ne suffisait plus, la voix l'accompagnait d'accens passionnés; le plaisir et le désir, confondus ensemble, se faisaient sentir à la fois: là fut enfin le vrai berceau des peuples; et du pur cristal des fontaines sortirent les premiers feux de l'amour. (*Essai,* p. 525)

There at the communal well is where the first ties were formed among families; there were the first rendezvous of the two sexes. Girls would come to seek water for the household, young men would come to water their herds. There eyes, accustomed to the same sights since infancy, began to see with increased pleasure. The heart is moved by these novel objects; an unknown attraction renders it less savage; it feels pleasure at not being alone. Imperceptibly, water becomes more necessary. The livestock become thirsty more often. One would arrive in haste and leave with regret. In that happy age when nothing marked the hours, nothing would oblige one to count them; the only measure of time would be the alternation of amusement and boredom. Under old oaks, conquerors of the years, an ardent youth will gradually lose its ferocity. Little by little they become less shy with each other. In trying to make themselves understood, they learned to explain themselves. There too, the original festivals developed. Feet skipped with joy, earnest gestures no longer sufficed, and were accompanied by an impassioned voice; pleasure and desire mingled and were felt together. There at last was the cradle of nations: from the pure crystal of the fountains flow the first fires of love.

Unlike the lone primitive, these young shepherds and maidens who meet at the well are caught up in the intersubjective relation that for Benveniste constitutes the core of linguistic exchange.

Rousseau, rather than carrying out an analysis of one couple, insists on a multiplicity of pairings that establishes this *prise de contact* between individuals as an event occurring many times and between many couples. In so doing, he underlines the well's generalized effect on the forms of social interaction. The multiplicity of responses, however, obeys a single form common to the experience of all: each pair of eyes and each impassioned heart reacts to the situation in the same way.

No doubt Rousseau's description of this scene includes a reciprocal, properly intersubjective moment during which each member of the pairs opens himself or herself to that redefinition by the other that Benveniste points to as the essence of linguistic exchange. For Rousseau, however, the implications of this intersubjective moment are entirely different. It is not the hallmark of a continuing interdependence concomitant with language but a limited, *prelinguistic* moment whose essential function is to overcome what precedes language: that same native fear that held the primitive at a safe distance from his fellows. The one sentence in Rousseau's description that refers explicitly to reciprocal action—"les uns avec les autres"—concerns only the couples' stepping beyond their almost animal-like uneasiness with any other human presence: "Une ardente jeunesse oubliait par degrés sa férocité: on s'apprivoisait peu à peu les uns avec les autres." The moment of intersubjectivity presented in this passage only sets the stage for an advance in expressivity that will itself take a different form. Instead of assuring a future, this fleeing moment of reciprocity obliterates a past.

After the impediment of natural ferocity has been removed, the first feasts take place around the communal well. For Rousseau, these festivities begin in dance, a language of bodily gesture that addresses itself to the sense of sight. The intense feeling triggered by this corporeal semiology initiates a desire for expression that pushes beyond the limits of gesture and demands the resources of voice as a more adequate form of self-expression. The ultimate importance of these festivities lies in their motivating man to acquire a new form of representation, a new language: "Le geste empressé ne suffisait plus, la voix l'accompagnait d'accens passionnés."

The affective intensity of the passions experienced by each individual loosens men's tongues, like an electric current finally animating a recalcitrant material. Contrasting these discoveries made around the well with the past they replace, Rousseau states: "Il n'y

avait là rien d'assez animé pour dénouer la langue, rien qui pût ar-
racher assez fréquemment les accens des passions ardentes pour
les tourner en institutions" (There would be nothing stimulating
enough in that to loosen the tongue, nothing to provoke accents
of ardent passion often enough to conventionalize them) (*Essai,*
p. 526). This transition from gesture to voice, although it occurs in
a collective festivity, nevertheless takes place, for each of the participants involved, as a resolutely individual experience of passion that
forces its way to expression—like the primitive's solitary use of the
word *giant.* In portraying this key moment, Rousseau uses a series
of three reflexives, establishing this process as one in which each individual subjectivity engages in self-directed experience: "en s'ef-
forçant de se faire entendre, on apprit à s'expliquer" (in trying to
make themselves understood, they learned to express themselves).

Even in this scene of lovers discovering their shared passion, a
scene Rousseau qualifies as the first acquisition of a truly socialized
language, the discovery takes place as an index of mental processes
that remain resolutely subjective. While these passions clearly have
another person as their object, Rousseau consistently presents them
as reflexive modifications of a self that is sufficient in its subjectivity.
Rousseau excludes from this moment any sense of man's entry into
language as a properly dialogic interdependence of subjectivities, in
which the self perceives itself as dependent for its place in discourse
on the other with whom it speaks. The individual's self-enclosed experience of a subjective passion, and it alone, pushes man toward
this new language of voice.

Rousseau's lovers experience their passion as the drive toward a
moment of pure declaration. Because "du pur cristal des fontaines
sortirent les premiers feux de l'amour," each participant struggles
toward a vocal representation adequate to the intensity of his or her
passion. The joy Rousseau describes here flows from the lovers'
shared experience, the simultaneity of one lover's voiced expression
and the other's answering swoon: "Le plaisir et le désir, confondus
ensemble, se faisaient sentir à la fois." Voice, once it has exteri-
orized this passion cosubstantial with the *I,* once it has communi-
cated its message, has no further function. The truth of passion
made manifest, the other has only to swoon in proof of its authenticity. Like a tool that has served its purpose and may now be cast
aside, the discovered voice remains closed to any temporality beyond that of a perfect present.

From Rousseau's statements on man's passage from gestural to vocal language emerges a concerted refusal of language that yields the speaker's identity to dialogic and dialectical redefinition through exchange with the other. In fact this refusal of mediation by the other is a leitmotif of the *Essay*. Rousseau finds a possible genesis of syllabic writing—the source of everything he most condemns in language—in the activities of those who have been redefined by the most promiscuous interplay of self and other: the traveling merchant peoples who sought in writing an instrument for regulating exchanges between a number of different linguistic communities. As when the Romans studied Greek or when any number of different language communities studied Hebrew, a vapid harmonization follows the introduction of accent and other diacritical marks into a language, degrading that native, melodic practice of the language that is unmediated by the knowledge of any other tongue.

This refusal of alienation explains why Rousseau's one explicit reference to a discursive relation structured as the mutual redefinition of an *I* and a *you* comes only in the last chapter of the *Essay*. For Rousseau, the intimate, interdependent, and always open-ended exchange of positions that characterizes a truly reciprocal use of the first and second persons is possible only in a society so vitiated by tyranny that all communication between individuals has become totally meaningless: "Les sociétés ont pris leur dernière forme: on n'y change plus rien qu'avec du canon et des écus; et comme on n'a plus rien à dire au peuple, sinon *donnez de l'argent,* on le dit avec des placards au coin des rues, ou des soldats dans les maisons. Il ne faut assembler personne pour cela: au contraire, il faut tenir les sujets épars; c'est la première maxime de la politique moderne" (Societies have assumed their final form: no longer is anything changed except by arms and cash. And since there is nothing to say to the people besides *give money,* it is said with placards on the streets or by soldiers in their homes. It is not necessary to assemble anyone for that. On the contrary, the subjects must be kept apart. That is the first maxim of modern politics) (*Essai,* p. 542). Within this context of universal submission to a single tyrant, the surviving vestiges of communication between individual slaves necessarily take the form of what Rousseau calls "*le bourdonnement des divans.*" Behind this image of huddled courtiers whispering together he asks us to see a society in which the addiction to false and debilitating luxuries— the scene takes place on a luxurious couch rather than in chains—

has blinded men to any goal of existence or language beyond the forging and betrayal, as the need arises, of hidden alliances. Life becomes a murky continuum of plots and counterplots carried out by fleeting groups of radically egotistical slaves, each of whom approaches the other only to maximize the power and privilege accorded him by their common tyrant: "Et qu'importe . . . de persuader le peuple, puisque ce n'est pas lui qui nomme aux bénéfices?" (And why . . . persuade the people since it is not they who dispense the benefices?) (*Essai*, p. 542).

□ □ □

Rousseau's condemnation of the *I–you* exchange, his refusal of the dialogic foundation of language, is in fact a function of his implicit but unswerving commitment to another, ideal form of communication. As a term adequate to the paradox represented by Rousseau's according primacy to the independent, self-sufficient speaker, I suggest *linguistic solipsism*. Solipsism, *solus ipse:* only the self, the self alone, myself alone, only to myself—this field of variants evokes the implicit utopia at work throughout Rousseau's delineations of his linguistic ideal.

The first properly transindividual form of such linguistic solipsism occurs, as we saw, during the scene at the well. The lover moves toward melodious voice to achieve the other-directed yet nondialogic expression of a subjective passion. Once the lover's song or poem has, as an index of passion, accomplished its purpose of self-expression, it neither expects nor awaits any linguistic response from the other to whom it is directed. Far from initiating any intersubjective redefinition of the self through the other, this exercise of voice leads instead to a fulfillment of desire in the beloved's swoon, the most adequate response to so eloquent an act of self-expression. The linguistic ideal of this golden age of human intercourse is that of solipsistic transition from an *I impassioned* to an *I expressed*.

In a second and more significant example of Rousseau's adherence to this ideal of linguistic solipsism, he discusses the situation of the individual who addresses himself not to one other person but to the collectivity, the community as a whole. At various points in the *Essay* Rousseau illustrates his claim that all languages as we know them have degenerated from a state of lost perfection. He points to various episodes, drawn either from antiquity or from descriptions of Oriental languages, that share common characteristics: a temporal or geographic distance from modern Europe and a constant reference to "speech situations" in which one individual addresses himself to and determines the actions of an entire group. These episodes, Rousseau insists, represent events that our own degraded languages prevent us from repeating or even understanding.

The first of these examples, one I will examine more closely in a later chapter, is taken from the biblical story of the Levite of Ephraim. Rousseau isolates for use in the *Essay* a single element of this story, the nonverbal message of the Levite's dispatching the pieces of his concubine's dismembered body to the twelve tribes of Israel. This action is pointed to as having the miraculous effect of unifying its audience in a unanimous desire to avenge the woman's rape and murder. Rousseau's reference to this biblical narrative opens with the single *I* of the Levite seeking to express himself to the collective *they* of the twelve tribes. The body as message elicits from each of the Israelites the recognition that, as a member of the community, he is as much a victim of this crime as the Levite himself. The collective *they*, in other words, is called upon to yield its multiple otherness to the Levite's redefinition of them as a unified group of individuals, all of whom are identical to the Levite as victim. The Levite's message establishes a new sense of the community as the divinely ordained instrument of vengeance. This optimal communication between the Levite and his nation takes place as each of those others making up the collective *they* finds himself redefined as one participant in a *we*, all of whose members now recognize themselves as identical to the *I* of the Levite who addresses them.

This same power of the single speaker to unify and mobilize the community again becomes paramount when, at the end of chapter 11, Rousseau makes his argument that Oriental languages are superior to European languages. "Le français, l'anglais, l'allemand, sont le langage privé des hommes qui s'entr'aident, qui raisonnent entre eux de sang-froid, ou de gens emportés qui se fâchent; mais les ministres des Dieux annonçant les mystères sacrés, les sages donnant des lois au peuple, les chefs entraînant la multitude, doivent parler arabe ou persan" (French, English, and German: each is a language private to a group of men who help each other, or who become angry. But the ministers of the Gods proclaiming sacred mysteries, wise men giving laws to their people, and leaders swaying the multitude, have to speak Arabic or Persian) (*Essai,* p. 528).

Rousseau's rationale for the superiority of the Orient's spoken languages, Arabic and Persian, over our own is their appropriateness to carry out what Georges Dumezil identifies, two centuries later, as the three functions that summarize society's duties in all Indo-European cultures.[6] The revelation of divine mysteries, the establishment of law, and the direction of military force (the three activities Rousseau alludes to in this passage) summarize, respectively, the community's organization of the sacred, of internal hierarchy and exchange, and of its protection from external threat. Significantly, Rousseau again approaches each of these functions from the perspective of the elected spokesman, the single *I* charged with enunciating a message that will ensure the community's carrying out the essential tasks: the minister, the sage, and the military chief. As with the Levite, Rousseau asks his reader to imagine these privileged individuals successfully addressing, now through verbal language, a collective *they* each will redefine as a community unified by a common faith, a common legislative ideal, and a common perception of menace as the single speaker enunciates it. Once again, each of these crucial acts of communication takes the form of a lone *I* addressing a collective *they,* all of whose members will ultimately be recast as a communal *we,* thanks to the identification of each with that speaking *I*.

Returning to Rousseau's condemnation of what he considered most evil, the *I–you* exchange in the servile hell of emasculated plotters, we see that it is made on the basis of the same ideal. He rejects the cowering whisperers because their very way of speaking opposes the ideal form realized only by languages whose acoustic properties make audible a message addressed by a single speaker to a large audience spread out over a great expanse: "Ce sont les langues sonores, prosodiques, harmonieuses, dont on distingue le discours de fort loin" (They are sonorous, prosodic, harmonious languages in which discourse can be understood from a great distance) (*Essai,* p. 542). These Oriental languages are, in other words, especially well suited to situations in which, as in Rousseau's preceding examples, one particularly persuasive, eloquent voice addresses the assembled society so that each listener, interiorizing the enunciated message, gains a new sense of self as a member of the community. For each listener, the regenerated *I* achieves its true identity in the *we* generated by the discourse of the single speaker.

The two situations Rousseau mentions in his closing chapter as counterexamples to the whisperings on a couch are likewise those of a general animating his troops and of a historian providing his listeners with an image of the community's collective identity over time: "Chez les anciens on se faisait entendre aisément au peuple sur la place publique; on y parlait tout un jour sans s'incommoder. Les généraux haranguaient leurs troupes; on les entendait, et ils ne s'épuisaient point. . . . Hérodote lisait son histoire aux peuples de la Grèce assemblés en plein air, et tout retentissait d'applaudissemens" (Among the ancients a speaker could easily make himself heard by the people assembled in the public place. One could speak for an entire day with no discomfort. Generals addressed their troops and they were understood without exhausting themselves. . . . Herodotus recited his history to the peoples of Greece assembled in the open air, and applause burst from everywhere) (*Essai*, pp. 542–43).

I have chosen the term *solipsism* to describe the ideal at work in these examples because each of them defines a successful community in which a single speaker persuades his audience to adopt his own position, perspective, and attitude on the message he enunciates. The speaking *I* is solipsistic not because he remains locked in some purely private and unshared subjectivity but because his message effectively makes his listeners his doubles. The solipsism at work here represents a *transitive* mode of communication: directed toward the other, acting upon the other, and transforming the other.

As paradoxical as *transitive solipsism* may appear, the term has the advantage of underlining the all-important fact that Rousseau's lone speakers, even as they address the community, remain outside it, free from any Benvenistian dependence on, or redefinition by, those to whom they speak. In each example considered, Rousseau portrays the situation of a single individual moving the entire community to some collective action. Implicit in this persuasiveness is the audience's conviction both of the speaker's sincerity and commitment to truth and of the impossibility of his either deceiving them or being mistaken in his statement.

At the center of his reflections on the abstract question of the suitability of language to communal action, Rousseau again asks, in another form, how we might imagine a discursive situation in which neither the sincerity of the speaker, nor the truth of what he says, nor its effect on those hearing it can be in doubt. The linguistic ideal at work in this essay corresponds to Rousseau's abiding dream of a truth capable of elaborating itself outside any threat of misinterpretation, misrepresentation, or distortion by the audience to which it is addressed.[7]

□   □   □

Something quite surprising happens in each of the examples Rousseau cites in this *Essay*. Only because the real possibility exists that the community will remain impiously indifferent to its creator, enslaved to an abusive authority, and incapable of defending itself from attack must the minister reveal the sacred mysteries, the sage institute just laws, and the general inspire his troops. To assume the importance Rousseau assigns the individual speakers responsible for their elimination, each of these possibilities must indeed have been a real alternative.

There is, in other words, a paradoxical disparity between the level of Rousseau's overall argument and the level of his supporting examples. Rousseau's intent in his argument is clearly to identify the various stages of the formal development of language and to delineate the implications of each for the community's political and social organization. We would expect, since all members of a given community share the same language, a certain homogeneity in the forms of discourse available to them. Each of Rousseau's examples demonstrates, however, the overwhelming preponderance of a speech act by one central figure whose utterance represents a major turning point in the community's history. In an essay that presents itself as an analysis of the formal properties of language, in other words, we find a surprisingly constant privileging of individual utterances that are somehow different from all others.

The ultimate object of Rousseau's fascination, this disparity seems to indicate, is not an abstract history of human communication approached from a disinterested and purely formal point of view. On the contrary, Rousseau grapples here with the distinctly personal and always more anguishing question how a particular individual might both enunciate his truth and guarantee its acceptance by the community as a whole. At the core of Rousseau's nostalgia for a lost language that assures the transparence of enunciated truth is his personal obsession with finding a means to force the recognition of his own word as truth. All his examples occur in societies already organized and already speaking, in which the symbolic, as law and as language, has long ago elaborated its systems of meaning, of exchange, and of signification. The Levite, the minister, the sage, and the general all address themselves to societies in which their statement of truth is a possible but certainly not an inevitable occurrence. Their interventions take the form of direct, delimited, and all-important utterances that speak through, yet at the same time redefine, an already existing symbolic order.

The paradox in Rousseau's linguistic ideal lies in the tacit accommodation of his position to those "handmaidens of deception," the mediating symbolic codes that must provide the context in which his ideal will operate. Rousseau's one additional demand, a demand reiterated in each of the examples he offers, is that the miraculous efficacy of the transitively solipsistic utterance be preserved—that the truth manifest itself and be recognized by one and all. In the very delineation of his linguistic ideal, Rousseau returns in a far more ambitious way to the same figure of the "disappearing code" we saw at work in his remarks on music and painting, on harmony and design.

□   □   □

My intention as I began this analysis of the *Essay on the Origin of Languages* was to investigate how Rousseau's relation to the symbolic manifests itself in his theoretical consideration of language as the most pervasive register of the symbolic. It becomes clear from this examination that Rousseau's linguistic theory elaborates itself on the basis of two distinct premises, one explicit, the other implicit, but each marked by its diametric opposition to the other.

On the one hand, Rousseau explicitly insists that language, in all its forms, is a secondary and ultimately disfiguring instrument created by man to express passions that existed before language. These passions occur as the subjective acts of a consciousness discovering itself in an unmediated relation to the object as object, that is, the object as a pure presence of the other. My analysis of the primitive's use of the words *giant* and *man,* as well as my contrasting of Rousseau's position with Benveniste's, has allowed me to examine the various corollaries of this explicit premise.

On the other hand, all the examples Rousseau points to as ideal moments of communication implicitly presuppose the existence of a symbolic order, a code, a law, and a language that, no matter how far back into history we recede, are already at work as a system to sustain the individual and to provide that individual with the only means he will ever have to signify his particular truth. As signs regulated by a system, these ideal utterances carry a hidden potential that Rousseau's examples must reject and deny: the terrifying threat that they might be lies. In a world already conceived in deception, Rousseau must elaborate the only vision of truth available to man.

Finally, then, Rousseau's vociferous rejection of language and writing as alienations from truth must be read as the preparation for and justification of an acceptance without which this anguished quest could never have begun. The ultimate form of Rousseau's linguistic ideal must be recognized as an instance of the symbolic capable, in spite of itself, of providing the double guarantee of solipsism: the guarantee that the speaker's words are an index of his feelings and the guarantee that his statement of truth will so move his audience that they will assume an attitude toward it identical to his own. The virulence of Rousseau's critique is not directed toward abolishing the symbolic, toward returning to some mute, unrepresented presence. The ideal informing Rousseau's *Essay* implies instead an imaginary doubling of the subject both in his act of representation and in the other's perception of that representation: I am what I say; and what I say is what the other believes.

Rousseau demands not that he step outside language but that he be recognized as speaking a language beyond language. His utterances, perceptible only through the already vitiated language of which they are instances, ask only to be received as the statements of a truth elaborated beyond the ruses and distortions of language.

4. The Freedom of Servitude

Mais restez le maître des jeunes maîtres.
—Rousseau, *Emile*

Taken from the work's closing paragraph, the quoted sentence summarizes Emile's final request of his esteemed tutor. Emile here addresses the one man who has scrupulously supervised every detail of his education, from the choice of a wet nurse to the designation of a bride who, as the text ends, will soon bear him a child.

It seems, when one thinks about it, a startling request on the part of someone groomed to personify independence and self-reliance. Even as he assumes the prerogatives of fatherhood, Emile subordinates his own authority over the child to the tutor's continuing authority over him. Speaking both for himself and for his bride, Emile closes this work inscribed under his name with a statement making the demand perfectly clear: "Conseillez-nous, gouvernez-nous, nous serons dociles: tant que je vivrai j'aurai besoin de vous. J'en ai plus besoin que jamais, maintenant que mes fonctions d'homme commencent. Vous avez rempli les vôtres; guidez-moi pour vous imiter, et reposez-vous: il en est tems" (Advise us and govern us. We shall be docile. As long as I live, I shall need you. I need you more than ever now that my functions as a man begin. You have fulfilled yours. Guide me so that I can imitate you. And take your rest. It is time).[1]

The reader of book 5, however, has been prepared for such docility. Once Emile has fallen in love with the young Sophie, his tutor abruptly tells him that he may marry her only after a two-year trip throughout Europe with the tutor. Emile's education, his preparation for marriage and fatherhood, will not be complete, the tutor insists, until he has examined firsthand Europe's political institutions. This study trip is important because, as Emile's first confrontation with a reality from which he has thus far been scrupulously protected, it will result in his profound and salutary distrust of all the illusions that sustain Europe's political systems. What is paradoxical about the skepticism Emile will acquire toward man's political delusions is that the pupil's independence of judgment has been, at every turn, studiously prepared and directed by the tutor. As his education draws to a close, Emile finds himself endowed with the singular freedom of someone who has been manipulated to a point where he is impervious to all further manipulation.

The whole history of Emile's careful formation by the tutor might be described as a mastery achieved through manipulation, an education carried out as a seduction. *Education* and *seduction* derive from the common root of *ducere:* to lead, to conduct. *Seduction,* with its prefix *se* meaning *to separate* or *to lead away from,* is certainly related to the pedagogy described in this work. More than anything else, Rousseau warns us again and again, an effective education demands that the tutor lead his pupil away from all the noxious influences of organized society. Like mastery and manipulation, education and seduction are synonyms in what they represent and antonyms in the value judgments they imply. The play of identity and difference between these terms takes us to the core of the ambiguous relation between authority and desire that sustains Rousseau's entire treatise on education.

□   □   □

The precariousness of Emile's freedom, its inevitable dependence on the education that sustains it, is a corollary to the tutor's position as master. The centrality of this master-slave model to the processes and goals of Emile's education is confirmed toward the end of book 5 when the tutor summarizes for Emile the ultimate result of the authority he has so long exercised over him: "Jusqu'ici tu n'étois libre qu'en apparence; tu n'avois que la liberté précaire d'un esclave à qui l'on n'a rien commandé. Maintenant sois libre en effet; apprends à devenir ton propre maitre; commande à ton coeur, ô Emile, et tu seras vertueux" (Up to now you were only apparently free. You had only the precarious freedom of a slave to whom nothing had been commanded. Now be truly free. Learn to become your own master. Command your own heart, Emile, and you will be virtuous) (*Emile,* 4 : 818). The precariousness of Emile's freedom, like that of all freedom sustained by education, is presented here as a corollary to the tutor's position as master. Should we wish to see in the tutor's use of the word *master* nothing more than an insignificant hyperbole for the many alternatives available to describe his relation to the pupil (the tutor as guide, protector, initiator, et cetera), this passage confirms the master-slave relation as a model relevant to both the processes and result of this education.

I call attention to this passage and its suggestion of a central metaphor for the education described in *Emile* because it provides a key phrase that functions both as a résumé of the successful education and as a definition of its goal: "Maintenant sois libre en effet; apprends à devenir ton propre maitre." If learning to be one's own master is the hallmark of the truly free man, then logically the ultimate acquisition of freedom must depend on, and dialectically define itself against, a prior and primordial perception of the self as slave and of the other as master.

The tutor's infinite discretion, his never having acted in such a way that Emile might feel himself compelled, poses a real problem for the completion of the education described here. From whom can Emile learn to become his own master when the tutor, the model master and the master model, has so scrupulously hidden from him all understanding of that imperium the pupil is now called upon to exercise over himself?

On the one hand, the tutor has scrupulously preserved for Emile the illusion that he acts outside all compulsion by any human agency. On the other, the tutor's explicit goal is to have exercised his authority so that he provides the model for his pupil's assuming a position of conscious mastery over himself.

□   □   □

In my earlier chapters, I tried to show how Rousseau's autobiographical, literary, and philosophical texts reveal a number of constants in the relation they assume between authority and desire. I spoke of them in terms of the individual's relation to what, because of the term's greater comprehensiveness, I called the symbolic. The ambiguities in Emile's "mastery" are important because they provide an ideal vehicle for extending my analysis to those specifically political texts in which the problem of the individual's relation to mastery, authority, and the symbolic becomes most explicit.

In *Emile*, Rousseau's extended consideration of how one individual might be prepared for an exemplary independence and self-mastery, we find most clearly stated the paradoxes and ambiguities that will reinscribe themselves at the core of the political writings. While the *Second Discourse* is imbued with a pessimism that extends to all forms of contemporary society and while the *Social Contract* prescribes a remedy applicable only to small and basically agrarian communities, *Emile*, because it is concerned with the education of one individual, represents the one alternative, the one possible ideal, available to modern man.

Looked at in this way, *Emile* is a key document confirming Rousseau's apparent optimism in the preface to *Narcisse,* where he states that man is not corrupted in his nature but by the effects of society on him. The secret of Emile's salvation, we remember, consists precisely in the tutor's insistence, up until their final study trip through the political inferno of contemporary Europe, that the pupil remain isolated from society's contaminating forces.

The thirty-page section of book 5 entitled "Des voyages" reads in great part like a severely abbreviated summary of Rousseau's *Institutions politiques,* the never-finished project he so long caressed and from which he finally separated the first part for publication under the title the *Social Contract.* Rousseau did insist that *Emile* and the *Institutions politiques* "font un tout complet"; [2] on the basis of that statement, the critic Otto Vossler has argued that the *Social Contract* might most profitably be read as a part of *Emile.* [3]

Such a reading, in spite of the elegant closure it establishes between the political and pedagogical writings, skirts a number of important problems. Emile's story, the destiny awaiting this perfectly educated man, clearly did not end for Rousseau with his final pledge of allegiance to the tutor. To the extent that we accept *Emile* as a response to the question of the alternatives available to an individual in a world whose political institutions are given over to dissimulation and corruption, we are obliged to include in our evaluation of that response a second text, a continuation of *Emile,* which Rousseau entitled *Emile et Sophie ou les solitaires.* Since we know that as early as 1762 Rousseau read to his friend Kirchberger a version of the two letters that make up this unfinished sequel, it is clear that he composed this text soon after *Emile* and that it represents a continuation of his struggle to deal with the problems at the core of the published work. *Les Solitaires* is one of the few indications we have of Emile's fate, the fate of a man whose ideal education led him inevitably away from the separate universe of his youth to contact with and devastation by the world of other men.

In insisting on the importance of this relatively short text (a first letter of thirty pages and a second, unfinished, letter of twelve), I am in no way disputing that Rousseau chose to publish *Emile* without this sequel and that he never completed *Les Solitaires* before his death in 1778. While these facts justify the decision made by most of Rousseau's modern editors to publish these pages as a separate work, they do not justify the claim that this sequel should be dismissed as irrelevant to the overall interpretation of the earlier text.

It is hardly surprising that Rousseau's critics have felt an enormous discomfort with a work that not only stops in midsentence but also has no fewer than three different but equally hypothetical endings.[4] I insist on its importance not out of regret for the melodramatic work that might have resulted had Rousseau completed it but because the very multiplicity of its endings, about which Rousseau thought even in the last months of his life, shows how long this project of finishing Emile's story continued to preoccupy him.[5]

Even the two letters Rousseau composed after finishing the main work suggest reasons for the systematic dismissal of this text. Any reader who has taken the tutor's self-assured didacticism at face value can only be discomforted by its embarrassing results for the star pupil. These two letters, written by Emile long after the events they recount, narrate what has happened to him since the marriage scene with which *Emile* ended. After the death of their second child, a daughter, Sophie fell into a lethargy that Emile set out to cure by leaving their rural solitude for the city. Once caught up in the corrupting influence of Paris, Sophie and Emile soon suffer the inevitable. Sophie, tricked into adultery by a woman jealous of her innocence, admits her sin to Emile. His world devastated by her revelation, Emile falls to pieces.

The standard interpretation of this letter, first offered by the editors Moultou and Du Peyrou in 1781, is that this unfortunate turn of events is the occasion for Emile's passage from untried innocence to tempered virtue. Hardened by adversity, Emile finds his passive apprenticeship to goodness transformed into unflinching virtue: "En mettant Emile aux prises avec la fortune, en le plaçant dans une suite de situations effrayantes, que le mortel le plus intrépide n'envisageroit pas sans frémir, il vouloit montrer que les principes dont il fut nourri depuis sa naissance, pouvoient seuls l'élever au-dessus de ces situations" (In surrendering Emile to misfortune, in placing him in a series of horrifying situations that even the most intrepid mortal could not face without shuddering, Rousseau wished to show that only those principles with which Emile had been nourished since birth could lift him above his fate).[6]

This interpretation overlooks the newly virtuous Emile's first act, which is to adopt, with no lessening of his claims to rectitude, a position that flies in the face of the overarching premise of the main text: the parent-tutor's sacred responsibility for the education of the child. Abandoning Sophie and his son, which becomes for Emile the one morally correct course of action, carries the added premium of edifying the fallen spouse in a way indistinguishable from revenge: "Qu'il lui reste seul pour ma vengeance; que chaque jour de sa vie il rappelle à l'infidelle le bonheur dont il fut le gage et l'époux qu'elle s'est ôté" (Let him remain with her as my vengeance. Let every day of his life recall to that unfaithful woman both the happiness of which he was the fruit and the spouse she has lost).[7]

The second letter is likewise a source of difficulty for Rousseau's critics. Here the problem arises from the sequel's treatment of individual liberty. While the defense and illustration of liberty are themes that run throughout Rousseau's works, the impassioned reader cannot help feeling uneasy at the dexterity with which Rousseau accommodates Emile's liberty to his status as a slave. In suggesting that *Emile,* when read through *Les Solitaires,* reveals a hidden dimension of Rousseau's vision of individual liberty, I am asking only that the reader remain open to the possibility that there were reasons why, on the one hand, Rousseau felt obliged to write so unexpected a sequel to *Emile* and why, on the other, he chose never to publish it.

□ □ □

Les Solitaires is, I would argue, a text far more essential to the central concerns of *Emile* than the rocambolesque *Afrikareise* to which it is often reduced. This period of Emile's real, as opposed to metaphoric, enslavement must be seen not as Rousseau's indulgence in some shoddy exoticism, but as his decision to offer the ultimate and inevitable stage of Emile's education as a free man, when the true slave finally becomes his own true master.

Unlike the tutor's suave manipulations, the iron rule of the Algerian slave driver provides the pupil with a vision of himself as the object of, and therefore as someone definable against, the most openly exercised control and rule. The Dey of Algiers and his lieutenants do nothing more inhuman to Emile than continue, but now in a straightforward and imperative mode, the treatment he had so long received from his devoted tutor. The only real change is that these new masters dispense with the well-intentioned charades that denied the pupil any real understanding of his situation. For this reason Emile's second letter makes the otherwise astonishing claim (and implicit reproach) that he has learned more about true freedom from these African slave masters than he had from all his tutor's elegant philosophizing: "Le tems de ma servitude fut celui de mon régne, et jamais je n'eus tant d'autorité sur moi que quand je portai les fers des barbares. Soumis à leurs passions sans les partager, j'appris à mieux connoitre les miennes. Leurs écarts furent pour moi des instructions plus vives que n'avoient été vos leçons, et je fis sous ces rudes maitres un cours de Philosophie encore plus utile que celui que j'avois fait près de vous" (The period of my servitude was that of my reign, and never did I have greater authority over myself than when I wore the irons of those barbarians. Subject to their passions but not sharing them, I learned to better know my own. Their extravagances were for me a more vivid instruction than your lessons, and I followed under those rude masters a course of philosophy even more useful than the one I took under your guidance) (*Les Solitaires,* 4:917).

In addition to this discovery of true freedom, a number of resonant echoes between *Emile* and its sequel establish the second work as effectively completing the first. Early in book 4 the tutor explains how the educator must handle the pupil newly arrived at the state of puberty. The essential thing here, the tutor insists, is to mold this new dimension of sexualized affectivity so that the attachment to one individual, which might easily become excessive, is redirected and expanded, becoming the basis of an attachment to all mankind. This ideal hardly seems to have been achieved in the final pages of *Emile.* What we find there is a bucolic vignette, in which Emile and Sophie consolidate their withdrawal from society in a conjugal hermitry.

To see this concern with teaching the pupil to love the whole of mankind as something more than a fleeting aside on Rousseau's part, abandoned in favor of the couple's comfortable eschewal of human folly, the reader must look beyond *Emile* to the second letter of *Les Solitaires:* "En rompant les noeuds qui m'attachoient à mon pays je l'étendois sur toute la terre, et j'en devenois d'autant plus homme en cessant d'être Citoyen" (In breaking the ties that bound me to my country, I extended them to the entire world. I became more a man as I ceased to be a citizen) (*Les Solitaires,* 4:912).

Again, because the tutor has insisted on the inherent illusion of all sexualized desire, *Emile*'s ending provides an incomplete and unsatisfying resolution. The tutor's entire psychology of desire is based on the premise that the beloved object exists only in the lover's mind. The actual person of the beloved is, in an almost Proustian sense, nothing more than a temporary and inevitably disappointing support for the fictive adornments projected by the lover's desire. The passage of time and continued possession will lead only to disillusion: "Qu'est-ce que le véritable amour lui-même, si ce n'est chimére, mensonge, illusion? On aime bien plus l'image qu'on se fait que l'objet auquel on l'applique. Si l'on voyoit ce qu'on aime exactement tel qu'il est il n'y auroit plus d'amour sur la terre" (What is true love itself if it is not a chimera, lie, and illusion? We love far more the image we make for ourselves than we love the object to which we apply it. If we saw what we love exactly as it is, there would be no more love on earth) (*Emile,* 4:656). Given this law of desire, one we have already seen dictating Julie's renunciation of Saint-Preux, it is difficult to accept *Emile's* ending as an authentic closure. We cannot, so long as we remember these statements, hypothesize Emile and Sophie's future as the uninterrupted conjugal bliss the novel's ending seems to imply. Sophie's fall from grace and Emile's despair, the subject matter of *Les Solitaires,* are already inscribed in *Emile's* given.

Perhaps the most intriguing echo of *Emile* in *Les Solitaires* results not so much from their thematic coherence as from their parallel and in many ways complementary treatment of a hidden natural force: magnetism. It is not surprising that, in elaborating his pedagogy, Rousseau should allude to the phenomenon of magnetism. It represents, each time it appears, a hidden yet irresistible force manipulated to create an illusion of mastery. Magnetism in this sense reconciles the otherwise dialectical relationship of transparency and obstruction that Starobinski has convincingly shown to be at work throughout Rousseau's writings. Magnetism is the unique exception to the opposition between these two terms. Floating in a basin at the fair, the wax duck with its hidden magnet creates the illusion that it follows the piece of bread molded around the bit of iron in the *bateleur's* hand precisely because the apparent obstacles of wax and dough in no way impede the magnetic attraction, which operates in a transparency untroubled by the materials masking it. At the same time, in a way more directly related to the pedagogical enterprise itself, the hidden force of magnetism, exercising its power through its various disguises, can be read as an archetype for the invisible patterns of manipulation through which the tutor controls his pupil's every act. In fact, only when we accept Emile's visit to the fair and the lesson he learns there as a key metaphor for the educational process can we account for the abruptly emphatic tone with which Rousseau ends that section of the narrative.

One day, as the story is told in book 3, Emile and his tutor go to the fair, where they come upon a juggler who ends his act with the duck-and-bread trick described above. Since, as it happens, Emile and his tutor have recently been conducting experiments on the magnetic attractions of various metals, Emile quickly understands that the juggler's gimmick is nothing more than a simple application of this natural phenomenon. That same evening a self-satisfied Emile returns to the fair with his own carefully prepared piece of bread and, stepping up to the basin, steals the show from the unsuspecting juggler. The showman, once he has regained his composure, suggests that the boy return the next day and, for the benefit of all his friends, repeat this demonstration of his marvelous powers. Emile's pride grows until that sad moment when, before all, the devious duck turns tail and speeds away from the bread he offers. The juggler, regaining his position of mastery, asks Emile if he might borrow his piece of bread; and so long as he holds it, the duck swims directly toward it. Even after the juggler, in full view of his audience, has disapprovingly removed the hidden piece of metal, the duck still goes after the bread. A series of similar tricks follows, adding up to the astonished pupil's total humiliation.

The following day the juggler visits Emile's house. He explains to the boy how he did the new version of his trick with the help of a small child, hidden under the basin, who controlled the duck's movements with a strong magnet. More important, however, he sternly reprimands Emile for his proud and cruel mistreatment of a poor vagabond who has done nothing more than earn his daily bread with the one harmless skill he possesses. Emile, now properly contrite, returns again to the fair and applauds the *bateleur-Socrate* from whom he has learned so valuable a lesson.

As Emile and his tutor stand together before the basin, the stakes, as revealed in the tutor's language, begin to mount: "Il [the juggler] fait ses tours comme à l'ordinaire, mais il s'amuse et se complaît longtems à celui du canard en nous regardant souvent d'un air assés fier. Nous savons tout et nous ne soufflons pas. *Si mon élève osoit seulement ouvrir la bouche ce seroit un enfant à écraser*"

(The juggler does his tricks as usual, but he entertains and indulges himself for a long time with the duck trick while looking often at us with a quite proud air. We know everything, but we don't breathe a word. *If my pupil dared so much as to open his mouth, he would deserve to be annihilated*) (*Emile*, 4:440; italics mine). As in the crescendo ending of the *Confessions*—"Quiconque . . . pourra me croire un malhonnête homme est lui-même un homme à étouffer" (Whoever . . . can believe me a dishonorable man is a man who deserves to be stifled)[8]—all the mountains of the earth are summoned to fall on the hapless pupil should he somehow not have gotten the point.

The lesson Emile must learn from this episode is the danger of vanity: "Que de leçons dans une seule! Que de suites mortifiantes attire le prémier mouvement de vanité! Jeune maitre, épiez ce prémier mouvement avec soin. Si vous savez en faire sortir ainsi l'humiliation, les disgraces, soyez sûr qu'il n'en reviendra de longtems un second. . . . et le tout pour nous faire une boussole" (How many lessons in this one! How many mortifying consequences are attracted by this first movement of vanity! Young master, spy out this first movement with care. If you know how to make humiliation and disgrace arise from it, be sure that a second movement will not come for a long time. . . . and all for the sake of making ourselves a compass) (*Emile*, 4:440).

Significantly enough, the apparently arbitrary reference with which the long episode ends—"le tout pour nous faire une boussole"—projects the reader to the second appearance of magnetism as a force determining Emile's destiny. Emile becomes a slave in Algiers because the ship on which he has taken passage as a sailor is manipulated by a similar magnetic illusion. The ship, instead of remaining in the safe waters of the French and Italian coasts on the way from Marseilles to Naples, sails directly to a point off the Algerian coast where it is intercepted by Barbary pirates. This happens because the renegade captain, a man secretly in the pirates' pay, has hidden a magnet on the bridge; even when the compass indicates a course of south-southeast, the ship is in fact moving south-southwest.

By the time the pirates intercept the ship, however, Emile is a changed man. Once he has discovered the trick and understood the captain's plan to sell the passengers and crew for a share of the ransom, he acts with the calm strength of a man in complete command of himself. Approaching the captain, Emile whispers in his ear that if they are taken by the pirates, the captain will pay with his life. Here Emile gives up his role as the always malleable dupe to manipulations that somehow contribute to his greater good and assumes complete responsibility for his fate. This resolute and decisive action reveals a new dimension of response to the whole series of tutors, jugglers, and captains who with good, bad, or indifferent intentions have led him to his present state.

Emile's act of justice, his beheading of the renegade captain with a single saber stroke, is carried out in full view of the pirates as they board the ship. Emile follows this apparently suicidal rebellion against one master, however, with an immediate submission to the new master, the new order and law represented by the Barbary pirates. The only condition of Emile's surrender is that he be recognized as having acted in the name of justice: "A l'instant, voyant le Chef des barbaresques venir impétueusement à moi, je l'attendis de pied ferme, et lui présentant le sabre par la poignée: *tien, Capitaine,* lui dis-je en langue franque, *je viens de faire justice; tu peux la faire à ton tour.* Il prit le sabre, il le leva sur ma tête; j'attendis le coup en silence: il sourit, et, me tendant la main, il défendit qu'on me mit aux fers avec les autres, mais il ne me parla point de l'expédition qu'il m'avoit vu faire; ce qui me confirma qu'il en savoit assez la raison" (In that instant, seeing the leader of the pirates closing in on me, I drew myself up and extended my saber to him hilt first. "So, Captain," I said to him in the lingua franca, "I have just executed justice. Now it is your turn." He took the saber and held it over my head. I awaited the blow in silence. He smiled and, extending his hand to me, forbade that I be put in irons with the others. He said nothing about what he had seen me do, which convinced me that he knew I had acted correctly) (*Les Solitaires,* 4:916).

Magnetism, the action of a hidden force, first manifests itself in Emile's life as the occasion of an all-important lesson on the dangers of vanity. What Emile learned at the fairground was that pride in his own knowledge might lead him to act with callous indifference to the effects of his actions on others who, unlike himself, depend on the limited skills they exercise in society. Much later, in the sequel's second letter, this same force draws Emile into a situation in which he demonstrates how well he has learned that lesson. During his captivity in Algiers, Emile's conduct is elaborately contrasted with that of two knights of Malta, the only two other characters developed as individuals in the sequel. Skilled in Latin and military tactics, they are paralyzed by their pride of rank, by their obsessive commitment to a definition of self through skills that, given their enslavement, represent pure vanity. Unlike Emile, who in this period of servitude discovers his true liberty, these two vain knights become, as Emile describes them, "moins que rien."

As the sequel to *Emile, Les Solitaires* reveals the fragility of Rousseau's attempt to appropriate to himself, and to coincide with, the voice of the master. Ultimately, it seems, he must adopt another voice, a radically different voice: that of the pupil-as-victim, the victim of even that best-intentioned care so lavishly heaped on him. As he portrays himself in the sequel, Emile is not only a victim but an eminently meritorious victim. His muted struggle against all that has been done for him transforms the letters to his tutor into a discourse that hovers between a plea to the master and an implicit inculpation of that master.

□ □ □

The ambivalent feelings toward the tutor revealed in Emile's last testament should come as no surprise. Numerous critics have noted that the tutor's basic idea of education, the pedagogue's approach to his pupil, comes uncomfortably close to a minutely organized and vigilantly executed conspiracy. At every moment of Emile's life, the tutor is there watching and counseling, anticipating and controlling.

Emile's education lends itself to a comparison with conspiracy because the tutor readily enlists and carefully prepares any number of third parties to act in the various morality plays he stages for his pupil's edification. Real people may step onto this stage, but only as characters whose every line has been dictated by the omniscient tutor's script. Robert, the gardener, puts in a superb cameo in the Parable of the Beans and Melons. All the passersby on a busy street have been assigned their parts should the child's tendency toward domestic tyranny make the timing of his daily outings a subject of dispute.

The cardinal rule of any pedagogy worthy of the name demands that, as in Julie's garden, the manipulating hand everywhere erase the traces of its intervention. The child must never suspect the constant effort being made to control every element of his universe. The tutor's imperatives, it is made clear, must always cloak themselves in necessity. Since the young pupil cannot distinguish between the forbidden and the impossible, the tutor must disguise the first as the second: "On l'enchaîne, on le pousse, on le retient avec le seul lien de la necessité sans qu'il en murmure" (You may fetter him, prod him, and restrain him without any protest so long as you do so in the name of necessity) (*Emile,* 4:321).

□   □   □

There is little doubt that as he wrote *Emile* Rousseau knew well what he was saying. A child's education, Rousseau insists, can be assured only when, in complete lucidity, we exercise a correct and judicious control over his actions. Rousseau remains unperturbed by objections to the tutor's easy assumption of conspiratorial postures because the potential liabilities of this control will be more than adequately compensated. An effective education, Rousseau states over and over again, must take place in stages: stages corresponding to the child's physical and mental development, stages that may be postponed or anticipated only at great risk to the pupil's ultimate well-being. Yes, up to a certain point, education may be a tutor's plot. But there comes an all-important moment when the effects of such deception are redefined by their positive contribution to the child's welfare. This moment, an antidote to all the possible poisons of the past, occurs as a carefully prepared revelation. It involves the disclosure to the child of everything the tutor has previously held hidden. It is a moment that arrives during puberty.

As described in book 4, puberty is a time of crucial and counterbalancing adjustments. As Emile undergoes his potentially dangerous adjustment to a burgeoning sexuality, so also the tutor must adjust every aspect of his relation to his pupil. In the complementarity of these adjustments to authority (the natural authority of Emile's maturing body and the arbitrary authority of the tutor's continuing pedagogy) and in their effect on the pupil's experience of his newly autonomous consciousness, we begin to see not only why *Emile*'s sequel was written as it was but also how the outcome proposed there—the necessary accommodation of freedom to authority—presupposes an ideal at work in the political texts.

The tutor's first task in approaching the potential problems of puberty is to present his pupil with a "full accounting" both of his past education and his present situation. Everything is revealed. The master's authority, wielded until this moment by reason of the pupil's weakness, must now be validated by the adolescent's free choice. Emile, overcome with feelings of gratitude for everything the tutor tells him, responds in a way that establishes a metaphor for the act of social allegiance that has always been perceived as the critical interpretive problem of the *Social Contract:* "Défendez-moi de tous les ennemis qui m'assiégent, et surtout de ceux que je porte avec moi et qui me trahissent; veillez sur votre ouvrage, afin qu'il demeure digne de vous. Je veux obéir à vos loix, je le veux toujours, c'est ma volonté constante; si jamais je vous desobéis ce sera malgré moi; rendez-moi libre en me protégeant contre mes passions qui me font violence; empêchez-moi d'être leur esclave et forcez-moi d'être mon propre maitre en n'obéïsant point à mes sens, mais à ma raison" (Defend me from all the enemies who besiege me, and especially from those whom I carry within myself and who betray me. Watch over your work that it remains worthy of you. I want to obey your laws, I want to do so always. This is my steadfast wish. If ever I disobey you, it will be in spite of myself. Make me free by protecting me from my passions. Prevent me from being their slave; force me to be my own master and to obey not my senses but my reason) (*Emile*, 4:651−52).

This image of the child who, presented with an exact accounting of the past, makes the fully conscious decision to exist as an incarnation of the paternal ideal transcribes in the tutor-pupil relation the more generalized societal act of allegiance Rousseau defines as the essence of the social contract. The carefully reasoned alignment of the individual's *volonté particulière* to the collective *volonté générale* is for Rousseau the indispensable act that transforms man into citizen. The declared intentions in Emile's affirmation of filial loyalty are all corollaries to the attitudes motivating the true citizen: in exchange for allegiance, he asks protection, but, above all, protection from the self as the potential seat of desires preferring the individual over the collective good. Once and forever Emile, like the citizen, renounces all those inordinate, unbridled, and potentially destructive mirages of a self imagined apart from or in opposition to the community. Should he ever, in a moment of weakness, surrender to such passions, he asks only that he be compelled to return to the true freedom of reason.

Emile's response is important because, as a central moment in the story of pupil and tutor, child and paternal order, individual and symbolic, it reveals so profound a similarity between the ideals informing Rousseau's pedagogical and political works that each might be read as a version of the other.

The importance of this passage and its disturbing implications for a certain reading of Rousseau's political works cannot be minimized. Emile pleads with his tutor to protect him from himself, to watch over and control him so that he can avoid the dreaded fate of becoming a slave to his own passions.

Emile's most important encounter with the dangers of passion comes as he first meets his beloved Sophie: "Il s'agit d'un jeune homme dont c'est ici, non seulement le prémier amour, mais la prémiére passion de toute espéce; que de cette passion, l'unique, peut-être, qu'il sentira vivement dans toute sa vie, dépend la derniére forme que doit prendre son caractére. Ses maniéres de penser, ses sentimens, ses gouts fixés par une passion durable vont acquérir une consistance qui ne leur permettra plus de s'altérer" (I am dealing here with a young man for whom this is not only his first love, but his first passion of any kind. On this passion, perhaps the only one he will feel intensely in his whole life, depends the final form his character is going to take. Once fixed by a durable passion, his way of thinking, his sentiments, and his tastes are going to acquire a consistency which will no longer permit them to deteriorate) (*Emile*, 4:778).

Rousseau's insistence on both the axial role of this first passion and its relation to the tutor's exercise of reason brings into focus one of the most puzzling aspects of Emile's adjustment to puberty. How, we might ask, can the interiorizing of a paternal superego I referred to in discussing the tutor's "full accounting" apply to a work in which childhood is characterized by the complete absence of any maternal figure? In Emile's confrontation with the paternal/tutorial/symbolic order, at least from his point of view, no maternal object of desire is disputed. No moment of paternally enforced eviction establishes Emile's consciousness in opposition to the father/tutor as a metonymy of symbolic authority. If Emile's education, or at least that part of it described in the main text, is successful, a large part of its success might be assigned not so much to the astuteness of the tutor's pedagogy as to the absence of any maternal object, whose loss constitutes a conflictual starting point for all tutorial interventions.

Puberty comes not as a rekindling of embers long smoldering under the ashes of repressed desire but as vulnerability, the discovery of a desire that is dangerous only because it is so easily misdirected. Sexual desire enters this text not as a resurrection of the past but as the utilitarian anticipation of a future defined by death:

"Le vrai moment de la nature arrive enfin, il faut qu'il arrive. Puisqu'il faut que l'homme meure, il faut qu'il se reproduise, afin que l'espéce dure et que l'ordre du monde soit conservé" (The true moment of nature comes at last. It must come. Since man must die, he must reproduce in order that the species may endure and the order of the world be preserved) (*Emile*, 4 : 639).

At the moment when passion, in the form of sexual desire, might pose a threat to Emile's continuing education, the tutor becomes a subliminal pornographer, flashing before his pupil's mind images that both excite and direct his desire: "En lui peignant la maitresse que je lui destine, imaginez si je saurai m'en faire écouter; si je saurai lui rendre agréables et chéres les qualités qu'il doit aimer; si je saurai disposer tous ses sentimens à ce qu'il doit rechercher ou fuir? Il faut que je sois le plus maladroit des hommes si je ne le rends d'avance passionné sans savoir de qui" (Imagine whether I shall know how to get his attention when I depict the beloved whom I destine him for. Imagine whether I shall know how to make agreeable and dear to him the qualities he ought to love, whether I shall know how to make all his sentiments properly disposed with respect to what he ought to seek or flee. I would have to be the clumsiest of men not to be able to make him passionate in advance of his knowing about whom) (*Emile*, 4 : 656). Oblivious to the forces determining the pathways of his desire, Emile is dispatched on a quest whose goal will be valorized only as it corresponds to this ideal so carefully molded by the tutor.

The tutor predetermines Emile's feminine ideal with the highest moral intent. The imposed ideal will, on the one hand, have the happily prophylactic effect of holding the pupil safe from the dangerous charms of all women but one.[9] On the other hand, as the instrument of a carefully calibrated sexual orthopedics, this ideal, instead of being conventionally perfect, will be marked by imperfections chosen to delightfully correct those of the pupil. In so deftly molding Emile's feminine ideal and in giving her the hypothetical name of "Sophie," the tutor effectively programs his pupil as a Manchurian Candidate of desire, ready to be activated as soon as he happens into the right farmhouse.[10]

Given his careful preparation of Emile's desire, it is not surprising that when his love story actually begins, the tutor should continue to play an important role. There is, in fact, something profoundly ambiguous about the whole narrative sequence of book 5, from

Emile and Sophie's first meeting to their engagement on the eve of Emile's study trip. On the one hand, this section is the most traditionally romanesque of the entire novel: for the first time we leave the abstract, nonconflictual chronology of a pedagogical practice that spans over twenty years to follow a precise, day-to-day sequence of events in which wishes are expressed, obstacles encountered, and solutions found. On the other hand, one could hardly imagine a love story with less suspense and fewer surprises than that of these two beings who discover, each in the other, the person to whom their entire pasts have rigorously directed them. The real interest of this sequence lies not so much in whether Emile and Sophie fall in love as in how the tutor mediates and remains at the center of the lovers' relationship.

When Emile first hears Sophie's name, his reflex amid the psychological disarray that word triggers is to rivet his attention on the tutor as someone who holds the answer to the question of his desire: "Il me regarde inquiet et troublé; ses yeux me font à la fois cent questions, cent reproches. Il semble me dire à chaque regard: guidez-moi tandis qu'il est tems; si mon coeur se livre et se trompe, je n'en reviendrai de me jours" (Uneasy and troubled, he looks at me. His eyes put a hundred questions to me and make a hundred reproaches all at once. He seems to say to me with each glance: "Guide me while there is time. If my heart yields and is mistaken, I shall never recover all of my days") (*Emile*, 4:776). To the extent that Emile can experience a desire he recognizes as his own, it must be doubled by a parallel desire on the part of the tutor: "Déja Sophie lui paroit trop estimable pour qu'il ne soit pas sur de me la faire aimer" (Already Sophie appears too estimable for him not to be sure of making me love her) (*Emile*, 4:778).

It is not surprising that since Emile's desire can exist only as a mirror image of the tutor's, Sophie should embark on a seduction of the tutor. Speaking affectionately to him, always careful to please him, Sophie expresses a constant solicitude for the all-important model. The tutor is correct when he assumes that the difficult first conversation between Sophie and Emile during the family's afternoon walk will have no subject other than himself.

Sophie and Emile's entire courtship will be played out as a children's plot to seduce the master—and this with a complexity of motivation as yet unsuspected by the young conspirators: "Je comprends qu'Emile lui a parlé de moi; on diroit qu'ils ont déja

complotté de me gagner: il n'en est rien pourtant, et Sophie elle-
même ne se gagne pas si vite. Il aura peut-être plus besoin de ma
faveur auprès d'elle que de la sienne auprès de moi" (I understand
that Emile has spoken to her about me. One would say they have
already plotted to win me over. Nothing of the kind has happened,
however, and Sophie herself is not won over so quickly. He will perhaps need my favor with her more than hers with me) (*Emile*,
4:785). Emile, meeting resistance on Sophie's part (her misgivings
about the disparity between their fortunes), counters it by pleading
for the intervention of that all-powerful version of himself situated
at the apex of the triangle linking the three parties: "Vous qu'elle
honore, vous qu'elle aime et qu'elle n'osera faire taire, parlez, faites-
la parler; servez votre ami, couronez votre ouvrage; ne rendez pas
vos soins funestes à votre élève: ah! ce qu'il tient de vous fera sa
misere, si vous n'achevez son bonheur" (You, whom she honors, you
whom she loves and whom she would not dare to silence, speak,
and make her speak. Serve your friend. Crown your work. Do not
make all that care fatal to your pupil. Ah, what he has gotten from
you will cause his misery if you do not complete his happiness)
(*Emile*, 4:787).

The actual process of this courtship—it follows a scenario that
Rousseau might have imagined for a less suicidal Anet, had he but
accepted the starring role offered him by the young Jean-Jacques's
unpossessive adoration of Madame de Warens—generates an affective paradise in which all three parties draw maximum pleasure
from oscillating between the ambiguities of their respective positions. The tutor, thanks to his continued mediation, finds himself at
the confluence of two distinct sources of joy: "Me voila donc le con-
fident de mes deux bonnes gens et le médiateur de leurs amours! . . .
cet emploi ne laisse pas d'avoir ses agrémens: je ne suis pas mal venu
dans la maison; l'on s'y fie à moi du soin d'y tenir les amans dans
l'ordre: Emile toujours tremblant de me déplaire ne fut jamais si
docile. La petite personne m'accable d'amitiés dont je ne suis pas la
dupe" (Now I am the confidant of my two good young people and
the mediator of their loves! . . . This employment does not fail to
have its agreeable aspects: I am not unwelcome in the house. Emile,
who is constantly trembling for fear of displeasing me, was never so
docile. The little girl overwhelms me with a friendliness by which I
am not deceived) (*Emile*, 4:788–89). For Sophie, the presence of
so discreet an intermediary allows an ideal reconciliation of affec-

tion with decorum. Using the tutor as her go-between, she can afford herself the pleasure of voicing feelings for Emile that she would blush at revealing to him directly. And, finally, Emile, an Eternal Husband well before marriage, discovers that even the most direct contact with his beloved never carries with it the same anxious intensity as that mediated by the tutor in his role as model and double: "Il se console quand elle refuse son bras à la promenade et que c'est pour lui préférer le mien. Il s'éloigne sans murmure en me serrant la main et me disant tout bas de la voix et de l'oeil: ami, parlez pour moi. Il nous suit des yeux avec intérêt. Il tâche de lire nos sentimens sur nos visages et d'interpréter nos discours par nos gestes: il sait que rien de ce qui se dit entre nous ne lui est indifferent" (When she refuses his arm in walking, he consoles himself with the fact that it is to prefer mine to his. He leaves without complaint, grasping my hand, and saying softly to me with his eyes as well as his voice, "Friend, speak for me." His eyes follow us with interest. He tries to interpret our speeches by our gestures. He knows that nothing of what is said between us is inconsequential for him) (*Emile*, 4:789).

Throughout this love story paternal figures initiate, direct, and approve every act of desire as it elects its object. The emotional intensity of Emile and Sophie's first encounter (even before he learns her name) arises from Emile's reaction to the father's narrative of his and his wife's mutual devotion in adversity. Moved to tears by that story, Emile takes their hands in his and squeezes them convulsively. Meanwhile, these actions, which evoke Telemachus's reaction to the misadventures of Philoctetus, allow Sophie to identify Emile with her own masculine ideal as her father has carefully implanted it.

Given this overwhelming preponderance of parental and tutorial mediation, it comes as no surprise either that the young husband should implore the tutor to remain with them or that once the tutor has departed—once we have entered the period narrated by *Les Solitaires*—Emile and Sophie's desire, as well as their marriage, becomes part of a lost past.

Emile's passage through puberty allows us to see an intriguing parallel between a desire that can survive only so long as it imitates its model and the tutor's demand that his pupil achieve the very liberty and self-determination that his entire pedagogy has compromised. The parallelism between the problem of desire and the problem of liberty is reflected in the two separate letters Rousseau composed for the sequel to *Emile,* the story of the pupil separated from his tutor, the first narrating the sad truth that desire must be mediated by a third party and the second narrating the equally sad truth that liberty must accommodate servitude. I have argued for the importance of this sequel to the reading of *Emile* because it forces us to confront the interdependence of the passional and the political, the sexual and the social.

The first of the two letters making up *Les Solitaires,* the story of Sophie's infidelity and Emile's exile, recounts the transformation of Emile's vision of liberty into one of absolute negativity. Obsessed with the past and all he has lost, Emile sees freedom as little more than resignation to his status as someone with nothing more to lose. His becomes the classically stoic posture defining life as a series of radical beginnings. In ending, each day dies, leaving the future undetermined by the past.

As Emile moves away from his past, as we proceed to the second letter, a new tone appears. Emile's exercise of freedom becomes less a frantic denegation of his past than a free-flowing acceptance of the present. Because he carries in him all that he expects of life, each new day dawns as a fresh discovery of liberty.

Against the background of this newly discovered self-sufficiency, Emile's condition is abruptly redefined by his capture and sale as a slave in Algiers. This apparent absence of all freedom, this encounter with a mastery far more devastating than that exercised by the tutor, as we saw earlier, affords him his ultimate lesson in the true nature of liberty. Emile's two key statements about his captivity, "Je suis plus libre qu'auparavant" (I am freer now than before) (*Les Solitaires,* 4:916) and "Le tems de ma servitude fut celui de mon régne" (The period of my servitude was that of my reign) (*Les Solitaires,* 4:917), provide the introduction and conclusion to the carefully reasoned argument he offers to substantiate this, to say the least, provocative interpretation of his situation. He bases his argument on the premise that man, by definition, is born a slave to the physical laws of nature. To the brute physicality of, for instance, a falling boulder, human agencies of oppression add nothing more than a quantitative intensification of the servitude inherent in the human condition.

That a defined other exercises his oppression over Emile does not, however, have only negative consequences. Emile, like all men, is vulnerable to human passions. His own passions, as we have seen,

carry with them the greatest potential for suffering and enslavement. A tyranny exercised by the other, no matter how harsh, always brings with it a hidden benefit: it protects its victim from the
far more debilitating oppression of a surrender to the self's unbridled passions. Only when the other occupies the position of master does the master-slave relation become potentially surveyable and
governable by the calm law of reason: "Soumis par ma naissance
aux passions humaines, que leur joug me soit imposé par un autre
ou par moi, ne faut-il pas toujours le porter, et qui sait de quelle
part il me sera plus supportable? J'aurai du moins toute ma raison
pour les modérer dans un autre, combien de fois ne m'a-t-elle pas
abandonné dans les miennes?" (Subject by birth to human passions,
must I not, whether their yoke be imposed on me by another or by
myself, always wear it? And who can say which alternative is more
tolerable? At least when these passions are imposed by others, I
have all the power of my reason to moderate them. And how often
has reason abandoned me when I had to deal with my own?) (*Les
Solitaires,* 4:917). Unlike his necessary submission to nature and
unlike his past submission to his own passions in abandoning his
wife and child, this submission to the passions of the other is pal-
liated by his ability, since he is the object and never the subject of
those passions, to exercise against them the cool lucidity of untroubled reason. The slave's exercise of reason allows him to formulate and present to the master his own dispassionate and therefore
valid estimation of their common good.

The whole story of Emile's enslavement, the narrative content of
the second letter, illustrates this paradox. An almost Stakhanovian
worker, Emile finishes his assigned tasks in a fraction of the time
allotted by the foreman. He then devotes the rest of his day to help-
ing the older and weaker slaves, who could not otherwise complete
their own. The foreman, jealous, reacts by multiplying everyone's
assignments to the point where Emile can no longer help the others
and all are sure to die from exhaustion in the near future. When the
slaves, in desperation, refuse to work, the master comes to the site.
Speaking up over the foreman's protest, Emile presents the master
with a frank analysis of their common good: "Nous ne refusons
point d'employer nos forces pour ton service puisque le sort nous
y condanne; mais en les exédans ton esclave nous les ôte et va te
ruiner par notre perte. . . . Mieux distribué ton ouvrage ne se fera
pas moins et tu conserveras des esclaves laborieux dont tu tireras

avec le tems un profit beaucoup plus grand" (We are not refusing to use our force in your service since we are condemned to that by fate. But in demanding more than we can give, your slave is destroying us and will ruin you through our loss. . . . Better apportioned, this work will be done just as surely and you will preserve the service of laborious slaves from whom in time you will derive a far greater profit) (*Les Solitaires,* 4:922–23). Moved by his slave's logic, the master orders that Emile and the foreman change places. Reason triumphs, profit increases, and Emile begins what promises to be a brilliant career.

From one perspective, Emile has at last achieved the tutor's definition of true liberty: during his captivity he has become his own master, a person able to wield authority over himself. From another perspective, this authority clearly presupposes a total submission: in accepting the other as master, Emile enters a realm that, although traced out according to the master's dictate, is ruled by a force he can understand (and potentially control) far better than the master. With submission defined as a tactic in the overall strategy of liberty, Emile applies to himself the law that guided all the tutor's benevolent manipulations: where the master's hand has intervened, the pupil must see only the inevitable dictates of nature. "Celui qui sait le mieux vouloir tout ce qu'elle [la nature] ordonne est le plus libre, puisqu'il n'est jamais forcé de faire ce qu'il ne veut pas" (He who knows best how to desire everything nature has ordained is the freest of men since he is never forced to do what he does not wish) (*Les Solitaires,* 4:917).

Most critics, instead of reading this second letter in relation to Emile's request that the tutor "remain the master of the young masters," dismiss it as Rousseau's unfinished attempt to illustrate the workings of despotism. Not only, however, does Rousseau refrain from using the term *despot* at any point in this second letter, but the Dey, who would logically deserve the name, in no way corresponds to Rousseau's definition of the despot as someone placing himself above all laws other than those of his own desire.[11] Rather than as a hereditary monarch long accustomed to the immediate acquiescence of all around him, the Dey began his career as a simple sailor. After rising through the military and political ranks, he was unanimously elected to his position. At the point where Rousseau's text breaks off, the Dey has chosen Emile as his political counselor precisely because he must, having ruled competently for twelve years but also having achieved no overwhelming successes, confront problems that scarcely seem those of a despot: governing an unruly nation and containing a mutinous military.

On the other hand, the term *despot* does appear in book 2 of *Emile*. There it describes the child whose foolish tutor has complied with his every wish: "Heureux, lui! C'est un Despote" (Happy! He! He is a Despot) (*Emile*, 4 : 3 1 4). Such a child, dependent because of his age, imperious because he is spoiled, inspires Rousseau to enunciate a maxim whose wisdom can be read as the obverse of everything Emile will learn during his captivity in Algiers: "La foiblesse et la domination réunies n'engendrent que folie et misère" (Weakness and domination joined engender only folly and misery) (*Emile*, 4 : 3 1 5). Reversing both cause and effect, we arrive at a second law, implicit in the first, that summarizes all of Emile's hard-earned wisdom: "Strength and submission joined engender reason and happiness."

□   □   □

Emile's newly acquired talent to seduce the master through the calm exercise of his many talents manifests itself repeatedly in *Les Solitaires*. When Emile takes work as a carpenter's assistant on the outskirts of Paris, people quickly notice that he "faisoit tout mieux que le maitre" (does everything far better than the master) (*Les Solitaires*, 4 : 906). After Emile kills the renegade captain in full view of the approaching pirates, their chief, we saw, treats him with a deference extended to none of the other prisoners. When first put to work as a slave in Algiers, Emile quickly realizes that his master can see that "j'étois le sien dans son métier" (it was I who was his as far as the trade was concerned) (*Les Solitaires*, 4 : 918). As *Les Solitaires* breaks off, everything indicates that Emile will have an equally astounding success as the counselor to the Dey of Algiers.

This pattern is important because it establishes a paradox that extends far beyond this posthumously published manuscript. In each instance cited, the manifestation of Emile's superiority initiates a redefinition of the intersubjective positions of master and servant. While the master may recognize in his servant someone who is effectively his master, he does so outside any movement toward resentment. While the servant is aware that he has mastered the master, he remains untouched by any desire to evince or take the place of the master. Superiority and inferiority, reversing yet at the same time preserving the socialized positions of master and servant, manifest themselves in an intersubjective forum held safe from resentment, violence, and the will to power.

To analyze *Emile* in isolation from its sequel, to ignore that essential postscript, truncates and distorts the implications of Rousseau's pedagogy for his properly political writings, in which his treatment of the relation between the individual and the community is equally paradoxical. To make Rousseau the untroubled and unsuspecting spokesman for the most egregious tutorial manipulation opens *Emile* to the misreading of critics who see in Rousseau's parallel disquisitions on the workings of the social contract only a tawdry apologetics of totalitarianism. To read *Emile* through *Les Solitaires,* on the other hand, is to recognize in that postscript Rousseau's abiding identification with the voice of the victim, his abiding desire to seduce that far greater master of whom he asks only that his truth be recognized.

5. The Victim's Sacrifice

Although Rousseau has been enshrined by literary history as the apostle of self-determination, the most eloquent spokesman for an ethos of authenticity and independence, the shape of his life and writings resulted from a constant, relentless, and often agonizing dialectic between himself as an individual and a social order that he felt impinging on, disfiguring, and attempting to silence him. From his earliest memories of childhood, Rousseau was conscious of a self that was passive, innocent (*in-nocere:* unable to do harm), unjustly victimized by forces for which he bore no responsibility: the death of his mother, the spanking for the broken comb, the apprenticeship to Ducommun, et cetera, et cetera. Perhaps for this reason, both in his representations of the self in the autobiographical writings and in his representations of history and society in the political writings, Rousseau accorded particular importance to what I would call the *event:* the sudden eruption of forces beyond human control but irresistibly and devastatingly affecting all they touch. Understanding the *event*—its occurrence, impact, and implications—allows us to identify an abiding structure of Rousseau's textuality: a singularly complex interplay of proclaimed innocence and passivity that is nonetheless founded on and orchestrated toward an active and continuing inculpation of the other.

I would like to examine a work that, although unpublished in his lifetime,[1] was particularly important for Rousseau from the time he first composed it in 1762 to the year of his death, when he took great pleasure in reading it to Bernardin de Saint-Pierre. In book 11 of the *Confessions,* speaking of *The Levite of Ephraim,* Rousseau goes so far as to say "s'il n'est pas le meilleur de mes ouvrages, il en sera toujours le plus chéri" (if it is not the best of my works, it will always be the most cherished.)[2] In addition to declaring his purely personal pleasure in writing, and later rereading, this text, the short preface of 1762 declares the work's relation to society as a whole, assigning it a function that as the years pass will become uppermost in his mind: "Si jamais quelque homme équitable daigne prendre ma defense en compensation de tant d'outrages et de libelles, je ne veux que ces mots pour éloge: Dans les plus cruels momens de sa vie, il fit *Le Lévite d'Ephraïm*" (Should some just man one day take my defense against so many outrages and libels, I ask only these words of praise: "In the cruelest moments of his life, he wrote *The Levite of Ephraim*") (First *Préface*, 2: 1205–6).

This work's intimate connection to the *event* of *Emile*'s condemnation and the order for Rousseau's arrest makes *The Levite* singularly important, not only for understanding Rousseau's immediate reaction to that event but also for grasping the idiosyncratic relation between such an event and its representation in the literary text. *The Levite* is simultaneously the story of Rousseau's persecution, the imaginary avenging of that persecution, and Rousseau's proof that he remained totally unconcerned with such vengeance.

As the preface of 1762 makes clear, Rousseau asks the reader to relate *The Levite*'s genesis to "les plus cruels momens de sa vie": the order for his arrest and the ensuing flight to Switzerland. Book 11 of the *Confessions*, however, offers a more complex and intriguing description of the work's circumstances—a description, in fact, so detailed and so nuanced that it seems to tell more about the writing of this short text than we know about most of the major works, in which, more often than not, we sense a strong element of retrospective justification in everything Rousseau has to say.

In early June of 1762, having lived for almost five years at Montlouis, the small country house provided by the Duc and Duchesse of Luxembourg on their estate at Montmorency, Rousseau has taken to combating his nightly insomnia by reading from the Old Testament. On the evening of June 8, finding it more difficult than usual to fall asleep, Rousseau extends his nocturnal reading to the whole of what he calls "le livre qui finit par le Lévite d'Ephraim et qui si je ne me trompe est le livre des Juges" (the book that ends with the Levite of Ephraim and which, if I am not mistaken is the Book of Judges) (*Confessions*, 1: 580). Finally falling asleep, yet at the same time drawn back to the story he has been reading, Rousseau begins to dream: "Cette histoire m'affecta beaucoup, et j'en étois occupé dans une espéce de rêve, quand tout à coup j'en fus tiré par du bruit et de la lumiére" (That story greatly moved me, and I was pondering over it in a sort of dream when suddenly I was aroused by a noise and a light) (*Confessions,* 1 : 580).

At two o'clock in the morning, tearing apart a dream fabric woven around the story of the Levite, the event erupts in Rousseau's life. Opening his eyes, he finds La Roche standing at his bedside with a note from the Duchesse enclosing a letter she has just received from the Prince de Conti. The message is as simple as it is alarming. Nothing more can be done. Tomorrow morning, in a few hours, the Grand' Chambre will not only issue its condemnation of *Emile* but will decree Rousseau's arrest and dispatch *huissiers* to Montmorency. Maneuvering as best he could in overwhelmingly hostile circumstances, Conti could obtain only the assurance that if Rousseau is not at Montmorency when the *huissiers* arrive, he will not be pursued.

Rousseau decides immediately to flee, insisting, however, that concern for his own safety does not motivate his decision. He so readily accepted the idea of flight to spare his hosts, the Duc and Duchesse, the embarrassment of harboring a man whose arrest had been ordered by legitimate civil authority: "Cela me décida à sacri- fier ma gloire à sa [the Duchesse's] tranquillité, à faire pour elle en cette occasion ce que rien ne m'eut fait faire pour moi" (That de- cided me to sacrifice my reputation for the Duchesse's peace of mind and to do for her, on this occasion, what nothing would have in- duced me to do for myself) (*Confessions,* 1 : 580). Rousseau makes only one demand: that his sacrifice be acknowledged as such. His hosts, at least in the final moments of his stay with them, are asked to recognize in their guest their benefactor. Stupified by the Du- chesse's apparent inability to grasp so obvious a truth, Rousseau is ready to retract his decision and stay on. Finally, however, the Duc and Madame de Boufflers arrive, comporting themselves with a def- erence sufficient to convince him that he should actually carry out his decision to leave.

The rest of the morning is taken up with an incredible scene in which the aged Duc helps Rousseau sort through his accumulated papers, deciding what will be burned, what Rousseau will take with him, and what will be left at Montmorency. During these frantic preparations, when Thérèse is finally summoned to receive the news of his departure, Rousseau first interprets this event as separating his life into two distinct parts: a *before,* now recognized as lost fe-

licity, and an *after,* announcing itself as relentless woe: "Mon enfant, il faut t'armer de courage. Tu as partagé la prosperité de mes
beaux jours; il te reste, puisque tu le veux, à partager mes misères.
N'attends plus qu'affronts et calamités à ma suite: le sort que ce
triste jour commence pour moi me poursuivra jusqu'à ma dernière
heure" (My dear, you must arm yourself with courage. You have
shared the good days of my prosperity. It now remains for you, since
you wish it, to share my miseries. Expect nothing but insults and
disasters henceforth. The fate that begins for me on this unhappy
day will pursue me till my last hour) (*Confessions,* 1:583).

With the same lamentation, addressed not to Thérèse as a premonition but to all his readers as a factual résumé of the period
from June 1762 to the time he wrote the *Confessions,* Rousseau begins book 12: "Ici commence l'oeuvre de tenebres dans lequel depuis huit ans je me trouve enseveli, sans que de quelque façon que je
m'y sois pu prendre il m'ait été possible d'en percer l'effrayante
obscurité" (Here begins the work of darkness in which I have been
entombed for eight years past, without ever having been able, try as
I might, to pierce its hideous obscurity) (*Confessions,* 1:589).
As with his departure from Geneva, as with his separation from
Madame de Warens, Rousseau once again organizes his life around
a radical break separating past happiness from future suffering, a
break caused by an event over which he has no control.

Rousseau's long stay with the Luxembourgs culminates in a scene
of particular intensity that recalls the moment of perfect happiness
Rousseau experienced at the royal premiere of the *Devin du Village.*
Preparing to take leave of his hosts, to bestow on them the gift of his
sacrifice, Rousseau finds himself surrounded by a group of women
who are moved to tears by their shared admiration of him. Unlike
the women at Fontainebleau, each of the women here actually approaches and embraces him. Given the extraordinary circumstances,
however, the scene is colored far more by the absence the women
prefigure than by any presence they incarnate. After the Duchesse
and Madame de Boufflers, Madame de Mirepoix embraces Rousseau. This last good-bye remains most vividly inscribed in his memory when he writes the *Confessions.* A woman Rousseau has always
judged to be cold, reserved, and particularly haughty because she
has accorded him no attention, Madame de Mirepoix makes a final
gesture that has the special value of a long-delayed recognition: "Je
trouvai dans son mouvement et dans son regard je ne sais quoi d'én-

ergique qui me pénétra" (I found in her look and her gesture a certain intensity of feeling which touched me deeply) (*Confessions,*
1 : 584).

□   □   □

Once alone in the coach, Rousseau returns, as it were, to the abruptly
interrupted dream of the previous night: the story of the Levite of
Ephraim. In fact, he spends the first days of his journey to Yverdon
in an ambiguously motivated prolongation of this singularly pleasant dream. To understand both how *The Levite* functions as a text
and why it is far more significant than the secondary, supposedly
pedestrian variation on a biblical story to which critics often reduce
it, we must examine how the conscious continuation of the dream
work responded to the trauma of Rousseau's flight.

Rousseau offers two different versions of the relation between his
flight and the composition of *The Levite*. In book 11 of the *Confessions,* the global narration I have been following, he insists that he
wrote *The Levite* without concern for his personal situation. The
story of the Levite, Rousseau claims, returned to his mind only *after*
he had completely forgotten the events of the previous day: "Dès le
lendemain de mon départ j'oubliai si parfaitement tout ce qui venoit
de se passer . . . que je n'y aurois pas même repensé de tout mon
voyage, sans les précautions dont j'étois obligé d'user. Un souvenir
qui me vint *au lieu de tout cela* fut celui de ma derniére lecture la
veille de mon départ" (The day after my departure I so completely
forgot all that had just happened . . . that I should never have given
it another thought during my whole journey if it had not been for
the precautions I was obliged to observe. One memory which came
to me *in place of all these* was that of the book I had been reading
on the eve of my departure) (*Confessions,* 1 : 586; italics mine). By
what might be called a process of total substitution, Rousseau
presents the decision to rewrite the end of *Judges* as replacing and
excluding all sterile handwringing over his personal fate.

Should we hesitate to suspect a strong element of denegation in
Rousseau's insistence on a complete forgetting, we have only to examine the other version of the same scene, in a text published in the
Pléiade edition as the *Second projet de préface* to *The Levite* and
usually dated June or August 1768. This second preface makes clear
that rewriting the Levite's story provided Rousseau with a gratifica-
tion of desires born of his misfortune, but even more important, it

reveals a form of substitution whose implications extend far beyond this single text: "Ces tristes idées me suivoient malgré moi, et rendoient mon voyage desagréable. Je les chassois de tout mon pouvoir, il n'y en a point dont mon coeur s'occupe moins volontiers que celle des torts qu'on peut avoir avec moi, et je m'irrite bien plus des injustices dont je suis le témoin que de celles dont je suis la victime. J'imaginai de donner le change à ma reverie en m'occupant de quelque sujet" (Those sad ideas pursued me in spite of myself and made my trip an unpleasant one. I tried as hard as I could not to think of them since there is nothing my mind less willingly concerns itself with than wrongs done me. I am far more upset by the injustices I witness than by those I suffer. I decided it would be wise to end my daydreaming by forcing myself to think of other things) (Second *Préface*, 2:1206). Obsessed by a particularly painful series of mental representations, trying to force them from his mind, Rousseau substitutes for them an even more strongly cathectic image of his fate: "Je m'irrite bien plus des injustices dont je suis le témoin que de celles dont je suis la victime." Taken in its total context, then, this passage suggests that the force and importance of Rousseau's consciously elaborated status as a *witness* who denounces social injustices derives from the sublimation of a more profound, properly unconscious, need to consolidate his status as *victim*.

This second preface, a short text of roughly one printed page, alerts the reader to the question why, in the *Confessions*, Rousseau so strongly insists on a radical break between his anxiety as a fugitive and the writing of *The Levite*. In a sense, we have already seen the beginnings of an answer to this question in the short quotation from the first preface, the one written at the same time as *The Levite*, in which Rousseau asserts the best refutation of his detractors: "Dans les plus cruels momens de sa vie, il fit *Le Lévite d'Ephraïm*." In book 11 of the *Confessions*, however, the other narration of *The Levite*'s genesis, the rationale for this break is most extensively developed.

In the midst of various details on his journey by postal coach, Rousseau abruptly steps back from his circumstantial account and offers his reader a self-portrait, elaborating it as a comparison of his reactions to happiness and unhappiness, to the good and ill fortune he has experienced. Rousseau draws his portrait so that his writing of *The Levite* during those days in the coach proves all the contentions he will make concerning himself. Rousseau presents himself as a *Janus bifrons,* endowed with two separate and distinct visions, one looking only to the happiness of the past, the other seeing only the suffering and unhappiness of the future. Memory and anticipation, the registers of past and future, are so distinctively forceful and so vividly present for Rousseau that any material allocated to one ceases to be in any way available to the other. Unhappiness exists for Rousseau only as the subject matter of anticipation, as a dread of something in the future. The actual experience of ill-treatment in the present provokes only fleeting anger, an irritation quickly forgotten: "Il est étonnant avec quelle facilité j'oublie le mal passé, quelque récent qu'il puisse être. Autant sa prévoyance m'effraye et me trouble tant que je le vois dans l'avenir, autant son souvenir me revient foiblement et s'éteint sans peine, aussi-tôt qu'il est arrivé. . . . j'épuise en quelque façon mon malheur d'avance; plus j'ai souffert à le prévoir, plus j'ai de facilité à l'oublier" (It is astonishing how easily I forget past ills, however recent they be. When they lie in the future, anticipation disturbs and alarms me. But the memory of them comes back to me only dimly and it no sooner comes than it fades. . . . I exhaust my misfortune in advance. The more I suffer in anticipation, the easier I find it to forget) (*Confessions,* 1:585). Happiness, the less developed of the two alternatives, is, on the other hand, assigned exclusively to the register of memory. It becomes part of an indelible and nourishing past, readily recalled with intense pleasure: "Sans cesse occupé de mon bonheur passé, je le rappelle et le rumine, pour ainsi dire, au point d'en jouir derechef quand je veux" (Continuously preoccupied with my past happiness, I remember it and chew it over, so to speak, in such a way that I can enjoy it afresh at will) (*Confessions,* 1:585).

☐   ☐   ☐

Rousseau was a man willing to stake a great deal on a text. The stake in *The Levite,* however, unlike that in the *Dialogues,* in which what the text says is important, rides on what is absent from the text: anyone doubting Rousseau's obliviousness to the evil done him, his inveterate unconcern with resentment and retaliation, has only to read this text and think for a moment of when he wrote it.

And this claim is, to say the least, surprising. *The Levite of Ephraim,* a faithful retelling of the events narrated in the last three chapters of Judges, is, to summarize it briefly, the story of the gang rape and murder of an innocent woman whose body, cut up into twelve pieces and dispatched to the tribes of Israel, initiates a holy war of vengeance with no fewer than 65,000 casualties. Given what Rousseau recognizes as the "atrociousness" of his subject matter, the reader cannot help admiring the audacity of his claim that three days spent mulling over variations on these events irrefutably prove his irenic nature.

Rousseau's argument for this paradoxical interpretation, however, has a certain logic. He insists that, without eliminating a single episode from this macabre story, he has managed to transform the somber biblical diction into a "prose poem" characterized by "un style champêtre et naïf" in the manner of Salomon Gessner's *Idylles*.[3] He has, he continues, never written anything "où régne une douceur de moeurs plus attendrissante" (where there reigns a more touching sweetness of manners). The point, then, is that in circumstances justifying paralysis in a dark despondency he was able, with astounding facility, to meet the challenge he had set himself and transform his own rendition into something radically different from the original: "Il n'étoit guére à presumer que ma situation présente me fournit des idées bien riantes pour l'égayer. Je tentai toutefois la chose, uniquement pour m'amuser dans ma chaise et sans aucun espoir de succés. A peine eus-je essayé que je fus étonné de l'amenité de mes idées, et de la facilité que j'éprouvois à les rendre" (It was hardly to be supposed that my situation at that time furnished me with such cheerful ideas as might enliven it. I made the attempt, however, simply to amuse myself in my carriage and without any hope of success. The moment I began it I was astonished at the pleasant flow of my ideas and the facility I found in expressing them) (*Confessions*, 1 : 586).

In a sense, the logic at work here is like that of Proust's suggestion that beautiful women should be left to men without imagination. How simple it would have been, and how insignificant, to have taken as his point of departure an innocent, lighthearted story whose characters and situations would have set the tone for his own text. But with such a choice the possibility of drawing a firm boundary between the influence of the source and the specific creative impulse of the author would have disappeared. The real test of an author's serenity, Rousseau seems to claim, comes not when he is asked to tell a story that portrays and solicits such calm but when, setting himself to telling the most violent and somber tales, he suffuses even such recalcitrant material with a spirit of peace and benevolence. In fact, precisely this baroque challenge that he sets for himself transforms what began as a justification of self into an implicit accusation of others: "Qu'on rassemble tous ces grands philosophes, si supérieurs dans leurs livres à l'adversité qu'ils n'éprouvèrent jamais, qu'on les mette dans une position pareille à la mienne, et que dans la prémière indignation de l'honneur outragé on leur donne un pareil ouvrage à faire: on verra comment ils s'en tireront" (Let all those great philosophers be brought together who, in their books, are so superior to the adversities they have never sustained. Let them be put into a position like mine. Let them try to undertake a work like mine in the first violence of their outraged honor. We should soon see what they would make of it) (*Confessions*, 1 : 587).

□   □   □

It is not surprising that Rousseau found himself fascinated by the story of the Levite. Even my rapid summary suggests why Rousseau, a man whose life was marked by the death of a woman, should have been drawn to this story of a man whose own fate, along with that of his entire nation, is redefined by the death of a much-loved woman, which he was powerless to prevent.[4] Only by examining the strange logic of Rousseau's psychic investment in this text can we hope to evaluate what he has actually done in his variation on the biblical narrative of violence and retribution. The four chants of Rousseau's *Levite* represent, in the fullest sense of the term, a return of the repressed: the reappearance, in a significantly transmuted form, of precisely those desires whose absence the work is presented as proving. As a microtext, this short work of roughly fifteen printed pages reveals a structure of denegation centering on victimage and violence that informs the macrotext of all Rousseau's writings: the pedagogical and the political as well as the literary and the autobiographical.

A short summary of the Levite's story as told in Judges 19–21 will help us identify and evaluate Rousseau's additions, deletions, and transformations. Rousseau breaks the first chapter at the couple's departure from Bethlehem; otherwise his four chants parallel the chapter divisions of the Bible. In the valley of Mount Ephraim, chapter 19 begins, there lived a Levite and his concubine from Bethlehem. When she returned to her father's house, the Levite went there to bring her back. On their return they stopped in the Benjaminite town of Gibeah. An old man living there with his daughter took them in, but that evening the townsmen surrounded the house and demanded that the Levite be given to them for their sexual pleasure. After refusing the old man's offer of his virgin daughter, they took the Levite's concubine, abused her, and killed her. The Levite brought her body back to Mount Ephraim, cut it into twelve pieces, and sent one to each of the tribes of Israel. Chapter 20 opens with the Israelites assembled at Mizpah, where they decided to form an army to punish the evildoers. Since the Benjaminites refused to turn them over, a war ensued. On the third day of the war, after losing forty thousand men, the Israelites were victorious and killed all but six hundred of the twenty-five thousand Benjaminites. With the war over, chapter 21 shows the Israelites realizing that the oath they had taken before the battles never to give their daughters in marriage to a Benjaminite has condemned an entire tribe of Israel to extinction. Since, however, the town of Jabesh had shirked its duty to send soldiers for the holy war, the Israelites destroyed it and took its four hundred virgins as wives for the surviving Benjaminites. The remaining two hundred were sent to Siloh to kidnap an equal number of maidens. All retaliation by the men of Siloh was prevented when the Israelites explained to them that this was the only way to avoid breaking the collective oath while assuring that the tribe of Benjamin survive.

Even this summary allows us to recognize a number of elements that explain, at least on a conscious level, Rousseau's fascination with the story. Judges is so named because it describes a period of Israel's history when the twelve tribes were not subjugated to a single monarch. The biblical text ends with a statement sure to appeal to the author of the *Second Discourse:* "In those days there was no king in Israel and each man did what was right as he saw it" (Judges 21.25). Rousseau, in fact, transposes to the very beginning of his narrative an expanded version of this Thelemic observation— with other implications nowhere present in the biblical text: "Dans les jours de liberté où nul ne régnoit sur le peuple du Seigneur, il fut un tems de licence où chacun, sans reconnoitre ni magistrat ni juge, étoit seul son propre maitre et faisoit tout ce qui lui sembloit bon. Israël, alors épars dans les champs, avoit peu de grandes villes, et la simplicité de ces moeurs rendoit superflu l'empire des loix" (In those days of freedom when no man reigned over the people of the Lord, there was a time of liberty when each man, recognizing neither magistrate nor judge, was himself his own master and did all that seemed right to him. The nation of Israel, spread out over the fields, had no large towns, and the simplicity of its ways made laws superfluous (*Le Lévite,* 2:1209). As much as it is the story of a crime, the episode of the Levite is also the story of an entire community arriving at its point of greatest unity, discovering a unanimous general will, in the declaration of war made by the assembled tribes. The biblical text is punctuated by phrases such as "all as one" (Judges 20.1) and "all the people rose as one man to say . . ." (Judges 20.8). On yet another level, we have already seen how the Levite's dispatching a piece of the concubine's corpse to each of the tribes drew Rousseau's attention when, in the *Essay on the Origin of Languages,* he argued that "le langage le plus énergique est celui où le signe a tout dit avant qu'on parle" (the most energetic language is that in which what is seen says everything before anyone speaks).[5] The story of the Levite taken from Judges serves as one of Rousseau's most important examples in that text.

It would be easy to continue this list of themes and incidents from the last chapters of Judges that echo preoccupations in all of Rousseau's work. The point, however, is clear: Rousseau's obsession with this story justifies our approaching his text as an overdetermined symptom condensing into one short narrative elements at work in all the "major" texts.

My principle in discussing Rousseau's version is that we can best apprehend his own purposes and preoccupations at those points in his narrative that most deviate from the story told in the Bible. As it happens, the most substantial and significant deviations occur at three points: at the beginning of the story, where Rousseau describes the Levite and his concubine before their arrival in Gibeah; in the middle section, where he deals with the discovery of the crime and its social ramifications; and at the close of the narrative, where Rousseau adds an entire cast of characters to the biblical given.

□   □   □

The first chant represents that part of *The Levite* in closest harmony with Rousseau's argument that his treatment proves his unconcern with hatred or revenge. The biblical text begins with four short, purely narrative sentences, free of descriptive detail, that introduce the two characters and bring us to the Levite's arrival in Bethlehem to retrieve his concubine. Rousseau expands this sober statement of events into a pastoral love story in four acts. Act 1 opens with the Levite, well before the start of events in Judges, passing through Bethlehem and discovering there a young girl whose beauty moves him to a declaration of love passionately made and quickly accepted. She does not become the Levite's "wife," Rousseau points out in the text's sole footnote, only because the injunctions of the Mosaic Law regarding the intertribal circulation of property forbid her that legal status. Act 2 takes the couple to the valley of Mount Ephraim where their life consists of love songs accompanied by the Levite's golden zither and gifts of wild honey, roses, and turtle doves pressed to the girl's bosom. Act 3 casts a shadow over the idyll as the girl surrenders to her growing nostalgia for the childhood joys of her father's house. Rousseau motivates her departure with the observation that "la jeune fille s'ennuya du Lévite, peut être parce qu'il ne lui laissoit rien à desirer" (she grew tired of the Levite, perhaps because he left her nothing more to desire) (*Le Lévite*, 2 : 1210). This is, it should be pointed out, a substantial deviation from the biblical explanation. The Ostervald Version offers "elle commit une impureté," whereas André Chouraqui, in a recent translation that prides itself on fidelity to the original Hebrew, gives "sa concubine putasse."[6] Act 4 focuses on the Levite, now desolate, who assumes the romantic posture of one who lives in a world that has become a poeticized memorial to his absent beloved.

I enumerate these elements of Rousseau's first chant because, aside from the bare statement of facts, none of them is present in Judges. Rousseau emphasizes the simple joys of rustic family life with the Levite's stay in Bethlehem and the attempts by the girl's loving father to prolong it by stretching out meals until it is too late in the day to travel. The biblical text mentions only the father, whereas Rousseau adds a mother and a number of *folâtres soeurs*. Moreover, Rousseau heightens the melodramatic potential of the ultimate departure so that the father's grief—"ses muettes étreintes étoient mornes et convulsives; des soupirs tranchans soulevoient sa poitrine" (his mute embraces were lugubrious and convulsive; piercing sighs lifted his breast) (*Le Lévite*, 2 : 1211)—functions as a premonition of his daughter's fate.

We might tentatively conclude from this first cluster of deviations that Rousseau identifies with the character of the Levite. All his expansions derive from a clearly pleasurable imagining of what might have been the Levite's actions and reactions in the bare skeleton of the biblical narration. A period of shared happiness abolished by the woman's longing for reintegration in the paternal order is not, of course, a theme to which the author of *Julie* was indifferent. As a corroboration of this identification, it should be noted that the Neufchâtel manuscript contains, in Rousseau's hand, instructions for a series of illustrations he intended for this text. All three of them, even though they are destined for a story that continues far beyond the Levite's disappearance from it, have this character as their central focus: the Levite offering a turtle dove to his beloved, the Levite discovering her body in Gibeah, the Levite addressing the assembled Israelites. The longest and most detailed of the three is, in fact, the only one that has no biblical counterpart: "Une vallée agréable traversée par un ruisseau et pleine de rosiers, de grenadiers et autres arbustes. Un jeune et beau Lévite offre à sa jeune bien aimée une tourterelle qu'il vient de prendre au piége. La fille charmée caresse la tourterelle et la met dans son sein" (A pleasant valley traversed by a stream and lush with roses, pomegranates, and other bushes. A young and handsome Levite has offered to his beloved a turtle dove that he has just caught in a net. The delighted maiden caresses the dove and clasps it to her bosom.) (Notes to *Le Lévite*, 2:1926).

□ □ □

The second cluster of modifications occurs in the sequence beginning with the Levite's discovery of his concubine's body and extending to the transformation of the murder into the gravamen of a holy war. This cluster in *The Levite*, a text turning on the relation of the individual to the community, reveals with a clarity unique in Rousseau's works how the operation of the general will as a process relies on an act of expulsion and victimage. *The Levite*, in other words, speaks directly of what might be called the "dark side" of the general will, a side that the political texts repress in favor of a uniformly irenic view of achieving unanimity in the ideal society.

This second cluster opens and closes with significant departures from the biblical text. At the end of Rousseau's second chant, the Levite, having brought his concubine's body back to Mount Ephraim, dissects it and sends one piece to each of the tribes of Israel. In and of itself this is a message whose immediate eloquence convokes the tribes to the assembly at Mizpah: "D'une main ferme et sure il frappe sans crainte, il coupe la chair et les os, il sépare la

tête et les membres, et après avoir fait aux Tribus ces envois effroya-
bles, il les précéde à Maspha, déchire ses vétemens, couvre sa tête de
cendres, se prosterne à mesure qu'ils arrivent et réclame à grands
cris la justice de Dieu d'Israël" (With a firm and sure hand, he cuts
the flesh and the bones, separating the head from the limbs. After
having dispatched these terrifying gifts to the twelve tribes, he goes
before them to Mizpah, rends his garments, strews ashes on his
head, prostrates himself as they arrive and, with great lamentations,
demands justice from the God of Israel) (*Le Lévite*, 2 : 1215–16).
Judges, on the other hand, has the Levite sending the tribes not only
the dissected body but also emissaries carrying a message that defines the corpse's significance. Whereas in Rousseau's text the body
alone is a supremely eloquent and self-sufficient message, the biblical account presents it as a token, a proof, a particularly horrifying
answer to the habeas corpus the Israelites are expected to formulate
as a response to the emissaries' narrations: "And the men whom he
sent he commissioned as follows: 'Thus you shall say to every man
of Israel, "Has there ever been such a thing as this from the time the
Israelites came up from the land of Egypt to this day? Put your mind
to it! Take counsel and speak!"'" (Judges 19.29–30).

The assembly at Mizpah listens to the Levite's story and, responding to his cry for justice, resolves unanimously to punish
Gibeah. At this point the Levite disappears from the biblical text,
never to be mentioned again as the narrative takes up the story of a
holy war. Judges is the story of a particular period in the history of
Israel as a nation; the Levite is one of a number of characters, always
secondary to the nation as such, who fade from view once they have
played out their limited roles in that history. Rousseau, on the other
hand, adds a final and particularly important scene centered on the
Levite as an individual: his falling dead before the assembled Israelites and his burial beside the reconstituted body of the concubine.
"Alors le Lévite s'écria d'une voix forte: Beni soit Israël qui punit
l'infamie et venge le sang innocent. Fille de Bethléem, je te porte une
bonne nouvelle; ta mémoire ne restera point sans honneur. En disant ces mots, il tomba sur sa face, et mourut. Son corps fut honoré
de funérailles publiques. Les membres de la jeune femme furent
rassemblés et mis dans le même sepulcre, et tout Israël pleura sur
eux" (The Levite then cried out in a loud voice: Blessed be Israel as
she punishes infamy and avenges innocent blood. Maiden of Bethlehem, I bring you good news: your memory shall not be dishon-

ored. In saying these words he fell forward onto his face, dead. His body was accorded a public funeral. The pieces of his wife's body were brought together and placed in the same tomb. And all Israel shed tears upon them) (*Le Lévite*, 2 : 1216). The literal and figurative reunion of these two bodies in their burial, an act carried out as a public ceremony, reaffirms a threatened social order. The affective charge of this added scene for Rousseau is confirmed by an earlier variant contained in the notes but dropped from the final text— dropped most probably because Rousseau sensed that it departed too radically from the biblical given. In the variant, instead of the woman's being dead when the Levite finds her on the old man's threshold, she is still alive. As her dying words, she whispers a request that not only excludes any question of the Levite's responsibility for what had happened to her but also anticipates and motivates the burial scene to come: "O mon mari, mon corps est souillé, mais mon coeur est pur. Ne refuse pas un cercueil à ta malheureuse épouse" (O my husband, my body is sullied, but my heart is pure. Do not refuse a tomb to your unhappy spouse) (Notes to *Le Lévite*, 2 : 1924). Suppressed or not, the concubine's request confirms the importance Rousseau placed on having the Levite's story end with a collective act of burial rather than the character's unnoticed disappearance from the text.

Rousseau's text, in other words, tells the story of an individual who finds himself the focal point of a criminal and profoundly transgressive desire shared by the men of Gibeah. From their midst emerges only one person, himself a foreigner—the Levite's host— who opposes that group. His opposition, however, fails and the crime is committed. The Levite, in the person of the concubine with whom he will be buried, is its victim.

The men of Gibeah, by reason of their shared desire, form a community. But, Rousseau makes clear, this community is a sham, an anticommunity leagued in common transgression, first, of the law of hospitality, and, more profoundly, of the law of Israel. Their crime reduces them to a level below the human. The men become a horde or, as Rousseau's metaphor tells us, a pack of predatory animals: "Tels dans leur brutale furie qu'au pied des Alpes glacées un troupeau de loups affamés surprend une foible genisse, se jette sur elle . . . vos hurlements ressemblent aux cris de l'horrible Hyene, et comme elle vous devorez des cadavres" (In their brutal fury they are like a pack of famished wolves as they surprise a weak heifer at the foot of the frozen Alps and throw themselves upon her. . . . Your cries are like those of the horrible hyena, and like it you devour cadavers) (*Le Lévite*, 2:1214–15).

But this, of course, is only part of the story. In reaction to the crime committed by the men of Gibeah, all the Israelites assemble at Mizpah. The criminal conspiracy by a subgroup is referred to the community in its entirety. Once brought before this court of last appeal, the narrative, the crime as narrative, becomes itself a force ensuring a true, just, and effective unification that animates the community in its just punishment and elimination of the subset of conspirators.

Rousseau fulfills in *The Levite*, in other words, the same abiding and constantly reiterated wish that motivates the *Confessions* and the *Dialogues*. He presents before the court of posterity, before the court of society as a whole, his denunciation of a criminal conspiracy leagued against him, its elected victim. No matter how large that conspiracy might become, no matter how closely it might coincide with society as a whole, his denunciations testify to his unswerving faith that a larger community will render an informed judgment of him and, recognizing his truth, will denounce and avenge the violence of which he has been the victim.

Only by distinguishing these two movements and understanding their complementarity can we begin to grasp the full implications of Rousseau's claim that hatred and vengeance were the emotions farthest from his mind as he composed *The Levite of Ephraim*. In writing this work, Rousseau identified fundamentally with the Levite, the innocent victim. And, strictly speaking, the Levite does not carry out an act of vengeance. That will be the concern of the community as a whole, the nation of Israel, once it knows the truth. The Levite's story is a story of unshakeable faith in the community, in the collectivity of all as capable of righting the wrongs suffered by an innocent victim who finally has only to speak and to die.

This act of faith in the community's capacity to recognize truth and avenge wrong manifests itself from the text's opening words. The first paragraphs of the first chant form a prologue, invoking the muse of virtuous anger, defining, as it were, the lesson to be drawn from the story that will follow. The diction of these two paragraphs, standing outside of yet summarizing the narration to come, is curiously ambiguous. At some points the paragraphs read like quotations from the Levite addressing the assembled Israelites at Mizpah.

At others, however, we hear Rousseau's voice speaking to his readers of their duty to look upon the spectacle of his own persecuted innocence and to judge, to punish, to avenge: "O vous, hommes débonnaires, ennemis de toute inhumanité; vous qui, de peur d'envisager les crimes de vos fréres, aimez mieux les laisser impunis, quel tableau viens-je offrir à vos yeux? . . . Peuple saint, rassemble-toi; prononce sur cet acte horrible, et décerne le prix qu'il a mérité. A de tels forfaits, celui qui détourne ses regards est un lâche, un déserteur de la justice" (O you men of meekness, enemies of all inhumanity; but who, for fear of looking upon your brothers' crimes, prefer to leave them unpunished, what horrors shall I offer your eyes? . . . O sacred people, come together, judge this horrible act and accord it the response worthy of it. The man who turns away from such crimes is a coward, a deserter from the service of justice) (*Le Lévite*, 2:1208).

This prologue is also important because it focuses attention on the story's crucial moment, when the innocent victim of a conspiracy represents himself to the community as a whole. If, as is clear in a text like the *Essay on the Origin of Languages,* Rousseau was obsessed with the problem of semiology, his obsession arose from his acute need for some *other* system of signs that, breaking through the endless lies spoken and written about him, might at last figure forth and adequately represent the full truth of his victimization. Rousseau's abstract reflections on the degeneration of human sign systems in progressively more elaborate forms of social organization must be read, as I argued earlier, as an attempt to explain coherently why in spite of his many and repeated messages, his truth continued to go unrecognized.

Rousseau's fascination and identification with the figure of the Levite comes at least in part from that character's ability to achieve a perfect act of self-representation. A theoretical text like the *Essay* makes clear that for Rousseau the Levite had access to a system of representation no longer conceivable in French society as he knew it. Immediately after the Levite's dispatching of the dismembered body, which exemplifies how eloquent purely visual signs can be, Rousseau remarks: "De nos jours, l'affaire, tournée en plaidoyers, en discussions, peut-être en plaisanteries, eût traîné en longueur, et le plus horrible des crimes fût enfin demeuré impuni" (In our day this affair, recounted in court pleadings and discussions, perhaps in jest, would be dragged out until this most horrible of crimes would in the end have remained unpunished) (*Essai*, pp. 502–3). For Rousseau, contemporary society offered only a vitiated language, which had long ago accommodated itself to a political organization where relations of force and domination had become sclerotic. His contemporaries, a debased hierarchy of interlocking masters and slaves, needed only a language suited to the whispered consolidations of self-interest: "Les nôtres sont faites pour le bourdonnement des divans. . . . Or je dis que toute langue avec laquelle on ne peut pas se faire entendre au peuple assemblé est une langue servile; il est impossible qu'un peuple demeure libre et qu'il parle cette langue-là" (Our languages are made for murmuring on couches. . . . I say that any language with which one cannot make oneself understood to the people assembled is a slavish language. It is impossible that a people remain free and speak that language) (*Essai*, p. 543).

□   □   □

The third cluster of Rousseau's modifications comes at the end of his narration. It involves, as I mentioned, the addition of an entire cast of characters, none of whom have specific equivalents in the biblical text. Judges ends with the attempt to resolve the problem of finding wives for the two hundred Benjaminites still without women after the four hundred virgins from Jabesh have been handed over to the six hundred survivors at Rimmon Rock. Judges presents this solution in two moments. The first is a general council of the elders. They decide that the abduction of the daughters of Siloh by the two hundred Benjaminites is the best way of getting around their oath. Anticipating the one problem sure to arise, they assure the Benjaminites that they will head off any counterattack by explaining to the men of Siloh that the abduction was the only way to save the tribe of Benjamin while avoiding anyone's breaking his oath. The second moment is a rapid "And thus it was done" that leads directly to everyone's return to his home and clan.

Rousseau segments this ending into a number of distinct scenes, in each of which specific characters embody the major conflicts. At the council of the elders, one man, the Old Man of Lebona, presents the plan to have the Benjaminites kidnap the maidens at Siloh. Following this scene is a direct narration of the ambush in the vineyards. The tumult as the maidens are overpowered by the Benjaminites brings the entire population of Siloh to the vineyards; and another general assembly is formed. Moved by the fathers' indignation at their daughters' being carried off like slaves by the Moabites, the assembly relents and decides that the captured maidens are free to do as they wish. At this point Rousseau focuses his narrative on one couple: Axa and her fiancé Elmacin, who is among the men just arrived from the town. Axa's choice seems obvious; however, Axa's father, the man who had chosen Elmacin as his daughter's fiancé, steps forth. He is, Rousseau points out, none other than the Old Man of Lebona, the same elder who first suggested the kidnapping of these women by the Benjaminites. Taking his daughter by the hand, he calls upon her to accept her duty to the nation of Israel as twelve tribes. Closer to death than life, Axa lets herself fall into the arms of the Benjaminite who had captured her. Elmacin, the fiancé, then steps forward and, taking a vow of chastity, consecrates the rest of his life to the service of the Lord. Following this example, all the maidens choose their Benjaminite abductors and the people raise a cry of joy.

The importance of this final reconstitution of the nation becomes clear when we contrast it with the earlier variant, in which Rousseau affirmed his faith in the capacity of the community to ensure justice once it knows the truth. Justice for the crime of Gibeah took the form of denunciation: the larger community, the assembled tribes of Israel, denounced as criminal the conspiracy of a smaller group to appropriate authority through violence. This final scene, however, presents a different situation. The problem the community confronts cannot be resolved by perceiving a truth thus far hidden. The moments of truth and justice are past. The crime of Gibeah has been punished and we are now in the phase of pity and pardon for the surviving Benjaminites.

The community finds itself in a double bind: because all have taken a collective oath, none may give his daughter to a Benjaminite; because all are the chosen people of the Lord, none may tolerate the extinction of an entire tribe. If the community is to survive, some element in it must step outside the already established law and, as an anomaly, provide a solution that will ensure the continued existence of the whole. The Old Man of Lebona, in presenting his plan to the council of elders and in overcoming his own paternal affection, becomes a variant of the ultimate foundation of the community in Rousseau's political works. The Old Man of Lebona, as he sets about organizing the just community, represents the same incarnation of the impossible in the possible as the Lawgiver de-

scribed in book 2 of the *Social Contract:* "Pour découvrir les meil-
leures regles de société qui conviennent aux Nations, il faudroit une
intelligence supérieure, qui vit toutes les passions des hommes et qui
n'en éprouvât aucune, qui n'eut aucun rapport avec notre nature et
qui la connût à fond, dont le bonheur fût indépendant de nous et
qui pourtant voulut bien s'occuper du notre" (The discovery of the
best rules of society suited to nations would require a superior intelligence, who saw all of men's passions yet experienced none of them,
who had no relationship at all to our nature yet knew it thoroughly;
whose happiness was independent of us, yet who was nevertheless
willing to attend to ours).[7] The Old Man of Lebona, the final avatar
of the father in *The Levite,* is an agent of continuity and equilibrium. Through his extraordinary action, upon himself as much
as upon the community, the social order is preserved, the tribe of
Benjamin is resurrected, and this entire narration of crime and vengeance draws to a close in peace and justice enforced and protected
by symbolic authority.

The importance of the Old Man of Lebona should not, however,
lead us to overlook the equally significant role played by another of
Rousseau's added personae: Elmacin, Axa's fiancé. As described in
this text, Elmacin's situation is a rapidly drawn recapitulation of all
those elements making up what we saw in the earlier chapters to be
the ideal form of Rousseau's relation to a cherished woman. For
Elmacin the beautiful Axa is an object of desire both designated by
the symbolic order (he is the fiancé chosen by her father) and, as
events develop, placed by that same symbolic order at an insuper-
able distance from him. Axa accords him ultimate recognition as
the true object of her love by pronouncing his name in a voice
broken by tears and by signifying the inevitability of their separation. The father ordains the rigors of this separation both to recognize Elmacin's superior merit and to offer him the occasion to prove
his allegiance to a duty beyond desire, a duty extending, via Axa's
father, to the entire community for which he will now sacrifice
himself.

Faced with the impossibility of any real possession of his beloved,
Elmacin chooses to accept and perpetuate that separation, not as a
depravation, but as the apotheosis of an original purity and innocence that will now be preserved both as the uneffaceable memory
of their love and as the consecration of his person to a higher principle. Unable to become her husband, he vows eternal chastity and

devotes the rest of his life to the service of the living God as the Nazarene of the Lord.

This final scene might, in fact, be read as a free transposition of the central conflict in *Julie:* out of deference to a social order that designates a preferred substitute, a paternal figure declares impossible the union of his daughter with her originally chosen beloved. At the same time, the reader cannot help noticing a number of echoes linking this final sequence to the earlier part of *The Levite*. Both the Levite as he faces the men of Gibeah and Elmacin as he arrives before the Benjaminites are marked by an initial passivity before the ongoing spectacle of violence. Both the Levite's concubine and Axa are characterized by similar turns of phrase in their respective plights: "Aussi-tôt ils entourent la jeune fille à demi-morte" (They immediately surround the half-dead young girl) (*Le Lévite*, 2:1214) and "se retournant à l'instant demi-morte, elle tombe dans les bras du Benjamite" (turning around half-dead, she falls into the arms of the Benjaminite (*Le Lévite*, 2:1223). Elmacin's final decision to become a priest likewise has him assuming the function normally assigned to the tribe of Levy.

□   □   □

When these three clusters are brought together, it is clear that Rousseau's modifications of the biblical text turn on the expansion or addition of elements grouped around two central figures: the Levite and the Old Man of Lebona. Each of them, as we saw, has one or more doubles in the narrative: Elmacin for the Levite; the old man at Gibeah and the concubine's father for the Old Man of Lebona. This proliferation of doubles both undermines any treatment of these characters as distinct psychological presences and justifies our reading them as successive representations of two primordial figures: the son and the father. The son, in other words, is son only because he continues to address himself to the father, because he preserves his faith in a paternal and symbolic order from which he asks only justice.[8]

What this configuration reveals, then, is that *The Levite of Ephraim* is a synthesis. On the one hand, as Rousseau's almost immediate response to the order issued by parliament for his arrest, the text is firmly grounded in and determined by the precise historical event in which a legally constituted authority most explicitly and most aggressively decided what would be his place (or lack of place, his implicit expulsion) in the community. On the other hand, this concise, overdetermined narrative weaves together, in a fabric as intriguing as the dream it continues, strands linking it to other texts traditionally designated as Rousseau's major works.

As in the *Second Discourse,* the past from which everything begins is an idyllic pastoral marked by self-sufficiency and immediately gratified desire. Abolished by an event "which might well never have taken place" but that, once having happened, irremediably separates him from his past, the Levite, like the author of the *Confessions,* addresses himself to and asks justice of a higher tribunal of the symbolic that he identifies with society as a whole, a totality from which his truth cannot remain forever hidden. In order, however, to preserve the social order once justice has been administered, one axial figure, as in the *Social Contract,* a human yet superhuman Lawgiver, must step beyond and restructure the laws of that society to incorporate the truth revealed by the innocent victim's act of self-representation. Finally, as in the *Dialogues* and the *Reveries,* the sacrifice of this secular Christ, the Nazarene, is never intended as a radical defiance of the social order, a calling into question of its ultimate authority to judge. His plea is instead that it recognize and punish the wrongs done him. The victim himself, like Elmacin, may linger on, but as one for whom felicity exists only as a cherished, ineradicable memory to sustain a life lived in recollection.

6. The Lawgiver's Paraclete

Few writers have influenced modern political thought as crucially yet ambiguously as Jean-Jacques Rousseau. During his lifetime, however, Rousseau was not thought of primarily as a political writer. The *Social Contract,* now looked on as Rousseau's *summa politica,* was, at the time of its publication in 1762, all but an *échec de librairie.* Compared with *Julie* and *Emile,* both enormous and immediate successes, this work provoked little comment or reaction outside the various administrative bodies that dutifully saw to its condemnation. Simply stated, the *Social Contract* did not at the time of its appearance significantly inflame any quadrant of the public imagination. It was not until twenty years later, when a whole new generation of readers had arrived to discover it, that Du Peyrou's first posthumous edition of Rousseau's complete works began with a volume including not only the *Social Contract,* but, for the first time in easily accessible form, the two *Discourses,* the *Encyclopédie* article entitled "Political Economy," and the *Considerations on the Government of Poland.* Even then, only seven years before the Revolution, these texts were not read as primarily political statements. The audience that welcomed this first volume of the complete works had been inspired by the recent publication of the *Confessions* and by the long-standing success of Rousseau's novels. Thus even in 1782, Eric Weil points out, Rousseau's readers approached his political works with expectations different from our own: "Nous lisons aujourd'hui les oeuvres du *penseur* Rousseau; la génération de la Révolution a trouvé chez un grand *écrivain* des idées, et elle les admirait, non parce que ces idées lui paraissaient prouvées, mais parce que c'étaient les idées d'un héros, d'un saint, d'un être adorable et adoré. Ce qui a produit des conséquences. Rousseau n'était pas grand parce qu'il avait formulé des principes justes; ces principes devaient être justes parce qu'ils venaient de lui, et la nouvelle forme de la sensibilité importait plus que ce qu'elle renfermait de contenu 'idéologique'" (Today we read the works of Rousseau the *thinker*. The generation of the Revolution looked instead to a great *writer* who also happened to have ideas. They admired those ideas not because they seemed irrefutable but because they were the ideas of a hero, a saint, someone who was adorable and adored. And this is not without consequence. Rousseau was not a great man because he had formulated just principles; these principles had rather to be just because they came from that great man. The new form of sensibility he represented was far more important than any "ideological" content it might contain).[1]

Only after the Revolution, in programmatic political objectives inconceivable at the time Rousseau wrote and published these works, did they begin to assume the implications we now read into them. History—and not only at the time of the Revolution—has consistently reworked what Rousseau's readers would perceive as the "real meaning" of his political writings.

□   □   □

In an attempt to step outside the patterns of distortion to establish some contact with the original impetus of Rousseau's political writings, I return to the first of them, the work marking Rousseau's emergence into the world of Parisian letters: the *First Discourse,* the *Discours sur les sciences et les arts.* I extend this return even beyond the text, however, to the engraving, the visual sign, the frontispiece with which the eighteenth-century reader made his first contact with Rousseau's thought. Although Diderot actually commissioned this engraving (he supervised the entire printing of the *Discourse* once its publication had been assured by the prize offered by the Dijon Academy), its subject is rooted in Rousseau's important note to the opening sentence of part 2 of the *Discourse,* a note in which he draws from antiquity a single image that epitomizes his relation to the world around him: "Le satyre, dit une ancienne fable, voulut baiser et embrasser le feu, la premiere fois qu'il le vit; mais Prometheus lui cria: Satyre, tu pleureras la barbe de ton menton, car il brûle quand on y touche" (The satyr, an ancient fable relates, wanted to kiss and embrace fire the first time he saw it. But Prometheus cried out to him: "Satyr, you will mourn the beard on your chin, for fire burns when you touch it").[2]

Toward the end of his somewhat exasperated response to Lecat's "refutation" of the *Discourse,* Rousseau returns to this frontispiece.

He not only refers to it as an integral part of his essay but also offers an interpretation that establishes it as an icon of his position as the author of this, his first political text: "J'aurois cru faire injure aux Lecteurs, et les traiter comme des enfans, de leur interpréter une allégorie si claire; de leur dire que le flambeau de Prométhée est celui des Sciences fait pour animer les grands génies; que le Satyre, qui voyant le feu pour la première fois, court à lui, et veut l'embrasser, représente les hommes vulgaires, qui séduits par l'éclat des Lettres, se livrent indiscrétement à l'étude; que le Prométhée qui crie et les avertit du danger, est le Citoyen de Geneve. . . . Que doit-on penser d'un Ecrivain qui l'a méditée, et qui n'a pu parvenir à l'entendre?" (I would feel I were insulting my readers, and treating them like children, in interpreting an allegory whose meaning is so clear. Prometheus's torch is that of the sciences as they are destined to inspire men of great genius; the Satyr who sees fire for the first time and runs toward it wishing to embrace it represents those vulgar men who, seduced by the brilliance of learning, devote themselves indiscriminately to its study; the Prometheus who cries his warning against that danger is the Citizen of Geneva. . . . What must we think of a supposed writer who pondered that image, but did not manage to understand it?) (*Arts et Sciences*, 3 : 102).

Rousseau's identification of himself with one of the figures in this mythological scene is not without ambiguity. Prometheus, the central character, seems to play, if we examine Rousseau's wording carefully, two contradictory roles. On the one hand, he has stolen fire from the gods and offers it to mankind as a gift. On the other hand, he warns the satyr, a symbol of vulgar humanity, of the dangers that accompany his exploitation of that gift. In his first function as the bearer of fire, Prometheus is Prometheus. In his second, as counselor and Cassandra, he is Rousseau: the Citizen of Geneva. Rousseau's casting himself in the role of Prometheus carries another implication as well: splayed out on Mount Caucasus where the eagle of Zeus will feed on his liver, Prometheus will soon become the victim of his benefaction.

Rousseau, as he interprets this image, implicitly casts himself as a victim sacrificing himself for all mankind: for the wise because he braves for them the vengeance of the gods; for the vulgar because he, the Citizen of Geneva, "cries his warning" to them and interposes himself between their violent desires and the sacred flame.

The surprises of this engraving, however, do not stop with this ambiguous duality. When we examine the frontispiece itself, we discover that it is different from what a cursory reading of Rousseau's description would lead us to believe. Instead of *two* figures (the satyr and Prometheus), there are three. On the right in the engraving is the satyr, half man, half goat, his eyes glistening with cupidity as he stands ready to leap toward the billowing torch. To the extreme left is Prometheus, a muscular, bearded, and decidely paternal figure, who holds the torch in his right hand and extends it toward the satyr. Between them, standing on a marble pedestal in the center of the engraving, is a third figure: a naked, angelic boy, whose body, unlike the satyr's or Prometheus's, is drawn with an almost epicene lack of line and detail. Prometheus holds the extended torch directly above the boy's head. This third figure may stand between the fatherly fire bearer and the impetuous satyr, but his posture is hardly one of admonition or dissuasion. His arms beseechingly extended, he assumes an almost crucifixional stance. His eyes look toward neither the satyr nor the flame. His gaze is fixed instead on the hand of the father as it holds the torch above him. Prometheus's other free hand, the left, rests on the boy's right shoulder in a gesture of confirmation and encouragement. If, as Rousseau would have it, he himself, the Citizen of Geneva, is represented in this scene, it can only be as this pubescent figure transfixed by the frightening magnitude of the father's gift. Beside him the vulgar, concupiscent world of the satyr bustles impatiently with desire and violence.

As we compare this engraving with Rousseau's description of it, it is difficult not to feel that something astounding enunciates itself in this separation between image and interpretation. Rousseau's reading of this engraving is so selective and so tendentious that it must reveal something far more important than he conveys in his petulant admonition of Lecat.

Such ambiguities—the use, for instance, of the single name "Prometheus" to refer *both* to the paternal figure bestowing the gift *and* to the innocent son obliged to struggle against its abuse—parallel what we have seen to be Rousseau's most consistent relation to authority and the symbolic. Everywhere, it seems, there is a satyr, a vulgar usurper, an illegitimate and abusive power to be denounced. And everywhere that denunciation depends for its effectiveness on a victim who appeals to a higher, ultimately just, and fundamentally righteous instance of authority. This appeal, changing the venue

Frontispiece to the first edition of *Le Discours sur les sciences et les arts.*

from the tribunal of the satyr to the tribunal of the father, can be carried out, however, only by immolating that innocent voice that would speak the truth.

My goal in this chapter is to examine the ambiguities of this relation to authority as they inform Rousseau's most historically virulent texts. Throughout his political works Rousseau is acutely aware that writing and publishing, addressing his fellows, is never a simple act. On the one hand, as both the theme and form of the *First Discourse* make particularly evident, he finds himself writing for a readership made up of an elite, of "academicians": a small, select group constituting an authority that he calls on to judge his work. In addressing such readers, Rousseau must, by definition, speak as a man of knowledge, a man of science, a savant—even when he indicts the very sciences that sustain this community of self and audience. On the other hand, beyond these bestowers of the prize, this group of recognized authorities, lies another audience, made up of mankind in general, that is far more vast and for Rousseau far more important. In relation to this second audience, the one at which he aims the full force of his persuasion, Rousseau must speak not as a savant but as a citizen—the Citizen of Geneva who accepts responsibility for his writings as messages intended to inflect the fundamental workings of the human community.

This double readership generates the dilemma Rousseau must face in his first political statement. He must speak both as a savant, asking to be recognized by those qualified to accept or reject his claim to that title, and as a citizen conscious of a higher duty to mankind in general. These poles, difficult to reconcile and ultimately contradictory, define a tension at work throughout Rousseau's political writings. It is hardly surprising, then, that the frontispiece of his first political statement, at least as Rousseau interpreted it, represented an innocent young man caught between the bearer of the flame and an impetuous humanity. And it is equally significant both that the greater humanity to whom he is responsible is portrayed as a satyr and that the *First Discourse* systematically challenges, even to the point of disqualification, the very assembly of savants called upon to adjudicate its author's credentials.

□　□　□

This opposition between value defined as abstract knowledge and value defined as a concrete contribution to human conviviality is the central issue of the *Discourse on the Arts and Sciences*. Rousseau insists that we judge the sciences as they contribute to man's life in society. Rousseau addresses this issue by seemingly renouncing all allegiance to the audience of savants: man's sciences must be denounced because they have had everywhere an altogether catastrophic effect on man's life in society. If we honestly evaluate how we live together, Rousseau claims, we must reject our sciences as sources of evils that far outweigh any benefits they might bring.

In their motivations as well as in their effects, the sciences have initiated, intensified, and at the same time cleverly hidden a universal intercourse of violence and exploitation. They are, as his opening metaphor would have it, "garlands hiding our chains." Does it not follow that the sciences themselves are utterly without merit? In their specific applications, they may ameliorate the quality of an individual's life or extend a man's strength beyond the limits of his physical nature. They are evil not because they are sciences but because they are practiced in a society whose idolatry of them has redefined both man's being and his desire. Like the value of Prometheus's gift, their value depends on man's use of them and their influence, in turn, on man's collective destiny. The sciences are to be condemned because as human creations they inevitably establish themselves as handmaidens of pride, amplifiers of all that sets man against man.

In the *First Discourse* we witness both a recognition and a universalizing of the motivations that we saw leading Rousseau to write from afar. Alone able to speak the truth, he must protect his voice from a society threatening to silence it. What Rousseau once described as his "timidity," the idiosyncratic anguish and paralysis of one individual, he now projects as a universal corollary of the human condition. Instead of one man painfully out of step with mankind's proud advance, we find a single lucid consciousness able to see both where we began and where we are headed in that forced march that calls itself civilization. Precisely because the arts and sciences have generated a wholly distorted system of values that fosters ebullient optimism where only the bleakest pessimism can be justified, Rousseau feels it inevitable that the great majority of his readers will blind themselves to the sobering truth of violence and devastation all around them.

The shift from a painful consciousness of the self as singularly deviant to an exaltation of its deviance as the very touchstone of his truth establishes the author of the *First Discourse* as the unique spokesman for a suffering and misled humanity. For the first time Rousseau proclaims that all the "failures" of his past must be taken as tokens of his uncorrupted vision.

The *First Discourse* signals a profound shift in Rousseau's attitude toward the anguish he felt so acutely whenever he was forced to submit himself to judgment by established authority. What he had experienced as humiliation now becomes the irrefutable proof of his truth. For everyone everywhere, Jean-Jacques is somehow other than what men expect because he alone, in his otherness, has remained uncorrupted by the forces of depravation at work throughout the society to which he must speak.

In this shift of Rousseau's attitude and in the different dictions that express it we might best understand the relation between the *First* and *Second Discourses*. The *First Discourse* condemns the arts and sciences entirely because of the changes they have wrought on human society. Born in superstition (astronomy), ambition (rhetoric), or, at their least noxious, vain curiosity (physics), they have fostered indolence and intellectual pride in their practitioners, setting each against all, jeopardizing our fraternity, and sapping our strength. Presupposing and multiplying luxury, they have extirpated virtue, leaving in its place a superficial urbanity that only disguises our enslavement. Throughout this work Rousseau elaborates his argument as a series of highly rhetorical juxtapositions of present depravity with a virtuous past situated in ancient Sparta, republican Rome, or pre-Columbian America. All human history seems to turn on the opposition between two primordial moments—a past and a present, a then and a now—in which the second moment always reveals itself as a vitiated parody of the first. Like a group of wizened, senile old men before whose eyes Rousseau would thrust a portrait drawn at the peak of their adolescent force, his audience is asked to compare its past with its present and, in comparing, to admit the bleak truth of its degeneration. The rapid and implacable movement from comparison to comparison allows Rousseau to amplify his argument while he avoids explaining what happened between these historical moments. This text makes no attempt to explain *how* we have moved from so glorious a past to so enfeebled a present.

The *Second Discourse,* the *Discourse on the Origin of Inequality,* extends and rationalizes the position Rousseau takes in the first.

Rather than a paratactic rhetoric, Rousseau here offers his readers a carefully reasoned, provocative explanation of mankind's transit from past to present. This essay confronts the reader with a historical anthropology of depravity. Rather than Sparta or Rome, the point of origin in the *Second Discourse*—and the subject matter of its entire first part—is that absolute beginning of the lone, self-sufficient primitive wandering the primeval forest. Rousseau analyzes the psychological and technological forces motivating each catastrophic choice, each stage of the primitive's encounter with other men, each step toward his slowly granted consent to link his own with his fellows' fate. Whereas in his prizewinning essay of 1750 Rousseau issued a strident, sometimes hysterical rejection of every possible value we might attribute to the realm of human endeavor in which he had once sought to establish himself, now, five years later, he has transmuted that abrupt *prise de position* into an all-inclusive and radically unorthodox reading of human history.

In the *Second Discourse* Rousseau isolates two distinct moments as crucial in shaping human history. The first, the simultaneous yet accidental discoveries of metallurgy and agriculture, represents this work's most cogent illustration of the thesis expressed in the *First Discourse*. The second, the striking of the pact inaugurating man's entry into a properly civil state, indicates not only how this text relates to the later stages of Rousseau's political thought but also how a particular pattern of personal motivation reclaims its place in his vision of man's universal history.

The concurrent development of agriculture and metallurgy, a historical accident Rousseau sees as having happened only on the European continent, is described toward the middle of the second section of the *Discourse*. Here we see most clearly the relationship Rousseau would establish between technological change and the transformation of individual consciousness. These two discoveries not only end the happiness of *l'état familial* but also, in civilizing man, condemn him: "Pour le Poëte, c'est l'or et l'argent, mais pour le Philosophe ce sont le fer et le bled qui ont civilisé les hommes et perdu le Genre-humain" (For the poet it is gold and silver, but for the philosopher it is iron and wheat which have civilized man and ruined the human race) (*Inégalité*, 3 : 171). As he defends this contention, Rousseau's precise sequencing of the causes and effects associated with the development of these two sciences allows him to offer his most intellectually cogent restatement of the thesis at the heart of the *First Discourse*.

The Promethean secret of fusing and separating metals could only have been discovered, Rousseau argues, by a particularly intrepid individual who dared to approach and study the workings of a volcano in eruption. To transform that secret into a usable technology, this man must call to his aid a number of men who, since they can no longer carry out their daily tasks of hunting and food gathering, need to be fed. The first practical application of this secret stolen from nature is for that reason the invention of the plow and other tools that allow workers of the land to multiply the fruits of their labors. The application of a more advanced technology to farming in turn makes it possible for those cultivating the fields to elaborate a true science of agriculture, for they now have the leisure necessary to analyze and plan their daily efforts. Over an extended period of time, this scientific agriculture will yield harvests far surpassing their collective needs.

The transformations of communal life brought about by these apparently simple changes are, Rousseau insists, devastating. When a multiplication of output follows a division of labor, men lose their independence: metal workers depend on the farmers for food just as farmers depend on the metal workers for tools. Time itself is redefined as men consider the present in relation to a later harvest or output. The simultaneous development of agriculture and metallurgy likewise implies a new human consciousness of private property, an articulation of the land and its resources into a series of distinct possessions that belong to some rather than to all. In all this transformation man loses nothing less than the freedom and equality that characterized the earlier organization of his efforts in a state of nature: "Dès l'instant qu'un homme eut besoin du secours d'un autre; dès qu'on s'apperçut qu'il étoit utile à un seul d'avoir des provisions pour deux, l'égalité disparut, la propriété s'introduisit, le travail dévint nécessaire, et les vastes forêts se changérent en des Campagnes riantes qu'il falut arroser de la sueur des hommes, et dans lesquelles on vit bientôt l'esclavage et la misére germer et croître avec les moissons" (From the moment one man needed the help of another, as soon as they observed that it was useful for a single person to have provisions for two, equality disappeared, property was introduced, labor became necessary, and vast forests were changed into smiling fields which had to be watered with the sweat of men, and in which slavery and misery were soon seen to germinate and grow with the crops) (*Inégalité*, 3 : 171). As we review this carefully argued rationale, we are far from the rhetoric of the *First Discourse*.

Rousseau's arguments no longer depend on a shrill denunciation of luxury as the destroyer of martial fortitude or on a facile comparison of man's encounter with the arts and sciences to a child's use of a gun placed in his hands. Yet the judgment is the same.

In extending and refining the thesis of his *First Discourse*, Rousseau articulates for the first time a distinction between *natural* inequality (men's differences from one another when judged by their varying sizes, strengths, and dexterities) and *moral* inequality (men's differences from one another when judged by arbitrary social values). This key distinction allows Rousseau to present human history as a unified movement of displacement and multiplication of the first by the second, of natural inequality by moral inequality. The arts and sciences are to be condemned because they amplify to catastrophic proportions the otherwise insignificant bases of man's natural inequalities. They consolidate and disguise, Rousseau argues, an ever more despotic rule of the strong over the weak, the rich over the poor.

The second axial moment of the *Second Discourse*, the moment marking the inauguration of man's civil existence, results inevitably from the mutations implicit in growing mutual dependence. Moral inequality, transforming the consciousness of self into a violent demand for recognition by the other, has exacerbated man's natural inequalities to the point where all social intercourse, every meeting of man with man, becomes an implacable and unregulated struggle for dominance and mastery. The private possession of land, of things, and even of other men has become a reality, a reality sustained, however, by nothing more than the prerogatives of force. One man's designating something as his own depends on his always precarious ability to repel and defeat those who would challenge that claim: "L'égalité rompüe fut suivie du plus affreux désordre: c'est ainsi que les usurpations des riches, les Brigandages des Pauvres, les passions effrénées de tous étouffant la pitié naturelle, et la voix encore foible de la justice, rendirent les hommes avares, ambitieux, et méchans" (The destruction of equality was followed by the most frightful disorder; thus the usurpations of the rich, the brigandage of the poor, the unbridled passions of all, stifling natural pity and the as yet weak voice of justice, made men avaricious, ambitious and evil) (*Inégalité,* 3 : 176). Every encounter of man with man repeats a universal scenario of violence. Life in society soon becomes indistinguishable from what Rousseau calls a state of general warfare. All men, puppets of the rapacious desires they share with their fellows, can now be described in the same metaphor Rousseau later uses to describe the evil men of Gibeah. They are an enraged, self-devouring species: "Ils ne songèrent qu'à subjuger et asservir leurs voisins; semblables à ces loups affamés qui ayant une fois goûté de la chair humaine rebutent toute autre nourriture, et ne veulent plus que dévorer des hommes" (They thought only of subjugating and enslaving their neighbors: like those famished wolves which, having tasted human flesh, refuse all other food and thenceforth want only to devour men) (*Inégalité,* 3 : 175–76).

This condition of universal and self-propagating violence leads to an all-important moment when the richest and the most cunning, those best able both to recognize the precariousness of their positions and to take measures to protect them, conceive a ploy, a scheme, a nefarious ruse to make their adversaries their protectors: "Le riche pressé par la nécessité, conçut enfin le projet le plus réfléchi qui soit jamais entré dans l'esprit humain; ce fut d'employer en sa faveur les forces même de ceux qui l'attaquoient, de faire ses défenseurs de ses adversaires, de leur inspirer d'autres maximes, et de leur donner d'autres institutions qui lui fussent aussi favorables que le Droit naturel lui étoit contraire" (The rich, pressed by necessity, finally conceived the most deliberate project that ever entered the human mind. This was to use in his favor the very force of those who attacked him, to make his defenders out of his adversaries, to inspire them with other maxims, and to give them other institutions which were as favorable to him as natural right was adverse) (*Inégalité,* 3 : 177).

In particular detail and with particular pleasure, Rousseau then, for the first and last time in this text, offers his readers a verbatim rendition of what he imagines must have been the clever ruse with which the conspirators perpetrated on their fellows the universal hoax of justice, law, and peace:

"Unissons-nous," leur dit-il, "pour garantir de l'oppression les foibles, contenir les ambitieux, et assûrer à chacun la possession de ce qui lui appartient: Instituons des réglemens de Justice et de paix auxquels tous soient obligés de se conformer, qui ne fassent acception de personne, et qui réparent en quelque sorte les caprices de la fortune en soûmettant également le puissant et le foible à des devoirs mutuels. En un mot, au lieu de tourner nos forces contre nous-mêmes, rassemblons les en un pouvoir suprême qui nous gouverne selon de sages Loix, qui protége et défende tous les membres de l'association, repousse les ennemis communs, et nous maintienne dans une concorde éternelle." (*Inégalité*, 3 : 177).

"Let us unite," he says to them, "to protect the weak from oppression, restrain the ambitious, and secure for everyone the possession of what belongs to him. Let us institute regulations of justice and peace to which all are obliged to conform, which make an exception of no one, and which compensate in some way the caprices of fortune by equally subjecting the powerful and the weak to mutual duties. In a word, instead of turning our forces against ourselves, let us gather them into one supreme power which governs us according to wise laws, protects and defends all the members of the association, repulses common enemies, and maintains us in an eternal concord."

Rousseau insists on offering the verbatim transcription of this moment, the precise tissue of what he calls its *raisons specieuses*, because it both reenacts and ironizes what he sees as the fundamental lie his contemporaries have chosen to believe so fervently. Speaking to an opulent and sophisticated society, Rousseau organizes his history of mankind so that at the point where his audience would least like to hear it, one of the principal players in the drama steps out of the faraway forest of time gone by and confronts the reader with a speech echoing what he hears everywhere around him. Conceding his reader an excuse, but an acutely embarrassing excuse, Rousseau continues his description of this moment with what might be called a portrait of the reader as dupe: "Il en falut beaucoup moins que l'équivalent de ce Discours pour entraîner des hommes grossiers, faciles à séduire, qui d'ailleurs avoient trop d'affaires à démêler entre eux pour pouvoir se passer d'arbitres, et trop d'avarice et d'ambition, pour pouvoir longtems se passer de Maîtres" (Far less than the equivalent of this discourse was necessary to win over crude, easily seduced men, who in addition had too many disputes to straighten out among themselves to be able to do without arbiters, and too much avarice and ambition to be able to do without masters for long) (*Inégalité*, 3 : 177).

After this crucial scene Rousseau returns to the narrative mode. In the closing pages of the *Second Discourse*, he sketches out a time after this original institution of civil society. Pseudodemocracy will yield to republicanism. Republicanism will yield to hereditary monarchy. Monarchy will yield to despotism. Mankind, by the end of the ride, will have come full circle to a second and far sadder equality: "C'est ici que tous les particuliers redeviennent égaux parce qu'ils ne sont rien" (Here all individuals become equals again because they are nothing) (*Inégalité*, 3:191). Immediately after his word-for-word, first-person transcription of this scene, however, Rousseau chooses to break his precise sequencing of consecutive historical stages. Over the space of nearly six pages Rousseau discusses on a purely theoretical level the other ways one might interpret this particular moment. As though having arrived at the key moment in mankind's long history, he takes great pains to refute the interpretations of it offered by Locke, Pufendorf, Barbeyrac, and Grotius. In a real sense, then, it is as though Rousseau's entire hypothetical history of mankind were intended to function as a frame, a background, a motivating context for this one crucial moment in which the reader finds himself called on to glimpse the essence not only of his past but of his present.

One effect of this procedure, the foregrounding and interpretation of the conspirators' hoax, is a refinement and redirection of the thesis common to the two *Discourses* of 1750 and 1755: rather than toward perfection, man has been led toward degradation by his encounters with everything summarized in the term *arts and sciences.*

Among man's many sciences, however, this argument seems to indicate that one in particular has played a crucial role; one science is, so to speak, the metascience. As a body of dangerous and prevaricating knowledge, its effects are not limited to any one area of man's activities but are spread out over the whole social fabric. To this queen science falls the task of motivating and justifying the entire context in which all other sciences and arts will develop and thrive. The science in question here, which offers us learned representations of the origin and structure of our societies, is political theory. It is a metascience because it rationalizes, motivates, and justifies the conditions necessary for the development of all other sciences. It is a pseudoscience because it invites us to imagine our chains as garlands. Blinding us to the most obvious reality of our situation, it is a consummate exercise of what, in the Marxist sense, will come to be called ideology.

Rousseau's indictment of political theory carries with it a number of paradoxes. He is writing and publishing a learned treatise on the origin of inequality among men. Adequate treatment of this question demands that he elaborate a radically iconoclastic theory of man's history. In elaborating such a theory and in repeatedly insisting on its indispensability to a proper understanding of our situation, he addresses himself to a readership made up of those who are informed about, concerned with, and able to evaluate the position he takes. He chooses, in other words, to speak to the existing community of political theorists: to those who know, and to the sum of their knowledge. Yet even as he addresses these readers, he denounces not only what they have said but their very right to speak. Rousseau's condemnation of his elected readership is "radical" because he is telling them not only that they are mistaken but that their very status and function render them incapable of even suspecting the truth they claim to speak so wisely. Rousseau's contact with that truth, his particular vision of man's history, he insists again and again, is not a result of bookishly acquired knowledge, of science, of his integration in the carefully woven web of accepted wisdom: "Plus nous accumulons de nouvelles connoissances, et plus nous nous ôtons les moyens d'acquerir la plus importante de toutes, et . . . c'est en un sens à force d'étudier l'homme que nous nous sommes mis hors d'état de le connoître" (The more new knowledge we accumulate, the more we deprive ourselves of the means of acquiring the most important knowledge of all, and . . . it is, in a sense, by dint of studying man that we have made ourselves incapable of knowing him) (*Inégalité,* 3 : 123). Because his own itinerary has led him to travel paths scrupulously hidden by the conspiracy everywhere determining his society, Rousseau, and Rousseau alone, has perceived the truth of what man is, where he began, and where he is headed. Instead of offering another illusion of civilized knowledge, Rousseau has confronted, reflected on, and adopted as the apodictic given of his analysis the simple and irrefutable fact that he, like all men, is a *victim.*

Thrown by birth into a society whose fate had been determined long before his coming, Rousseau experiences his obligation to take his place and to accept judgment by others as a form of intense suffering. Now in the series of works setting forth his political theory he adopts an attitude toward that suffering that distances him from those timid denegations and excuses we see at work in his autobiographical and literary texts. His suffering, instead of generating a desperate claim to recognition as a savant, becomes itself both the substance and guarantee of the truth he would enunciate as citizen.

Like that of all men before they were lulled by the masters' hoax,

Rousseau's treatment by his fellows, as he sees it, has been an implacable friction of violence, conflict, and deceit. His civilized judges, who have deluded themselves into believing the cynical promises of the conspiracy, may well glory in their ongoing collaboration with the forces that deprave them. Rousseau's position, as well as his every experience of that position, is radically different. And that difference, he insists, is the touchstone of his truth. What he refers to as timidity in the protective, absolving vocabulary of autobiographical introspection becomes in his political writings the very basis of his lucidity. This timidity, this awareness of his intense suffering at his every encounter with the social, becomes not something to be excused but something to be both proclaimed and exalted. Devastated by the violence of judgments he cannot hope to overcome, he calls on this shock of the other on the self to generate a spark: a spark of light in an overwhelming darkness, a spark of truth, a self-immolating spark with which it is his sadly Promethean duty to illuminate the world.

In this sense Rousseau is the first of the romantics. In his exposition of what he sees as the truth of the human condition, he addresses an audience that, quite literally, cannot yet exist. Disqualifying the positions taken by all established authority, Rousseau substitutes for them what seems at first glance an absolutely personal sense of his individual destiny. At the same time, however, the shape of this destiny presents itself to the imagined reader not as something unique, not as something singular, but as something that, once the debonair mendacities of social convention have been scraped away, all may discover to be the shared substance of their persecuted humanity. Their common status as victims ensures between writer and reader the communication of truth. In adopting this position, Rousseau's political writings place themselves outside the canons of readership recognized by his time. They attempt to fashion for themselves an audience made up of all those muted sufferers previously designated as incapable of comprehending. Whispering to everyman this explanation of his *patio ergo sum*, Rousseau offers to all who will listen a new knowledge based on understanding what it is to be a victim.

It is hardly surprising that Rousseau, from the beginning of the *First Discourse,* explicitly assumed the position of scapegoat to which his argument ultimately condemns him. Like Socrates, he must pay the supreme price for the truth he speaks. Unlike Socrates, however, he will suffer mockery and contempt instead of silencing hemlock because he lives in an age grown proud of its depravity: "Parmi nous, il est vrai, Socrate n'eût point bû la cigue; mais il eût bû dans une coupe encore plus amere, la raillerie insultante, et le mépris pire cent fois que la mort" (Among us, it is true, Socrates would not have drunk the hemlock; but he would have drunk from an even more bitter cup: insulting scorn and ridicule a hundred times worse than death) (*Arts et Sciences*, 3:15).

At the core of Rousseau's analysis, at the core of his knowledge as victim, is a message offering their rights to a potential readership made up of all those who come to recognize their own truth and their own victimage in a discourse that literally generates the audience it addresses. Rousseau is, in the most basic sense of the word, a paraclete. *Para-kalein:* he who calls out to, who exhorts from the side, who calls aside—and who strengthens. Even as he is condemned by the recognized authorities he so blatantly challenges, this condemnation strengthens the legions of other men, other silenced sufferers, who will come to recognize their own truth in his portrayal of socialized man as victim. The genius of Rousseau's political writings lies in their ability to initiate a discursive economy that both anticipates rejection and transforms it into a verification of the very truth the writings proclaim. The more he is anathematized and refuted, the more his truth as victim is confirmed. The call from aside, the voice of the paraclete, is audible only so long as its deviance is both recognized and amplified by the horrified clamor of consecrated authority.

Rousseau's covenant with his readers is based on a shared awareness of violence, a shared recognition of the readers' and the author's common status as victims of that violence. The Hobbeses, the Pufendorfs, the Grotiuses—all who would disguise or palliate our awareness of such painful truths—are little more than the hired spokesmen of those conspirators who have so long abused our weary agony.

Rousseau's primordial concern with violence (both the obvious violence of the general warfare preceding man's entry into the socialized phase of his history and the more insidious hidden violence of manipulation and control that claims to work only for the greater good of all) allows him to unify his political thought as a series of meditations on the strategies for its expulsion. The agony of a consciousness striving to imagine how it might escape this violence of the other serves as the common starting point for the two distinct versions of the ideal Rousseau will elaborate in his political works. Thus far, in speaking of the two *Discourses,* I have looked only at the first of these, the lost ideal of the past: that benign state of nature from which man's entire history has forced him to deviate. Characterized by desires born only as he encountered the means to satisfy them, natural man was marked by a consciousness unfissured by the conflicting demands and ensuing violence of any other impinging on the self.

Later, in the *Social Contract,* Rousseau proposes a different yet structurally similar reconciliation between individual freedom and the obligations of law. In this text, Rousseau's attention turns to the entire process by which the enunciation and enactment of the general will might protect the individual from violence inflicted in the name of the collectivity. A just law is nothing other than the application of the general will to a specific situation; as such, the law as discourse will be defined as both flowing from and guaranteeing the exact identity of individual and communal desire.

Each of these different ideals relies on a common redefinition of legitimate authority. In both cases Rousseau's goal is to disqualify an arbitrary rule of force, to depose a master who has set out to control violently the otherwise free individual. In the *First Discourse* the accrued authority of man's cultural values is transferred from the alienating anonymity of the other to an unmediated and utterly personal voice of individual consciousness. In the *Social Contract* the force of law is transferred from authorities, who place themselves above the dictates they impose on the community, to the general will, whose unifying processes ensure the exact identity of rulers and ruled.

Rousseau's political philosophy is innovative because of the way he resolves this fundamental question of the relation between violence and the organization of the state. Both Hobbes and Rousseau would have agreed, for instance, that man's various political unions, at least as they actually existed, were born in violence. For both of them, the generalized devastation of war led men to recognize the necessity of a common, regulating law. Hobbes believed that men consent to a ruler's comparatively minor violences on their individual wills for the sake of peace and of a union that preserves for all the inalienable rights to life and the pursuit of happiness. Individual and inalienable human rights did exist for Hobbes. They were simply, as it were, renegotiated at the birth of the state. Although in the abstract men might imagine that their rights have been limited, the scope of these rights nonetheless far exceeds what it was during the universal violence to which the birth of the state has put an end.

For Rousseau, the premises of this analysis are wholly unacceptable. Individual rights, he insisted, do not exist before society exists; they are born with it. They are not premiums to be negotiated and compromised in exchange for relative peace; instead they dictate an absolute criterion of individual liberty that the state must both express and preserve. The birth of the state must occur not as a minimizing of permissible violence but as an expulsion of violence, an eradication of all conflict between the individual and the society of which he is a part.

Rousseau's consistent abhorrence of violence as a generalized social praxis has, if anything, enabled conservative critics to present an interpretation of his work that is at least partially valid. These critics argue that the work is profoundly antirevolutionary and resolutely antithetical to the practices of those who have most stridently proclaimed themselves his designated progeny. Starting with a statement like that in book 2 of the *Social Contract,* in which Rousseau depicts the dangers of change in an established state— "Quand une fois les coutumes sont établies et les préjugés enracinés, c'est une entreprise dangereuse et vaine de vouloir les réformer" (Once customs are established and prejudices have taken root, it is a dangerous and foolhardy undertaking to want to reform them)[3]—these critics then point to the statements made by "the Frenchman" in the third *Dialogue* as representing Rousseau's fundamental position: "Les grandes nations ont pris pour elles ce qui [the *Social Contract*] n'avoit pour objet que les petites républiques, et l'on s'est obstiné à voir un promoteur de boulversemens et de troubles dans l'homme du monde qui porte un plus vrai respect aux loix, aux constitutions nationales, et qui a le plus d'aversion pour les révolutions et pour les ligueurs de toute espéce, qui la lui rendent bien" (Large nations have taken as directed at them what [the *Social Contract*] was intended only for small republics. They have persisted in seeing an incendiary and a troublemaker in the man who has the greatest respect for laws, for national constitutions, and who has the greatest aversion to revolutions and conspirators of every stripe—an aversion they have very much returned him in kind).[4] Although the critics distort Rousseau's meaning by extracting from its context a judgment made in a paroxysm of self-exculpation, the basic motivation referred to here, the fear of an uncontrollable violence waiting to be unleashed by any generalized overthrow of recognized authority, is certainly among the essential components of Rousseau's political thought.

□   □   □

The representation of violence in the *First* and *Second Discourses,* its consolidation of the author as victim, must be kept in mind as we consider what has always been the most invalidating accusation leveled against the *Social Contract:* that of totalitarianism. Those who would convict Rousseau on that charge argue that there, in his most explicitly political work, he becomes the apologist for a singularly pervasive political violence: the coercion of all not only to comply with but to believe in and espouse the dictates of the general will. Such readings point primly to what they see as Rousseau's justification of the community's sacred duty to enforce unanimity by all means possible: argument, coercion, banishment, and even death. How, these critics ask, could this political ideal be realized without the frequent use of an intolerable degree of violence on those who deviate from the communal orthodoxy?

As Rousseau describes the workings of the general will, he frequently mentions that he is here speaking of political processes for which our history has so ill prepared us that we lack even the most basic vocabulary for comprehending how they must work. Our efforts at understanding him are condemned from the start if when he uses such terms as *individuality, communication, conviction,* and *coercion,* we think only of what those words designate in the world around us. As Rousseau repeatedly insists, the political ideal set forth in the *Social Contract* is inapplicable to existing European states. Because of their past history, their physical size, and most of all their citizenries' epistemological inadequacy—their consciousnesses are corrupted by all that has gone before—these societies are beyond regeneration according to Rousseau's model. To argue otherwise is to ignore the entire historical and anthropological context Rousseau established for this ideal in the *Discourse on the Origin of Inequality.* The axial moment in man's history that I have called the conspirators' hoax is, for the whole of Europe as Rousseau saw it, something that actually happened, something that determined the ensuing development of those societies toward forms of individual and collective consciousness that exclude the option presented in the *Social Contract*. If the political processes described in this text—the intervention of the Lawgiver, the constitution of the general will, its incarnation in the sovereign—are to be realized, they must occur as alternatives to the conspirators' hoax, not as sequels.

When readers like J. L. Talmon and Lester Crocker present the *Social Contract* as a text speaking dangerously about what should be rather than what might have been,[5] they overlook its shadowy and always-imperfect evocation of an ideal that questions the deceits and impostures of the society in which we find ourselves. Moreover, they indulge themselves, with far more gravity but far less wit, in a judgment of this work like that of Voltaire, who feigned regret that in spite of his admiration for the *First Discourse,* he would refrain from crawling about on all fours and munching grass.

We can argue about Corsica, we can argue about Poland, we can argue about Geneva (the societies that, in various contexts and for various reasons, Rousseau saw as atypical and for which he suggested topical programs of reform), but none of these anomalies offers convincing proof that Rousseau envisioned applying the program proposed in the *Social Contract* to existing European states.

The crucial statement, as far as this question is concerned, occurs in chapter 8 of book 2, where Rousseau discusses what he sees as the decisive component of any established society: the quality of its citizenry, the tenor of its *peuple* formed by their entire history. Although no contemporary European states are mentioned here, Rousseau's statement leaves little doubt about his prognosis for those societies to which he had already addressed the *Second Discourse:* "Le sage instituteur ne commence pas par rédiger de bonnes loix en elles-mêmes, mais il examine auparavant si le peuple auquel il les destine est propre à les supporter. C'est pour cela que Platon refusa de donner des loix aux Arcadiens et aux Cyréniens, sachant que ces deux peuples étoient riches et ne pouvoient souffrir l'égalité" (The wise founder does not start by drafting laws that are good in themselves, but first examines whether the people for whom he intends them is suited to bear them. For this reason, Plato refused to give laws to the Arcadians and the Cyrenians, knowing that these two peoples were rich and could not tolerate equality) (*Du contrat social,* 3 : 384–85). Any community applying to itself the program set forth in the *Social Contract* must do so during the uncorrupted vigor of its youth. No community can apply this program, Rousseau insists, in the context of enslaved decrepitude that the *Second Discourse* attributes to every modern European state: "Mille nations ont brillé sur la terre qui n'auroient jamais pu souffrir de bonnes loix, et celles mêmes qui l'auroient pu n'ont eu dans toute leur durée qu'un tems fort court pour cela. Les Peuples ainsi que les hommes ne sont dociles que dans leur jeunesse, ils deviennent incorrigibles en vieillissant" (A thousand nations that have flourished on earth could never have tolerated good laws, and even those that could were only so disposed for a very short time during their entire existence. Most peoples, like men, are docile only in their youth. They become incorrigible as they grow older) (*Du contrat social,* 3 : 385).

In some circumstances Rousseau does allow for one other alternative, a rejuvenating revolution and civil war (for instance, in Sparta at the time of Lycurgus or in Rome after the Tarquins). But he describes the alternative so as to invalidate the argument that it applies to the highly cultured European mainstream: "Un peuple peut se rendre libre tant qu'il n'est que barbare, mais il ne le peut plus quand le ressort civil est usé. Alors les troubles peuvent le détruire sans que les révolutions puissent le rétablir, et sitôt que ses fers sont brisés, il tombe épars et n'existe plus: Il lui faut désormais un maitre et non pas un libérateur" (A people can liberate itself as long as it is merely barbarous, but can no longer do so when the civil machinery is worn out. Then disturbances can destroy it, but revolutions cannot reestablish it, and as soon as its chains are broken, it falls apart and no longer exists. Henceforth it must have a master and not a liberator) (*Du contrat social,* 3 : 385).

□   □   □

If we agree that Rousseau was not, like the Abbé de Saint-Pierre, composing a "Projet de contrat social pour la concorde perpetuelle," the real question becomes why he wrote, rewrote, and finally published this text, which he often referred to as the most important of his works.

The *Social Contract* is far less a program for practical political action than a refinement and development of the position taken in the *Discourse on the Origin of Inequality.* That earlier text, we remember, analyzed how man came to be what he is. Its purpose was to unmask the hidden forces at work in the history of civil society as we know it. It laid bare a precise and carefully reasoned genesis of the corruption inscribed at our society's core. The *Social Contract,* arguing for the same conclusion but approaching it differently, likewise sets out to provide a criterion against which we might judge the truth of our present situation. It does this, however, not by analyzing the past from which our present has come but by carefully delineating what might have been, the alternative untried. Choosing to situate his discourse outside the real as we know it, Rousseau offers instead an abstract morphology of political salvation. The *Social Contract* is a hypothetical blueprint that shows how, if only our catastrophic mistakes had been avoided, man's entry into civil society might have taken place as a prelude to his perfection rather than as a sealing of his doom. Like two distinct voices offering an antiphonal portrait of the human situation, the *Discourse on Inequality* and the *Social Contract* speak to us of a past that is sadly real and of an alternative that is tragically other.

The *Social Contract* can be read, in this sense, as Rousseau's long-pondered and painstakingly prepared answer to what had been since the publication of his *Discourses* the overwhelmingly negative and hostile response to the positions he had taken. From the moment he won the Dijon prize, Rousseau found himself accused of the bleakest pessimism and misanthropy. As a man who would reject the arts, the sciences, and even society itself, Rousseau had declared himself, his critics contended, an enemy of all that was best in the ongoing history of man's endeavors. To make matters worse, the most virulent of these critics were the very men he had once considered his friends, those who had designated themselves as the most progressive figures of their age: *les philosophes.* Voltaire, Grimm, d'Alembert, and even his once cherished friend Diderot seemed unanimous in their conviction that Rousseau's strictures of the forces they praised, his advocacy of a natural state somehow preferable to our own, only proved that he was motivated by a profound contempt for everything most promising in the human adventure, for all the powers of reason and enlightenment they themselves so brilliantly incarnated.

From this perspective, the *Social Contract* can be read as the most elaborate in the long series of Rousseau's attempts to stanch the gaping wound opened by those accusations. Everything this man has to tell us, his enemies claimed, is nothing more than a pathetic justification of his own cowardice in abandoning the very society he would counsel. The subtle chemistry linking political and psychological motivations in Rousseau's social thought reveals itself perhaps most clearly in his reaction to the most telling and certainly the most painful of the various forms this accusation took: what Rousseau saw as Diderot's gratuitously vicious insulting of him in his play *Le Fils naturel*. Rousseau's reaction to the reading of that play provides, I would argue, a particularly clear example of the many-layered and highly ambiguous elements at work in the dilemma his political statements set out to resolve.

In February 1757 Diderot sent Rousseau a copy of his play. It was hardly surprising that Rousseau should recognize at least a partial portrait of himself in the melancholy figure of Dorval. Much of this character's dialogue is in fact heavily colored by tonalities Rousseau had long appropriated to himself: "J'ai reçu du Ciel un coeur droit; c'est le seul avantage qu'il ait voulu m'accorder. . . . Mais ce coeur est flétri, et je suis, comme vous voyez, sombre et mélancolique. J'ai de la vertu, mais elle est austère; des moeurs, mais sauvages. . . . Je hais le commerce des hommes, et je sens que c'est loin de ceux-mêmes qui me sont chers que le repos m'attend" (I have received from heaven an honest heart; it is the only advantage with which it saw fit to bless me. . . . But that heart is withered, and I am, as you see, somber and melancholy. I am a man of virtue, but of an austere virtue; a man of morals, but of morals from another age. . . . I detest human society and I feel it is far from my fellows that peace awaits me).[6] The specific insult, what Rousseau saw as the proof of a sudden and inexplicable reversal in Diderot's feelings toward him, came in the way another of the characters, Constance, the sister of Clairville, responds to Dorval's very Rousseauian desire to separate himself from society: "Vous avez reçu les talents les plus rares, et vous en devez compte à la société. Que cette foule d'êtres inutiles qui s'y meuvent sans objet, et qui l'embarrassent sans la servir, s'en éloignent, s'ils veulent. Mais vous, j'ose vous le dire, vous ne le pouvez sans crime. . . . J'en appelle à votre coeur, interrogez-le, et il vous dira que l'homme de bien est dans la société, et qu'il n'y a que le méchant qui soit seul" (You have been blessed with the rarest gifts, and you owe an accounting of them to society. Let that mob of useless individuals who maneuver about with no real purpose, who trouble society without serving it, exile themselves if they wish. You could never do such a thing without committing a crime. . . . Examine your heart and it will tell you that honest men must remain in society and that only the evil man is alone) (Diderot, *Fils*, p. 62).

The last phrase of this reprimand, "only the evil man is alone," engraved itself in Rousseau's mind as an equation perversely threatening and misrepresenting everything he had done since his "reform," his decision to leave Parisian society and take refuge under the dubious patronage of Madame d'Epinay. This phrase became, in Rousseau's mind, an unpardonable affront: an insult not only ending his friendship with Diderot, but threatening the very meaning of that truth he had tried to communicate to his fellows.

Rousseau's obsession with this phrase set in motion an almost endless series of defensive reactions largely because, in the context of the play, that statement was closely associated with another, far more explosive, accusation: an accusation incriminating Dorval-Rousseau's reluctance to carry out his responsibilities even to those closest to and most dependent on him. In context, the lapidary "il n'y a que le méchant qui soit seul," is a tolerable and preferable substitute, a protective screen memory, for the decidedly more painful accusation Rousseau saw in Diderot's questioning his relation to paternity: how he had or had not fulfilled his duties toward the children left in the Parisian foundling home. Dorval, at the thought of becoming a father, exclaims: "Quand je pense que nous sommes jetés, tout en naissant, dans un chaos de préjugés, d'extravagances, de vices, et de misère, l'idée m'en fait frémir" (When I think that, at our very birth, we are thrown into a chaos of prejudices, extravagances, vices, and misery, the very idea of such a thing makes me shudder) (Diderot, *Fils,* p. 63). Constance's response is heavy with the scent of Diderot's own recriminations of Rousseau: "Dorval, vos enfants ne sont point destinés à tomber dans le chaos que vous redoutez. . . . Ils apprendront de vous à penser comme vous. Vos passions, vos goûts, vos idées passeront en eux. Ils tiendront de vous ces notions si justes que vous avez de la grandeur et de la bassesse réelles; du bonheur véritable et de la misère apparente. Il ne dépendra que de vous qu'ils aient une conscience toute semblable à la vôtre" (Dorval, your children are not necessarily condemned to become victims of the chaos you so fear. . . . From you they will learn to think as you do. Your passions, your tastes, and your ideas will be passed on to them. From you they will receive a perfect understanding of greatness and pettiness, of true happiness and apparent misery. It will be up to you to see that they acquire a conscience like your own) (Diderot, *Fils,* p. 63). The implicit reprimand in Diderot's dialogue, its calling into question Rousseau's refusal to assume the role of father, provides the only plausible explanation for the arguments with which Rousseau will go on to justify his own portrayal of his position as the one true source of political counsel.

Rousseau's immediate response to Diderot, his letter acknowledging that he had received the play, represents a moment of indecision about what attitude he might best adopt. It was, he insists, a controlled and civil letter, only mildly reproaching Diderot for having penned a maxim that the uninformed might mistakenly assume to apply to Rousseau. At least in the way Rousseau describes this subsequently lost letter, we are far from the judgment of "choquant et malhonnête"[7] that he makes of Diderot's gesture as he describes his first reading of the play in book 9 of the *Confessions*. Diderot, as though oblivious to the neuralgic point he had touched, goes blithely on, in his own reply of March 10, 1757, underscoring even more boldly his challenge to Rousseau's qualifications as someone who might speak to his fellows of their social duties: "Adieu, le Citoyen! C'est pourtant un citoyen bien singulier qu'un Hermite" (Adieu, Citizen! But how strange a citizen must be a hermit).[8]

One year later, in March 1758, the psychic hemorrhage occasioned by this insult shows its first textual symptoms. Outraged by the lapidary cast Diderot had given to his maxim, Rousseau, as though unable to rid his mind of this offending element, responds by offering his own corrected version of the same maxim. He does this in a text not specifically addressed to Diderot, but, via d'Alembert, to the whole group of *philosophes* Rousseau was convinced Diderot had now leagued against him. In the *Letter to d'Alembert,* a work warning his compatriots in Geneva of the grave dangers in Voltaire's plans to establish a theatre in their city, Rousseau manages to place his all-important correction: "Le plus méchant des hommes est celui qui s'isole le plus" (The most evil man is the one who most isolates himself).[9]

The unsuspecting reader might well wonder just what is the crucial difference between "only the evil man is alone" and the amended version, "the most evil man is the man who most isolates himself." The answer comes when we examine Rousseau's revision in its context. Discussing Racine, Rousseau makes the point that French theater exercises a particularly negative influence on public morals because it is obsessively concerned with representing passionate love: "Tout le Théâtre François ne respire que la tendresse: c'est la grande vertu à laquelle on y sacrifie toutes les autres, ou du moins qu'on y rend la plus chere aux spectateurs" (The whole of French theater is suffused with tenderness: it is the one virtue to which all others are sacrificed, or at least the one made to appear most admirable to its spectators) (*d'Alembert*, p. 157). The danger here, as Rousseau explains it, is that plays fostering passions for one supremely beloved individual necessarily atrophy the spectator's capacity to direct his emotions toward a more generalized, more socialized, more inclusive object such as, to cite Rousseau's examples, "the love of humanity, the love of country." To love one person or even a number of persons always entails, according to the same equation we saw at work in *Emile,* an implicit refusal to love mankind as a whole. The nadir of this movement occurs when, as in self-love, the subject and object of desire become one. At the acme of goodness, the point on the scale opposite "the most evil," a love once directed only toward individuals is transmuted into a universal love embracing all men: "Le meilleur est celui qui partage également ses affections à tous ses semblables. Il vaut beaucoup mieux aimer une maîtresse que de s'aimer seul au monde. Mais quiconque aime tendrement ses parens, ses amis, sa patrie, et le genre humain, se dégrade par un attachement désordonné qui nuit bientôt à tous les autres, et leur est infailliblement préféré" (The best person is the one who directs his affections equally toward all his fellows. It is better to love a mistress than to love only one's self. But whoever dearly loves his parents, his friends, his country, and the entire human race can only be degraded by an inordinate attachment to one person, an attachment which soon jeopardizes all others and which will always be preferred to them) (*d'Alembert*, p. 158).

Rousseau, then, as he rewrites Diderot's maxim, distinguishes carefully between physical separation, the person who is "alone," and emotional commitment, the person who, in terms of the object of his desire, "isolates himself." The semantic boundary between these two qualifications is crucial because—as Rousseau implicitly argues here and as he explicitly argues in the letters to Malesherbes—only when he is "alone," when he is protected from the society of other men, is he able to overcome his "isolation" and to extend the scope of his love to include not a few men, not most men, but all men.

This passage from the *Letter to d'Alembert* is important not only because it constitutes a second, delayed, response to Diderot's accusation as it appeared in *Le Fils naturel* but also because it articulates an argument and a justification to which Rousseau will return as he writes the *Social Contract* and addresses it to his fellows. There too, as we have seen, Rousseau constructs his argument so that the sincerity of his commitment to all mankind depends precisely on his being set apart from and rejected by the very community he sets out to address. The alternative, to be recognized by some rather than refused by all, would reduce his efforts to nothing more than an *esprit de parti*. His position would be that of someone inciting a conspiracy of the minority, a movement in the direction of "the most evil."

Instead of being motivated by pessimism or misanthropy, as his enemies claim, Rousseau's political theory is, he insists, a corollary of uncompromising optimism. His superior optimism, he points out, courageously eschews all contact with and contamination by the debilitating forces in the society around him. It is founded on his unswerving belief in a rule of law that, if only history had not happened, man might have followed toward a universal concord of liberty, equality, and felicity. More than anything else, Rousseau sets out to demonstrate in the *Social Contract* a faith in mankind so vast and so unqualified that he is willing to preserve it *in spite of everything*. His geography of the ideal, radically excluding the European real, paradoxically expresses his confidence in a truth so precious that it must accommodate none of the perversions to which it has everywhere been subjected.

Given so convoluted a position on Rousseau's part, readers of the *Social Contract* confront a highly ambiguous textual demand. On the one hand, the text denounces the cultivated audience most likely to interest itself in such political theory for collaborating with a social order that excludes the ideal presented by this text. In showing the way things might have been, the *Social Contract* explicitly condemns all who have found their place in the way things are. The audience that *necessitates* this text's being written is made up of those systematically duped by the powers that be into believing in the pleasant yet stultifying dream of enlightenment. The *Social Contract* asks its readers to recognize themselves as part of a world that, once they look up from the *Contract*'s pages, they can perceive only as a universal nightmare.

On the other hand, the text, given the hortatory mode in which this vision is described—all the ways the *Social Contract* is different from the *Second Discourse*—simultaneously appeals to readers potentially unlike their fellows, who perhaps number among the uncorrupted few who might one day recognize this truth for what it is. The *Social Contract* addresses readers who, should they sufficiently ponder this work's message, may one day understand the ideal to which it is dedicated. This second demand of the text projects each reader as a consciousness that, should it truly understand, may one day be stripped clean of society's disfigurements. Born anew, this reader may then assume a position alongside those mythical figures from antiquity who likewise caught sight of and strove to achieve the ideal.

At the intersection of these divergent demands the *Social Contract* makes on its readers, at their point of implied synthesis, we most clearly perceive the fundamental desire this political text expresses. Rousseau elaborates an ideal so radically antithetical to the real that in effect he provokes a reaction of refusal and persecution he can expect to be as unanimous as the evil he denounces. The *Social Contract* challenges not only established authority, the powers of the *ancien régime,* but also the opposition to that authority, the party of progress, the entire *philosophe* movement that had committed itself to an ideology of social change. Yet Rousseau's decision to publish this work, to offer it to the public, presupposes that the message it enunciates, the vision of the good it offers, will find readers of good faith who can still understand that something else is possible. Rousseau chose to publish this text because he felt he could not be alone in his desire to inaugurate a new order, a new freedom, and a new felicity intended for all men.

At first glance the two demands seem contradictory. The first calls both proponents and critics of established authority to a battle in which no quarter will be given or expected. The second, addressed to an only hypothetical readership that the text itself must generate, fervently appeals to everything its readers might one day come to understand.

This act of faith in a reader invited to be refashioned by his reading places the author in a position of epistemological superiority to the audience he sets out both to create and to save. The author, and the author alone, possesses a clear and unobstructed vision of the ideal. Even the reader moved by this text, convinced by it, remains, as someone weaned on an evil he is only now learning to reject, a consciousness that falters.

This implicit superiority of Rousseau's authorial voice has often been interpreted by his antitotalitarian castigators as proof of his intention both to identify himself with and to occupy the position of that one all-powerful, superhuman figure depicted in this work: the Lawgiver. In one sense, this accusation is understandable. As we have seen, Rousseau does assume that his own awareness of the ideal far surpasses that of his reader. At no point in this work, however, is this greater awareness negotiated into the pragmatically oriented directive we would expect from a voice appropriating to itself the full prerogatives of the Lawgiver. Although the authorial vision may well fix its greater acuity on a godlike presence, it at no point designates itself an incarnation of that presence. For the audience to which it was addressed, the *Social Contract* was marked instead by an insurmountable sense of loss, by nostalgia for an alternative no longer possible. In postlapsarian eighteenth-century Europe, author and reader could know both the Lawgiver and his salvation only through an indirect, negative theology that glimpsed the ideal only as it differed from the real.

Rather than becoming the Lawgiver, rather than committing himself and his reader to some definable program of political regeneration, Rousseau chooses to leave that reader in a state of unresolvable anxiety: once cut off from the text's ongoing movement, the reader can never surely deduce what might be done, what steps should be taken. Rousseau systematically frustrates readers who would become his lieutenants, acting on clear and binding orders. Rousseau instead asks of his readers an act of faith parallel to his own, an act of faith in the martyred paraclete cosubstantial with the author of this text. To lose faith—to cease to believe, to no longer be moved—leaves the reader with no alternative other than to accept his identification with the satyr, the vulgar multitude that would abuse and vituperate the precious gift being offered them.

In constructing his political ideal and defining its relation to the reality of European society, Rousseau continually confronts his reader with an impossible moral imperative: to understand what is by definition beyond comprehension. When Rousseau makes a statement like the famous "And in so doing we do nothing more than force him to be free," he is not, then, tipping his hand—revealing at last the totalitarian motivations at the core of his enterprise. On the contrary, he means his clearly paradoxical dictum to underline the corrupted, epistemologically vitiated status of the very concepts and logic through which his readers, thanks to the whole of their history, are forced to receive and evaluate his message.[10]

The publication of a text predestined to misinterpretation can only transform its author into a universally persecuted scapegoat who, enunciating so distant a truth, offers himself as the sacrifice that expiates his readers' unworthiness. A text like the *Social Contract* must be recognized for what it is: a carefully elaborated fail-safe device that defines the relative positions of both author and reader so that political salvation comes to depend on a leap of faith sustained by the redeeming sacrifice of the author as the martyred paraclete of the truth he speaks. In a sense, then, the most appropriate of "reader responses" to Rousseau's political works might be found in the curious closing of Adrien Rechastelet's inflamed introduction to the Charles Teste 1835 transcription of Etienne de La Boëtie's *Discourse on Voluntary Servitude:* "Votre frère en Christ et en Rousseau." [11]

□ □ □

Understanding the function of the *Social Contract* in the overall economy of Rousseau's works involves careful attention not only to the relation between violence and the political but also to the inevitable persecution of any writer who speaks of what is hidden, who states a truth that forces men to recognize their lies for what they are. In an essay entitled *Persecution and the Art of Writing,* Leo Strauss, one of Rousseau's most astute critics, takes a position that by contradistinction can help us grasp what is most singular about Rousseau's resolution of this problem. In speaking of censorship and interdiction as measures to silence a forbidden truth, Strauss makes the provocative claim that these practices generate writing that implicitly confirms the classical equation of knowledge with virtue. Considering the case of a writer like Spinoza who disguises his message by making it accessible only to those who are willing to read him carefully, he states: "An author who wishes to address only thoughtful men has but to write in such a way that only a very careful reader can detect the meaning of his book. But, it will be objected, there may be clever men, careful readers, who are not trustworthy, and who, after having found the author out, would denounce him to the authorities. As a matter of fact, this literature would be impossible if the Socratic dictum that virtue is knowledge, and therefore that thoughtful men as such are trustworthy and not cruel, were entirely wrong." [12]

As useful as Strauss's intuition is, it should be apparent that the position he describes is antithetical to Rousseau's. Rather than hide his truth behind a veil of erudition that only "careful" men might penetrate, Rousseau strives instead to proclaim it with an urgency and a directness that challenge his readers' most fundamental political concepts. Rousseau made that choice because his basic premise, his conviction about what men have become, forced him to adopt a working hypothesis diametrically opposed to Strauss's. Knowledge and virtue, far from going hand in hand, have become, Rousseau insists, irreconcilable enemies. This, we remember, was the explicit message of the *First Discourse.* For Rousseau, nothing is more dangerous than the "classical ideal" Strauss speaks of. This almost conspiratorial communication between "careful" writers and "careful" readers can represent for Rousseau only the monstrous marriage of established authority and self-seeking reformers whom he saw everywhere leagued against him, disfiguring his texts, misrepresenting his message. Rousseau insists that his truth not remain a secret to be shared only by the careful cognoscenti; instead it must address itself emphatically and openly to all. Only as a direct and denunciatory proclamation will it wrest from its audience the one confirmation of its truth they can accord it: their unanimous persecution of him as the scapegoat and immolated victim of a violence whose unmasking can be accomplished at no lesser price.

In this context we begin to see how a text like the *Dialogues,* far from representing a degeneration or perversion of Rousseau's properly political position, is in fact its corollary. Having said what he said, having addressed men as he addressed them, he, both as Jean-Jacques and as Rousseau, has no alternative but to proclaim a personal innocence whose most irrefutable proof is the very intensity of his persecution. More than anything else, the *Dialogues* trace the formation of a society unified by its common consensus of blame, its universal collaboration in silencing the truth and expelling its speaker. Approached in this way, *Rousseau juge de Jean-Jacques* becomes a text that instead of clinically confirming Rousseau's supposed insanity is, as Michel Serres has eloquently argued, another version of the *Social Contract:* "Il décrit en fait à la fin de sa vie ce qu'il avait posé en droit et abstraitement dans son exercice de philosophie politique. Les autres en bloc ont ensemble un pacte. Et ce pacte est issu de l'animosité générale, qui est la perversion ou la dérivation de l'ancienne volonté générale. Jean-Jacques dédoublé récrit le *Contrat social*" (Toward the end of his life Rousseau describes as fact what he had earlier, in his political writings, proposed as abstract theory. As a bloc, the others are bound together by a pact. This pact is the expression of their general hatred, a derivation from and perversion of what he had earlier called their general will. Jean-Jacques split in two rewrites the *Social Contract*).[13]

Above all else, the readers of the *Social Contract* are called on to recognize Rousseau's as a voice speaking from afar, a voice situated outside the congeries of violence and deceit, the voice of a man in every way "alone." Only by speaking from afar can he avoid the threat of compromise with the real. His status as the martyred paraclete is the precondition of his maintaining so absolute a vision of the good that he can denounce and unmask all the lies and stratagems that have systematically deceived mankind. The choice to constitute himself as victim becomes an act of love as all-encompassing as the hatred with which it must be greeted.

What is, is. And Rousseau sees it as no fault of his own that what he offers as an act of love, once sundered from an awareness of the ideal informing it, should be read as its opposite, an act of refusal and isolation. Readers who would choose their own present, refusing the nostalgia and sadness to which this text summons them, have no alternative but to respond in the currency of their blindness. The multitude hopelessly enslaved by the very illusions they have fabricated will declare themselves outraged enemies of this voice that utters so scandalous a truth. Rousseau must accept his fate as a messenger whose act of love, whose refusal of "isolation," will only initiate a process of violence and persecution aimed at reversing the very essence of his message. In elaborating his vision of the ideal, he offers himself to his contemporaries as a victim whose innocence provides the one suitable expiation of their guilt. In a world given over to the rule of the satyrs, the paraclete can be only a scapegoat.

Rousseau's insistence on the past conditional, on *what might have been* as the informing temporality of his ideal, is constant throughout his political writings. He calls upon a hypothetical reader somehow held safe from the corruption of our history to judge both the author and the ideal he expresses. The reader, however, must accept these two realities, author and text, as an irreducible amalgam joined in such a way that the second both exculpates and justifies the first. The *Social Contract* in this sense is a work that implicitly addresses one privileged reader, neither the satyr nor the man of science. Rousseau's decision to describe the perfect society as an ideal that radically excludes our real assumes its ultimate meaning when we realize that he has written for the one reader truly capable of understanding what he says. The Lawgiver himself, a hypothetical audience of one, is called on to recognize the voice of his paraclete, the voice of the one man who has kept faith with so rigorous a vision of what could have been.

The most singular discursive strategy within the *Social Contract* is this decision to address the work to a reader whose understanding and judgment must, by definition, far surpass those of the author's corrupted contemporaries. Rousseau's political theory is unique because it is informed by his decision to inscribe in its textuality his own supplication of the hypothetical reader. Rousseau's voice addresses itself to the very principle that sustains his ability to speak. Evoking and describing, through a glass darkly, an ideal order beyond the human as we know it, he implies that his work can be recognized for what it is only by the Lawgiver to whose judgment it addresses itself and in whose eyes it must find favor. As in the invocation of the sovereign judge in the opening pages of the *Confessions*, Rousseau ultimately treats his human audience, the wise and the foolish, the men of science and the satyrs, as intruders on his prayer, his *dulia*, which addresses an agency of judgment far superior to their own. *Dulia*: a veneration of the sacred; yet the word comes from the Greek *douleia* meaning servitude. It is a prayer uttered in servitude, the servant's prayer both to his Other and to the principle of that Otherness as the foundation of an ideal that radically surpasses our human condition.

☐   ☐   ☐

My intent in this chapter has been twofold. On the one hand, I have tried to show why we must reject what, starting even before Edmund Burke, has been the most consistent Anglo-Saxon interpretation of Rousseau's political works as an apology for totalitarian government. On the other, I have tried, as I made this argument, to underline how the most distinctive element in Rousseau's political works, the relation he assumes between authority, submission, and desire, is generated by the same vectors of paradox at work in his literary, autobiographical, pedagogical, and philosophical texts. In a work like the *Social Contract*, the authority the text ultimately addresses is its single elected reader: the Lawgiver himself. Rousseau can elaborate his refusal of the real, the uncompromising purity of his denunciation, only as he simultaneously expresses submission to that one exalted authority, away from whom the whole of history has so irremediably led mankind. The lost felicity in whose name Rousseau would speak is founded on the erasure of all distinction between desire and the submitting of that desire to an authority whose workings and dictates are defined as beyond the comprehension of his fellows. In this sense, the ideal delineated in the *Social Contract* must be read not only as an expression of what Rousseau would call his love for humanity but also as the token of his unswerving fidelity to the figure of the Lawgiver, the one redeeming agency of authority who can inaugurate and protect a social order that holds him in a perfect equilibrium of desire and submission. The fact of history, everything that has so compromised this ideal, implies for Rousseau the political theorist no alternative other than to see himself transformed into the martyred paraclete of that Lawgiver's impossible reign. Rousseau witnesses in his political works an ideal so divorced from the real that his contemporaries are implicitly summoned to make him as its spokesman a victim of the very truth he speaks.

7. Anthologies of Desire

> Il y a une logique du désir et c'est une logique du pari.
> A partir d'un certain degré de malchance, le joueur
> malheureux ne renonce pas, mais il mise des sommes
> toujours plus fortes sur des probabilités toujours plus
> faibles. Le sujet finira toujours par dénicher l'obstacle
> insurmontable, qui ne sera peut-être que la vaste indif-
> férence du monde, et il se brisera sur elle.
> —René Girard, *Des choses cachées depuis la
> fondation du monde*

During the last six years of his life Rousseau began two major
works: the *Dialogues* in 1772 and the *Reveries* in 1776—the second effort unfinished at his death on July 2, 1778. These two texts
represent a new and significantly different stage in Rousseau's understanding of his lifelong effort to write the truth. They both clarify and redefine the various beginnings of that undertaking.

In relation to Rousseau's political works, the *Dialogues* and the
Reveries constitute an extended, almost obsessive meditation on his
status as the innocent victim of the truth he sought to enunciate.
The first promenade of the *Reveries* opens with a self-portrait of the
author as the object of a universal, unjustified hatred: "Me voici
donc seul sur la terre, n'ayant plus de frere, de prochain, d'ami, de
société que moi-même. Le plus sociable et le plus aimant des humains en a été proscrit par un accord unanime. Ils ont cherché dans
les rafinemens de leur haine quel tourment pouvoit être le plus cruel
à mon ame sensible, et ils ont brisé violemment tous les liens qui
m'attachoient à eux" (I am now alone on earth, no longer having
any brother, neighbor, friend, or society other than myself. The
most sociable and most loving of humans has been proscribed from
society by a unanimous agreement. In the refinement of their hatred, they have sought the torment which would be cruelest to my
sensitive soul and they have violently broken all the ties which attached me to them).[1] In the winter of 1777, only six months before
his death, Rousseau reaffirms this conviction in the eighth promenade: "La ligue est universelle, sans exception, sans retour, et je
suis sur d'achever mes jours dans cette affreuse proscription sans
jamais en penetrer le mistére" (The league is universal, without ex-

ception, and past all hope. I am sure I will finish my days in this
dreadful rejection without ever penetrating the mystery of it) (*Rêveries*, 1 : 1077). This overwhelming hatred of one innocent victim, a
contagion touching all members of society, becomes, as Rousseau
sees it, the essential legacy of his generation—a duty that will be
passed on to all who follow.

What sets the *Dialogues* and the *Reveries* apart from Rousseau's
earlier works is his utter loss of faith in the possibility of speaking to
posterity. He no longer believes that they might one day recognize
his truth and, as a result, that he might be exculpated by those who
come after, those who were not themselves the organizers of the
conspiracy of defamation and persecution everywhere poised against
him. Rather than recognition and exculpation, Rousseau now realizes, he can expect from succeeding generations only that they will
vie for the honor of spitting on his grave.

The strident repetition of so dark a vision poses difficult problems for anyone trying to situate these last works in the overall
economy of Rousseau's writings. More often than not, the patent
"excess" of Rousseau's final meditations has led his critics to adopt
an attitude toward them that, paradoxically, confirms the very position they find so excessive. Labeling these texts as pathological delirium, most critics who choose to deal with them—and it is a relatively rare choice—repeat in their analyses a process of exclusion
that they simultaneously ask us to see as Rousseau's most obvious
paranoid symptom. They explain the *Dialogues* or the less placid
passages from the *Reveries,* with either embarrassment or glee, as
their author's lapses into clinical madness. Confronted with tirades
and pleas as extreme and as apparently beyond authorial control as
those in these works, critics understandably feel compelled to explain "scientifically" just what went wrong with the consciousness
behind them. The history of Rousseau criticism is punctuated by a
seemingly endless succession of autopsies taking us back to the
now-silent cadaver and, following the latest fashions in organic and
psychological pathology, offering yet another diagnosis of Rousseau's malady. For the more tactful, like Jean Guéhenno, this sick-
ness is a sad lesson in how far greatness can fall.[2] For others, like
Lester Crocker, it is the welcome confirmation that every phase of
Rousseau's work is shot through with this same noxious delirium.[3]

Such approaches to Rousseau's final works, whatever their sym-
pathies, share the disadvantage of placing the reader in an impos-

sible relation to the texts in question. Through whatever grid we read them and no matter how convincing the model of pathology through which we would pass from text to author, these final works never allow us to draw valid conclusions about Rousseau the man. To analyze these works as an index of the physical person behind them is to retrace the impossible journey of those who on December 18, 1897, finally obtained permission to exhume Rousseau's body to test their hypothesis that his crushed skull would reveal traces of the hammer blows with which they were convinced Thérèse had murdered him. Just as Rousseau's cranium bore no witness to so grisly a scene, all autopsical analyses of his final works likewise represent itineraries of judgment far more than itineraries of comprehension.[4]

However misleading and futile the hermeneutics to which such approaches might lend themselves, they have the far greater disadvantage of closing off the reader from the specifically textual and intertextual dimensions of Rousseau's works. In the case of the *Dialogues* and the *Reveries,* this is particularly unfortunate. In no other period of Rousseau's work was the act of writing more directly and explicitly determined by his relation to a whole network of texts outside his own. To write, for Rousseau, was both to respond to his anxious certainty that disfigured versions of his earlier works were circulating and to maintain contact with and consolidate the solace he found in reading such classical moralists as his beloved Plutarch. In these final works Rousseau redefines the entire shape of his enterprise through the organizing metaphors of the written text and the practice of botany. Writing and botany become for Rousseau homologous activities, for both result in a consignment of life to paper, of what is past to a book that preserves it for the future: "La vie que je méne depuis dix ans à la campagne n'est guéres qu'une herborisation continuelle" (The life I have been leading in the country for the last ten years is little more than a continual herborizing).[5]

I would like in this closing chapter both to examine the specifically intertextual dimension of these works and to isolate what is most singular about the "voice" we hear speaking through this final stage of Rousseau's attempt to write the truth. Toward that end I propose to consider these works according to an analytic model drawn from what linguistics has told us of a long forgotten "middle voice": a voice that in neither actively attempting to change the reader's mind nor passively imploring his judgment brings us particularly close to the tonalities of self-imposed sacrifice and victimage that inform these final works.

☐   ☐   ☐

In criticizing the lack of attention given to the intertextual dimensions of the *Dialogues* and the *Reveries*, I noted how most readings of these works ignore a series of explicit references to other texts whose processes and signification exercise a particular sway over Rousseau's elaboration of his own discourse.

The fourth promenade of the *Reveries* opens with one of Rousseau's frequent appeals to the figure of a snake twisted back on itself and grasping its tail between its jaws. Rousseau uses this image of an ending that recuperates its beginning to symbolize his reading habits during the last years of his life. Of the few authors he still reads, his favorite remains Plutarch, who provided the guiding illumination of his earliest youth: "Avant hier je lisois dans ses oeuvres morales le traité *Comment on pourra tirer utilité de ses ennemis*" (The day before yesterday I was reading in his essays the piece entitled *The Usefulness of Enemies*) (*Rêveries*, 1 : 1024). Significantly, Rousseau's reference to this essay can be read not only as a return of age to youth but as a looking back from reclusive solitude to that period of effervescence when he published the first of his political works, the *Discourse on the Arts and Sciences*. Rousseau drew from Plutarch's meditation on the usefulness of enemies, we remember, his quotation about Prometheus's gift of fire to the satyr—the scene that inspired the frontispiece to his first published work. At the same time, even the most cursory acquaintance with Plutarch's essay qualifies the assumption that the more paranoid aspects of Rousseau's last works are rooted only in his distorted imagination. On the contrary, Plutarch's discussion of those enemies from whom the wise man must learn to draw benefit is marked by an aggrandizement of the malefic other that is as stunning as anything Rousseau would ever write on the subject: "C'est que ton ennemy veille continuellement à espier toutes tes actions, et fait le guet à l'entour de ta vie, cherchant par tout quelque moyen de te surprendre à descouvert, pour avoir prise sur toy, ne voyant pas seulement à travers les chesnes, comme faisoit Lynceus, ou à travers les pierres et les tuyles, mais aussi à travers un amy, à travers un seviteur domestique, et à travers ceulx avec qui tu auras familiere conversation, pour descouvrir, autant qu'il luy sera possible, ce que tu feras, sondant et fouillant tout ce que tu delibereras, et que tu proposeras de faire" (Your enemy is constantly spying on your every act. He is like a watchman circling round your life, seeking out every possible occasion to catch you off guard, to find some hold over you. Not only can he see through oak trees like Lynceus, but he can see through stone and tile, through a friend, through a servant, through anyone with whom you have daily conversation. He does this to learn as much as he can about what you are planning to do. He plumbs and sifts through everything you deliberate, everything you propose).[6] The truly wise man, Plutarch continues, must learn to fix his attention on his enemies' words and gestures with a single-mindedness and resolution every bit as intense as Rousseau's helpless fascination with every whispered charge brought against him. Under Plutarch's influence Rousseau arrived at the conclusion that from his status as the innocent victim of a universal conspiracy he could draw an immense benefit. In response to the Plutarchian counsel that "Il n'y a doncques rien plus grave ne plus beau, que d'ouir un ennemy injurieux, disant injure, sans aucunement s'en passionner" (There is nothing more important nor more admirable than to listen to an unjust enemy stating his lies while never being moved by them) (Plutarch, *De l'utilité*, p. 197), Rousseau, in the eighth promenade, offers what must be recognized as a minimal variation on this *locus classicus:* "En me rendant insensible à l'adversité il m'ont fait plus de bien que s'ils m'eussent épargné ses atteintes. En ne l'eprouvant pas je pourrois toujours la craindre, au lieu qu'en la subjuguant je ne la crains plus" (In making me insensitive to adversity, they have done me more good than if they had spared me its blows. In not experiencing it, I might have always feared it; instead, by overcoming it, I no longer fear it) (*Rêveries*, 1:1081).

An acquaintance with Plutarch's essay not only limits the claim that Rousseau's last writings represent his retreat into an idiosyncratic world of total madness but confirms that his return to this key text of a favorite author initiated an important shift in his understanding of the violence he saw characterizing the society around him. Plutarch's insight about drawing benefit from our enemies rests on his contention that lies and defamation, like all violence, achieve their greatest destructive force only when all the parties involved, innocent as well as guilty, allow themselves to be caught up in a spiral of retaliation. The desire for revenge, the imitation of the attacking enemies, initiates an always-escalating mimesis of violence that ultimately obliterates all perception of individual moral valences. The wise man, to become something other than the victim of his victory, must respond to violence by seeking not the vulnerability of the other but the virtue of the self. As Plutarch puts it: "Mais la plus part de ceulx qui se sentent injuriez, ne regardent pas si le vice qu'on leur objice est en eulx, mais s'il y en a point quelque autre en celuy qui le leur objice: et comme les luicteurs ne secouent pas la poulciere dont ils sont saupoudrez, si ne font ils pas eulx les injures dont ils sont diffamez, ains s'entrepoudrent l'un l'autre, et puis en se saboulant s'entresouillent et s'entresallissent l'un l'autre" (When attacked, most people never ask whether they are guilty of the evil they are accused of but whether there isn't some greater evil in the person attacking them. They react to the charges leveled against them as though they were wrestlers who need pay no heed to the mud they are covered with. They dirty each other and, rolling over the ground on top of each other, only further sully and defile themselves) (Plutarch, *De l'utilité*, pp. 193–94). As a maxim, this same lesson appears in Diogenes's lapidary answer to the man asking what would be the best vengeance against his enemies: "En te rendant," Plutarch quotes him as replying, "toy-mesme vertueux et homme de bien" (By making yourself a man of goodness and virtue") (Plutarch, *De l'utilité*, p. 188).

Rousseau's own interiorization of this lesson entails a second level of elaboration. Convinced that even his studied eschewal of retaliation has failed to protect him from the community's violence, he finds himself forced to question the very rationality and humanity of his persecutors: "Je compris que mes contemporains n'étoient par rapport à moi que des êtres méchaniques qui n'agissoient que par impulsion et dont je ne pouvois calculer l'action que par les loix du mouvement. . . . Je ne vis plus en eux que des masses différemment mues, depourvues à mon egard de toute moralité" (I understood that, in relation to me, my contemporaries were nothing more than automatons who acted only on impulse and whose action I could calculate only from the laws of motion. . . . I no longer saw in them anything but randomly moved masses, destitute of all morality with respect to me) (*Rêveries*, 1 : 1078). The lesson Rousseau draws from his experience becomes a variant of the Plutarchian position, but one redefined by a degree of fatalism and passivity that all but obliterates the perception of any personal virtue to be strengthened.

Rousseau understood "qu'il falloit m'y soumettre sans raisonner et sans regimber parce que cela seroit inutile, que tout ce que j'avois à faire encore sur la terre étant de m'y regarder comme un être purement passif je ne devois point user à resister inutilement à ma destinée la force qui me restoit pour la supporter" (that I had to submit myself without reasoning and without struggling because that would be useless. I understood that, since all I had left to do on earth was to regard myself as a purely passive being, I ought not to use up, in futilely resisting my fate, the strength I had left to endure it) (*Rêveries*, 1:1079).

□   □   □

These quotations from the eighth promenade represent a refusal of violence and its mimetic reciprocity. They express a resigned understanding that as a process violence can never be ended by response and retaliation but only augmented and extended. In this sense, the *Reveries* are distinctly different from those other later works that are characterized by rebuttal and counteraccusation: the *Lettre à Christolphe de Beaumont*, the *Lettres de la montagne*, the *Confessions* and the *Dialogues*. These references to "The Usefulness of One's Enemies" do not, however, account for the motivation of the *Reveries* by a desire different from that in Plutarch to strengthen virtue by the attacks made on it. We find instead a desire to remove the self from all perception by the other. Shortly after the passage quoted above, Rousseau emphasizes even more strongly how his decision to "uproot" and "cut himself off" from judgment by other men has purified him of any tendency toward the enslavement of *amour propre:* "En se repliant sur mon ame et en coupant les relations extérieures qui le rendent exigeant, en renonçant aux comparaisons et aux préférences il [my self love] s'est contenté que je fusse bon pour moi; alors redevenant amour de moi même il est rentré dans l'ordre de la nature et m'a délivré du joug de l'opinion" (By withdrawing into my soul and severing the external relations that made it demanding, by renouncing comparisons and preferences, my self-love was satisfied with my being good in my own way. Then, again becoming a simple love of myself, it returned to the natural order and delivered me from the yoke of opinion) (*Rêveries*, 1:1079).

The ultimate object of Rousseau's desire, a desire for the absence of any desire that elects an object outside the self, establishes a metaphoric equivalence between the two major activities that occupy Rousseau's final years: the act of writing and the practice of botanizing. As Marcel Raymond has pointed out in his introduction to the Pléiade edition of the *Reveries*,[7] this equivalence is latent in the history of the French language. The verb *rêver* is derived from the late Latin form of *reexvagare:* "to wander about with no fixed goal," as in the modern *vagabonder.* Raymond offers a quotation dated 1300 in which, with a distinctly Rousseauian tonality, the verb *rêver* is used to describe those who set out in the name of a freedom sufficiently personal to find themselves called libertines: "les libertins resvoient toute la nuit hors parmi la ville." Rousseau himself, at the beginning of the seventh promenade, presents these two activities, writing and botanizing, as the polarities defining his entire affective life during his last years: "Le recueil de mes longs rêves est à peine commencé, et déja je sens qu'il touche à sa fin. Un autre amusement lui succede, m'absorbe, et m'ôte même le tems de rêver. . . . Me voila donc à mon foin pour toute nourriture, et à la botanique pour toute occupation" (This collection of my long dreams is scarcely begun, and I already feel it is near its end. Another pastime takes its place, absorbs me, and even deprives me of the time to dream. . . . Here I am with grass as my only nourishment, and botany as my only preoccupation) (*Rêveries*, 1 : 1060).

In the first promenade, Rousseau explains how he came to begin this work. He made his decision to resurrect the past, to dwell through his writing exclusively in his memories of a time now lost, both as a refusal of and an escape from the present he is forced to share with other men. Likewise, as his resuscitation of the past proves incapable of lifting him above the enmity of other men, Rousseau will discover in his fascination with vegetable nature, the world of plants, a far more effective means for achieving the same goal: "J'avois même à craindre dans mes rêveries que mon imagination effarouchée par mes malheurs ne tournât enfin de ce côté [my sad situation] son activité, et que le continuel sentiment de mes peines me resserrant le coeur par degrés ne m'accablât enfin de leur poids. Dans cet état, un instinct qui m'est naturel, me faisant fuir toute idée attristante imposa silence à mon imagination et fixant mon attention sur les objets qui m'environnoient me fit pour la prémiére fois détailler le spectacle de la nature, que je n'avois guére contemplé jusqu'alors qu'en masse et dans son ensemble" (Even in my reveries I had to fear lest my imagination, frightened by my misfortunes, might finally turn its activities to this side [my sad situation] and lest the continual sentiment of my troubles, gradually constricting my heart, crush me at last with its weight. In this condition an instinct which is natural to me, making me flee every depressing idea, imposed silence upon my imagination and, fixing my attention upon the objects which surrounded me, made me consider in detail for the first time the spectacle of nature which until then I had hardly contemplated except in a mass and in its wholeness) (*Rêveries*, 1 : 1062). Pondering this newly discovered remedy, Rousseau draws from his love of botany a conclusion exactly like that supported by his writing the *Levite of Ephraim* during those equally horrible days of his flight into exile. In the midst of universal animosity, to concentrate his attention on the plants of the fields is once again to display an absolute remove from all concern with vengeance and retaliation. This removal, Rousseau goes on to say, places him at a level of moral goodness far surpassing that to which his persecutors might pretend: "C'est le moyen de ne laisser germer dans mon coeur aucun levain de vengeance ou de haine, et pour trouver encor dans ma destinée du gout à quelque amusement, il faut assurément avoir un naturel bien epuré de toutes passions irascibles. C'est me venger de mes persecuteurs à ma maniére, je ne saurois les punir plus cruellement que d'être heureux malgré eux" (It is the means of not letting any germ of revenge or hatred spring up in my heart; and, given my destiny, to still find delight in an amusement, it is surely necessary to have a natural temperament quite purified of all irascible passions. I thus avenge myself on my persecutors in my way: I would not know how to punish them more cruelly than to be happy in spite of them) (*Rêveries*, 1 : 1061). In the practice of botany even more than in the actual writing of the *Reveries,* Rousseau coincides with the Plutarchian ideal of virtuous abstraction from the endless reciprocity of hatred and violence.

This equivalence of writing and botanizing is not, however, limited to their fulfillment of the negative desires of forgetting, escaping, and protecting oneself from the animosity of others. Rousseau's decision to consign to paper his joyful remembrances of various moments from his past had the positive effect of allowing him to reestablish contact with, to resurrect, the happiness those moments first brought with them: "Je fixerai par l'écriture celles qui pourront me venir encore; chaque fois que je les relirai m'en rendra la jouissance" (I shall fix in writing those which still come to me and each

time I reread them I will enjoy them anew) (*Rêveries*, 1:999). Describing himself as the opposite of someone like Montaigne, who
wrote so that others might read him, Rousseau now understands
that his writing is intended only for himself, that his own rereading
of his words will allow him to multiply the scant ration of joy and
happiness allotted him. To write for the self alone becomes the ultimate strategy for achieving a constant, autarkic access to all that
was best in a past only he can remember. Having written down in
the fifth promenade his memories of the happiness he knew during
his stay at the Ile St. Pierre, Rousseau can now and forever return to
that text as the promise of an integral resuscitation of the sentiments originally inspiring it. His pleasure is "de m'y transporter
chaque jour sur les ailes de l'imagination, et d'y gouter durant quel-
ques heures le même plaisir que si je l'habitois encor" (to transport
myself there each day on the wings of my imagination and to enjoy
for a few hours the same pleasure as if I were still living there) (*Rêveries*, 1:1049).

Following an exactly similar movement from negative to positive, from escape to recuperation, Rousseau, in the last of the eight
Lettres sur la botanique addressed to Madame De Lessert, describes the "text" of botany, the herbarium in which one must carefully preserve the flowers gathered from the fields, as a "*mémoratif*."[8] Rousseau explains the choice of this term, which refers to a
desire strikingly similar to that governing the composition of the
Reveries, when toward the end of the seventh promenade he describes what the specimens in his own herb book allow him to recall: "Toutes mes courses de botanique, les diverses impressions du
local des objets qui m'ont frappé, les idées qu'il m'a fait naitre, les
incidens qui s'y sont mêlés, tout cela m'a laissé des impressions qui
se renouvellent par l'aspect des plantes herborisées dans ces mêmes
lieux. . . . Maintenant que je ne peux plus courir ces heureuses con-
trées je n'ai qu'à ouvrir mon herbier et bientot il m'y transporte"
(All my botanical jaunts, the diverse impressions of the place where
the objects which struck me were located, the ideas that place
brought forth in me, the incidents which were mingled with it, all of
that has left me with impressions which are renewed by seeing the
plants that I looked for in those very places. . . . Now that I can no
longer roam about those happy regions I have only to open my
herbarium, and it soon transports me there) (*Rêveries*, 1:1073).

Rousseau's twin practices of "anthologizing" (a word designating a collection of texts but derived from the Greek *anthos:* "flower" and *legein:* "to choose") become the symbols of a desire that seeks to fulfill itself through the isolation and preservation of resurrective remnants from the past. As such, it can express itself equivalently through flowers consigned to a herbarium or through written descriptions of happiness inscribed in language. During his last years, just as Rousseau copied and distributed to carefully chosen friends certain of his manuscripts, so also he offered meticulously constructed herb books to such key figures in his life as Madame Boy de la Tour, Madame De Lessert, and Malesherbes.

The practice of botanizing, a redefining metaphorization of the act of writing, stimulates Rousseau to redeploy key themes from his earlier works. In a famous passage from the *Confessions,* for instance, the young Rousseau's undeserved punishment for the broken comb is described as casting a veil over and destroying the happiness he had previously found in the natural setting of Boissy. In the seventh promenade, as almost a direct response to that earlier episode, Rousseau describes a strange paradox: the injustices done him have reached a point of intensity where he can, even if only in the most precariously conditional mode, reestablish contact in solitary forays with a nature again capable of initiating the joyous metamorphosis of consciousness he had thought irretrievably lost. "Le plaisir d'aller dans un desert chercher de nouvelles plantes couvre celui d'échaper à mes persécuteurs et parvenu dans des lieux où je ne vois nulles traces d'hommes je respire plus à mon aise comme dans un azyle où leur haine ne me poursuit plus" (The pleasure of going into an uninhabited area to seek new plants blots out the pleasure of escaping from my persecutors, and having arrived in places where I see no trace of men, I breathe more at my ease, as though I were in a refuge where their hatred no longer pursues me) (*Rêveries,* 1 : 1070).

□   □   □

Even as he underlines botany's premium of the "mémoratif," however, Rousseau insists that this activity must be aimed at something more than the gathering of plants and the evocation of past happiness. As both a study and a field of knowledge on which Rousseau considered himself an authority, botany must also propose an organization and representation of its subject matter. Here in Rousseau's approach to the question of botany as a formal study, the crucial ambiguities of his enterprise once again begin to reformulate themselves. On the one hand, botany as a field of knowledge must make use of language. On the other, that reliance on language threatens botany's maintaining any real contact with the natural objects it sets out to represent. In the third of his letters to Madame De Lessert, Rousseau issues a stern warning: "Mais je vous préviens que si vous voulez prendre des livres et suivre la nomenclature ordinaire, avec beaucoup de noms vous aurez peu d'idées, celles que vous aurez se brouilleront, vous ne suivrez bien ni ma marche ni celle des autres, et n'aurez tout au plus qu'une connoissance de mots" (But I warn you: if you decide to follow the manuals and use the standard nomenclature, you will end up with many names but few ideas, and those you have will be confused. You will be unable to follow either my instructions or anyone else's. At most you will end up with a knowledge of words) (*Lettres sur la botanique,* 4 : 1161).

Rousseau rejects here the tradition of botanical nomenclature established by Joseph Pitton de Tournefort in his *Eléments de botanique ou méthode pour connaître les plantes* of 1694. Tournefort's system, assigning a long multiword Latin sentence as a name for each species of plant, came to symbolize for Rousseau the ultimately meaningless, self-enclosed logomachy that he saw lurking in every attempt to represent in language a nature whose most precious trait lay precisely in its being held safe from, and remaining unmediated by, the accretions and disfigurements of words. To counter this, Rousseau proposed as his major contribution to the science of botany what might be described as a nonlinguistic pasigraphy. Refusing even the much-simplified nomenclature proposed by Linnaeus in his *Systema plantarum* of 1753, Rousseau suggested a radically different approach to the problem. Employing no words at all, but only algebraic symbols (circles, dots, slashes, broken-line drawings), he assigned to each species of plant a sequence of these symbols meant to designate all its essential characteristics. The "name" of a given plant thus becomes not a string of words but a sequence of nonverbal symbols sufficiently numerous to isolate the species in question from all others like it.[9]

From our perspective, this project (which, it should be said, had as little practical success as Rousseau's similar ideas for a numerical system of musical notation) is important because it reveals Rousseau's insistence on establishing a mode of representation that would preserve for the botanist the direct, unmediated contact with vegetable nature that Rousseau saw as the real object of his solitary forays. Even as an object of formal study botany must be kept as isolated from man's symbolic accretions as the flowers of which it speaks. Thus Rousseau insists on an absolute break between *botany* as a pure, contemplative, nonutilitarian knowledge of plants and *herborizing* as a debasing subordination of that knowledge to the elaboration of a human pharmacopoeia. Pharmaceutical herborizing, for Rousseau, is not something complementary but something antithetical to any true knowledge and appreciation of vegetable nature: "Une autre chose contribue encore à éloigner du regne végétal l'attention des gens de gout; c'est l'habitude de ne chercher dans les plantes que des drogues et des remedes" (Yet another thing contributes to turning people's attention away from the vegetable realm: the habit of seeing only drugs and remedies in plants) (*Rêveries*, 1 : 1063).

To scrutinize nature with the eye of a pharmacist or herborist is to violate its essential purity, to abolish its saving otherness from everything human. The herborist inscribes on the surface of nature a second level of signification linking it to the whole of man's social and physical degeneration: "Je sens même que le plaisir que je prends à parcourir les bocages seroit empoisonné par le sentiment des infirmités humaines s'il me laissoit penser à la fiévre, à la pierre, à la goute et au mal caduc" (I even feel that the pleasure I take in wandering through groves would be poisoned by the sentiment of human infirmities, if I were led to think about fever, stones, gout and epilepsy) (*Rêveries*, 1 : 1065). Rousseau rejects the efficacy of herbal remedies because they subordinate the plants' salutary reality to what can only be a fallacious and meretricious exercise of fallible human authority: "Des gens qui passent leur vie à arranger savamment des coquilles se moquent de la botanique comme d'une étude inutile quand on n'y joint pas, comme ils disent, celle des proprietés, c'est-à-dire quand on n'abandonne pas l'observation de la nature qui ne ment point et qui ne nous dit rien de tout cela pour se livrer uniquement à l'autorité des hommes qui sont menteurs et qui nous affirment beaucoup de choses qu'il faut croire sur leur parole, fondée elle-même le plus souvent sur l'autorité d'autrui" (People who spend their life learnedly arranging shells ridicule botany as a useless study when we do not, as they say, combine it with the study

of properties; that is to say, when we do not forsake the observation
of nature, which does not lie at all, and yield to the sole authority of
men, who are liars who assert many things we must necessarily believe upon their word, itself most often founded on the authority of
others) (*Rêveries*, 1 : 1064). The thought of his cherished plants
being subjected to such debasement triggers Rousseau's eloquent
denunciation of herbal medicine as a movement of universal devastation and degradation: "Ces idées medicinales . . . fletrissent
l'email des près, l'eclat des fleurs, dessechent la fraicheur des boc-
cages, rendent la verdure et les ombrages insipides et dégoutans;
toutes ces structures charmantes et gracieuses interessent fort peu
quiconque ne veut que piler tout cela dans un mortier, et l'on n'ira
pas chercher des guirlandes pour des bergeres parmi des herbes pour
les lavemens" (Those medicinal ideas . . . wither the colors of the
fields and the splendor of the flowers, dry up the freshness of the
groves, and make our greenery and shady spots insipid and disgust-
ing. All those charming and gracious structures barely interest anyone who only wants to grind it all up in a mortar, and no one will
go seeking garlands for shepherd lasses amidst drugs intended for
an enema) (*Rêveries*, 1 : 1064).

In his defense of a resolutely nonpharmaceutical botany, Rousseau returns to the same argument that we saw him applying in the
Essay on the Origin of Languages to the arts of music and painting.
On the one hand, his praise for the botanical Theophrastus and his
condemnation of the herborizing Discorides parallels his earlier
preference for the directly expressive melodic line of Italian opera
over the systematically rationalized harmonics he saw as the insipid
essence of French opera. On the other hand, Rousseau's insistence
that the true botanist carry out his research in the full glory of wild
and uncultivated nature rather than on specimens collected in his
study is similar to his contention that true painting, relying on figure and line while excluding the abstract nonrepresentational play
of colors, must always be linked to a real scene drawn from nature.

The concluding paragraph of the seventh promenade, Rousseau's
single most extensive statement about the passion for botany that
became the most important occupation of his last years, explains
why he so adored this activity: "C'est la chaine des idées accessoires
qui m'attache à la botanique. Elle rassemble et rappelle à mon
imagination toutes les idées qui la flatent davantage" (I am attached
to botany by the chain of accessory ideas. Botany gathers together

and recalls to my imagination all the ideas which most gratify it) (*Rêveries*, 1 : 1073).

This notion of a "chain of accessory ideas" points to botany as a contact, a link, an affective resurrection of the specific past situation in which Rousseau first discovered the joys of that activity: his stay at Chambéry in the company of Madame de Warens and Claude Anet, which he consistently defined as the time of his greatest happiness. The mutually sustaining polarities of Rousseau's reflections on botany are a present and a past, much as in the opening sentence of the tenth and final promenade: "Aujourdui jour de paques fleuries il y a precisement cinquante ans de ma prémiére connoissance avec Madame de Warens" (Today, Palm Sunday, it is precisely fifty years ago that I first met Madame de Warens) (*Rêveries*, 1 : 1098). The present is happy only to the extent that it refers back to and grounds itself in a past plenitude so memorable that it communicates itself to everything with which it is associated. The past happiness associated with this final figure of the self as botanist depends, as we saw in the opening chapter, on Rousseau's position as the third and distinctly filial figure in the triangle made up of Madame de Warens and her servant-lover Claude Anet.

In book 5 of the *Confessions*, Rousseau describes how under Anet's guidance he first became acquainted with botany and recognized the happiness of that activity's direct relation to nature: "Le contentement que je voyois dans les yeux d'Anet revenant chargé de plantes nouvelles me mit deux ou trois fois sur le point d'aller herboriser avec lui. Je suis presque assuré que si j'y avois été une seule fois cela m'auroit gagné, et je serois peut-être aujourd'hui un grand botaniste" (The pleasure that I saw in Anet's eyes when he came back carrying new plants brought me two or three times almost to the point of going out to botanize with him. I am pretty sure that if once I had done so, the idea would have captured me, and today I might perhaps have been a great botanist) (*Confessions*, 1 : 180). During this same period, and in relation to the same affective triangle, the young Jean-Jacques's potential taste for botany was both confused with and jeopardized by his no less vivid dislike for herborizing and the medicinal use of plants. Anet set off so frequently in search of herbs because Madame de Warens was herself an avid practitioner of a purely utilitarian approach to those plants: "Maman, qui l'aimoit, n'en faisoit pas elle-même un autre usage; elle ne recherchoit que les plantes usuelles pour les appliquer à ses drogues"

(Mama carried it no further herself. She merely looked for the common plants she required for her medicaments) (*Confessions*, 1 : 180).

Rousseau's "mistake," the lost career he now so bitterly regrets, his confusion of Mama's pharmaceutical herborizing with the gloriously disinterested study of botany, was reinforced by his discovery that with his other newly discovered passion of that same period, music, he could tempt Mama away from her obsessive drug making and recenter her attention on himself. Somewhat later in book 5 a past promise tragically unkept reaffirms this same crystallization of desire around the practice of botany. With the help of Doctor Grossi, formerly the personal physician to King Victor of Sardinia, Madame de Warens launched the project of establishing both a Royal Garden and a College of Pharmacy at Chambéry. Once the funds were found, Anet would be named the official *démonstrateur* and Jean-Jacques, fixed in the filial position he so ardently desired, would have a place as his assistant. In this situation, Rousseau is quick to point out, he would surely have recognized and realized his potential as a botanist. This royal road to a life at the antipodes of the anguish and suffering that have been his lot was closed off when Anet fell ill and died of a fever brought on by an excursion to the mountains to find juniper for Doctor Grossi. Thus the loss of Anet becomes, in retrospect, the loss of both a revered paternal authority and a fragile and tragically unrecognized support of an order that would surely have assured Rousseau's own place: "Voila comment je perdis le plus solide ami que j'eus en toute ma vie, homme estimable et rare, en qui la nature tint lieu d'éducation, qui nourrit dans la servitude toutes les vertus des grands hommes, et à qui peut être il ne manqua pour se montrer tel à tout le monde, que de vivre et d'être placé" (In that way I lost the staunchest friend I have had in all my life; a rare and estimable man in whom nature supplied the default of education and who, though in the position of a servant, possessed all the virtues of a great man, only lacking, perhaps, in order to prove himself one to all the world, some more years of life and a suitable post) (*Confessions*, 1 : 205).

This "chain of accessory ideas" supporting both the privileged status of botany and its absolute difference from medicinal herborizing can be followed toward another, far less placid, register of Rousseau's recollections. Rousseau insists that his passion for botany excludes all concern with the pharmaceutical uses of plants because even in this text composed only a year before his death, he is implicitly refuting an accusation that had followed him for more than a decade. In the second *Dialogue,* a text dating from approximately three years earlier, the Frenchman, as soon as mention is made of the considerable time Jean-Jacques devotes to collecting plants, insists that there is only one possible explanation for that. Hasn't the innocent botanist also studied chemistry? And doesn't the combination of these two interests prove that he makes only the most sinister use of his many specimens? "Il sait, à force d'opérations, de manipulations, concentrer tellement les poisons des plantes qu'ils agissent plus fortement que ceux-mêmes des mineraux. Il les escamote, et vous les fait avaler sans qu'on s'en apperçoive, il les fait même agir de loin comme la poudre de sympathie, et comme le basilic il sait empoisonner les gens en les regardant" (He is able, thanks to any number of operations and manipulations, to so concentrate the poison of his plants that they act even more strongly than those of minerals. He hides them away, and makes you swallow them without knowing it. He can even make them work at a distance like a *poudre de sympathie.* Like a basilisk, he can poison people just by looking at them).[10] The almost burlesque tone of the Frenchman's accusation refers in turn to a far less comic, almost nightmarish, scene that took place during Rousseau's stay at Tyre-le-Chateau in mid-November of 1767. In a long letter to his protector of the moment, the Prince de Conti, Rousseau gives an almost hysterical rendition of the accusation by Du Peyrou, a man to whom he had repeatedly proved his most sincere friendship, that the simple broths Rousseau had prepared to ease Du Peyrou's chronic gout were, in fact, poisonous yeasts: "Le malade commença à s'inquiéter extrémement et d'une façon fort extraordinaire. Il parloit sans cesse des mauvais levains qu'il disoit être dans son estomac: ses regards, son air, ses mots entrecoupés avoient quelque chose de si étrange que m'en allarmant enfin tout de bon, je résolus d'en pénétrer le mistère. Que devins-je quand à force de l'examiner, de le presser, de le conjurer, d'expliquer son silence obstiné, je parvins à comprendre qu'il se croyait empoisonné, et par qui? . . . Mon Dieu!" (The sick man became extremely worried and in a most extraordinary way. He spoke incessantly of poisonous yeasts he was convinced were in his stomach. His looks, his whole air, his stifled words had something so strange about them that I became truly upset and decided to get to the bottom of the mystery. You can imagine my amazement when, after questioning him, pushing him to speak, and pleading with him to explain his obstinate silence, I finally understood that he thought he had been poisoned; and by whom? . . . My God!).[11] Finally, however, Du Peyrou does recover—either from his gout or, as Rousseau suspects, from the poison Du Peyrou's own servant, Grisel, had been administering to him—and Rousseau is even willing, begrudgingly, to discount the gravity of an accusation made under the influence of so painful and debilitating an illness. Although Rousseau may have considered the circumstances, the whole episode irrevocably modified his estimation of his supposed friend: "Je le [Du Peyrou] croyois au fond très sensible. Je me trompois; puisqu'il ne fut point ému de mes angoisses, il ne le sera jamais de rien" (I felt Du Peyrou was essentially a sensitive man. I was wrong; since he was not moved by my anguish, he will never be moved by anything) (*Correspondance,* 34 : 186).

Understanding how the memory of this scene darkens the otherwise effulgent "chain of ideas" associated with botany we can see how that study for Rousseau came to parallel the act of writing itself. Based in a love for uncorrupted nature, Rousseau's devotion to botany serves to refute an implicit accusation he senses: that no one but a poisoner would study both botany and chemistry. With its negative as well as its positive valences, botany is marked by a tension homologous to that of writing: Rousseau insists that the obvious innocence of his writings invalidates the repeated charge that their author's hypocrisy makes them a noxious poison in the body politic.

As he vehemently denies a toxicological dimension to his interest in plants, Rousseau's metaphor of botanizing crystallizes around itself all the paradoxical components we saw in his statements on his relation to mankind in general. Throughout the seventh promenade Rousseau presents the practice of botany, his excursions in search of specimens, as a necessary escape from others. At the same time, however, he insists that he *writes* about that passion, analyzing in words his predilection for a science in which he is neither an expert nor an authority, to extend a purely reflexive knowledge of self: "Il me semble que, bien eclaircie, elle pourroit jetter quelque nouveau jour sur cette connoissance de moi-même à l'acquisition de laquelle j'ai consacré mes derniers loisirs" (It seems to me that if it were thoroughly explained it could throw some light on this knowledge of myself I have consecrated my last moments of leisure to acquiring) (*Rêveries,* 1 : 1061). To preserve that "plein calme des passions" (*Rêveries,* 1 : 1069) that Rousseau sees as its essential charm, botany must be pursued in a way that consolidates his active renunciation both of all possible links to other men and of all concern with any value that depends on his recognition by a consciousness exterior to the self.

Even the slightest intrusion of the other in the world of the disinterested botanist reverses the polarities, imposing on the self a scenario of persecution generated by even the most passive presence of the other. In the closing paragraphs of the seventh promenade, Rousseau passes from the abstract analysis of his taste for botany to the evocation of one specific outing. While at Grenoble, Rousseau recalls, he was once accompanied on an excursion along the banks of the Isère by a certain Monsieur Bovier. This man, a local lawyer, had neither interest in nor knowledge of botany. He came along only because, as Rousseau would have it, there had fallen to him the task of keeping an eye on the suspect stranger. As it happened, Rousseau's attention was caught by a particular berry, which he was drawn to taste. Finding the taste slightly acidic but highly agreeable, Rousseau went on to eat a number of these berries. As he ate, Monsieur Bovier walked silently beside him. Suddenly a third person arrived who, horrified at what he saw, expressed his astonishment at Rousseau's unawareness of what everyone in that region knew: those berries were poisonous. Bovier suddenly becomes, by reason of what he did not do, a fiendish assassin, who would clearly have been delighted had the renegade botanist fallen into a death agony before his eyes: "Pourquoi donc ne m'avertissiez-vous pas? Ah! Monsieur, me repondit-il d'un ton respectueux, je n'osois pas prendre cette liberté" ("Why, then, didn't you warn me?" "Ah!, sir," he replied to me in a respectful tone, "I didn't dare take that liberty") (*Rêveries,* 1 : 1072).

Rousseau's decision to narrate this episode as the conclusion to his last and most extensive analysis of his love for botany must be read as a resurgence of the denegated underpinnings that always sustain his statements on the subject. He cannot implicitly equate himself with the innocence of nature or equate his autobiographical writing with an attempt to carry out a botanizing of the self without appealing to his primordial status as victim. Shadowed by the accusation that he is a poisoner, he consolidates in this phantasm of the self-become-plant a victimage dictating that his impugned innocence be ground to dust in the mortar of a world shared with other men.

□   □   □

The emergence of botany as a central metaphor for both conscious-ness and the act of writing signals a profound shift in Rousseau's self-projection before various agencies of authority. At the most im-mediate level, it demonstrates an almost stoic resignation to the in-evitable redefinition and perversion of his every act, word, and ges-ture by an infinity of conspiratorial reinterpretations over which he has no control. Lies have everywhere replaced the truth and a judg-ment has been passed. It is futile, Rousseau now realizes, to hope that in the world of men he might appeal for justice.

As readers of the *Reveries,* we enter a textual universe where all faith in others, even in ourselves as readers, has been abandoned. Unlike the *Confessions,* unlike the *Dialogues,* unlike the *Social Contract,* this text makes no appeal, implicit or explicit, to the con-sciousness of the reader as a potentially unprejudiced witness able to acknowledge and recognize the truth being written.

As Rousseau loses interest in his readers, he begins to describe his love for a nature from which man is absent with a distinctly theocentric tonality. The flowering earth to which he lowers his eyes becomes the mirror of an ultimately beneficent order held in place by a divine principle. The gathering of plants becomes a prayer in which simple homage to the creator is repaid with the intense joy accorded the adoring botanist who yields himself "au charme de l'admiration reconnoissante pour la main qui me fait jouir de tout cela" (to the charm of grateful admiration for the hand which lets me enjoy all of that) (*Rêveries,* 1 : 1069).

More important, however, than the often-debated question whether such statements should be read as evidence of a pantheistic, deistic, or quietistic tendency in Rousseau's religious posture is the incontrovertible fact that this joy of botany defines itself through a system of oppositions strikingly similar to those at work in Rous-seau's description in the *Social Contract* of the general will as the operative concept. In attempting to describe that blissfully con-templative state known only to the botanist, Rousseau speaks of the *rêverie* as a moment marked by the same movement from a particu-lar to a universal context of consciousness that defines the true citi-zen in relation to the community: "Une rêverie douce et profonde s'empare alors de ses sens, et *il se perd* avec une délicieuse ivresse *dans l'immensité de ce beau sistême avec lequel il se sent identifié.* Alors *tous les objets particuliers lui échappent; il ne voit et ne sent rien que dans le tout"* (A sweet and deep reverie takes possession of his senses; and through a delicious intoxication *he loses himself in the immensity of this beautiful system with which he feels himself one.* Then *all particular objects elude him; he sees and feels nothing except in the whole*) (*Rêveries*, 1 : 1062–63; italics mine). A few pages later, still describing the joys of botany, Rousseau makes even more explicit his appeal to the generative contrast between personal interest and a forgetting of the self, between what is exclusively individual and what depends on merging the self with the totality of which it is a part: "Non rien de personnel, rien qui tienne à l'interest de mon corps ne peut occuper vraiment mon ame. Je ne médite, je ne rêve jamais plus délicieusement que quand je m'oublie moimême. Je sens des extases, des ravissemens inexprimables à me fondre pour ainsi dire dans le système des êtres, à m'identifier avec la nature entiére" (No, nothing personal, nothing which concerns my interest can truly occupy my soul. I never meditate, I never dream more deliciously than when I forget myself. I feel ecstasies and inexpressible raptures in blending, so to speak, into the system of beings and in making myself one with the whole of nature) (*Rêveries*, 1 : 1065–66). Finally, as though confirming that only the solitary botanizing self can receive a felicity first fashioned as a gift for all mankind to share in a unified community, Rousseau explains how his rejection by other men, and it alone, forced him to turn his face to the ground and to grasp in solitude what he had once believed could be shared by all: "Tant que les hommes furent mes fréres, je me faisois des projets de félicité terrestre; ces projets étant toujours relatifs au tout, je ne pouvois être heureux que de la félicité publique, et jamais l'idée d'un bonheur particulier n'a touché mon coeur que quand j'ai vu mes fréres ne chercher le leur que dans ma misére" (As long as men were my brothers, I made plans of earthly felicity for myself. These plans always being relative to the whole, I could be happy only through a general felicity; and the idea of individual happiness never touched my heart until I saw my brothers seeking theirs only in my misery) (*Rêveries*, 1 : 1066). With no man as his judge, Rousseau looks instead to the one remaining authority by whom he might hope to be recognized in the full purity of his unmerited suffering: a God defined as being beyond what is human yet at the same time everywhere present in the simple glory of the fields: "Dieu est juste; il veut que je souffre; et il sait que je suis innocent. Voila le motif de ma confiance, mon coeur et ma raison me crient qu'elle ne me trompera pas" (God is just; He wills that I suffer; and He knows I am innocent. That is the cause of my confidence; my heart and my reason cry out to me that I will not be deceived by it) (*Rêveries,* 1 : 1010).

Rousseau's treatment of botany, his careful description of the joys it has brought him, reveals the enduring sway in his writing of a model, a structure, a relation to authority and desire, that has maintained itself in spite of the most radical transformations in the elements it must accommodate.

□   □   □

Rousseau's unconcern with his readers inevitably alienates them. They struggle to understand what is asked of them by a work that brands even the most fleeting concern with the other as a form of masochism Rousseau has forever renounced. Confronted with an act of writing that necessarily presupposes some *exchange* between author and audience, the reader discovers that he must find his way in a variant of that relation radically different from any encountered in Rousseau's earlier works. Rousseau here eschews all semblance of the didactic, reforming, or even *active* relation to his reader that informs the two *Discourses,* the *Social Contract,* and *Emile.*

At the same time, the *Reveries* are clearly concerned with something more essentially textual, more intimately linked to the act of writing itself, than were those portrayals of an exculpating *passivity* that make up so large a part of the *Confessions* and the *Dialogues.* Neither actively reforming nor passively excusing, Rousseau's diction in the *Reveries* is nonetheless motivated by an obvious urgency. It is urgent to put into words, to capture in language, a desire that depends for its fulfillment on an expression of self purified of all contamination by the other but at the same time demanding enunciation.

In trying to come to grips with this profoundly paradoxical message, we as readers find ourselves pushed beyond the categories through which we might normally understand the relation between literary work and authorial voice. As a way of describing the semiotic structure of this text and at the same time identifying what is specific to this highly eccentric discourse, I propose an interpretive model that I feel accounts for what is most distinctive in Rousseau's decision to write for a readership limited only to the self.

Emile Benveniste begins his study entitled "Actif et moyen dans le verbe" by pointing out that what seems the most unproblematic of verbal categories, "voice," is in fact highly complex: "La distinction de l'actif et du passif peut fournir un exemple d'une catégorie verbale propre à dérouter nos habitudes de pensée: elle semble nécessaire—et beaucoup de langues l'ignorent; simple—et nous avons grande difficulté à l'interpréter; symétrique—et elle abonde en expressions discordantes" (The distinction between active and passive provides an example of a verbal category which seems designated to confuse our usual habits of thought: it appears necessary, and yet many languages do not have it; simple, and yet we have great difficulty in interpreting it; symmetrical, and yet it abounds in conflicting expressions).[12] Benveniste goes on to explain that our very notions of active and passive—categories that seem particularly apt to describe this shift in Rousseau's relation to his reader—must, if we are to understand them at all, be related to a third voice, a voice that has disappeared from all contemporary languages: the middle voice.

The difficulties of discerning the effects in our languages of this now-absent voice form are considerable. On the one hand, we fashion our understanding of the "active" and "passive" voices only through their mutually differential relationship. On the other hand, in an earlier stage common to all Indo-European languages, the key opposition was not between "active" and "passive" but between "active" and "middle." Our "passive," Benveniste points out, is in fact only a later transformation of that middle. Given this state of affairs, how can we move from our present notion of the active, a notion generated by the opposition of active to passive, to a different notion, one generated by the opposition of active to the now-lost middle voice?

In attempting to resolve this dilemma, Benveniste analyzes a number of single verb forms (*either* active *or* middle) drawn from Sanskrit, Greek, and Latin. Summarizing his findings, he isolates the specific difference between the active and middle voices in the way each characterizes the single relation morphologically posited by all Indo-European verbs: the precise way in which the verb refers its action back to the subject and never to its object. The active voice, he finds, describes an action that originates in the subject but whose effects extend beyond that subject. The middle voice, on the contrary, describes an action whose effects remain interior to its subject.

As Benveniste goes on to insist that this opposition must not be reduced to a difference between "verbs of action" and "verbs of being," we begin to see how his description of the middle voice can help in analyzing the particular semiology of the *Reveries:* "Ici [in the case of the middle voice] le sujet est le lieu d'un procès, même si ce proces . . . demande un objet; le sujet est centre en même temps qu'acteur du procès; *il accomplit quelque chose qui s'accomplit en lui*" (Here [in the case of the middle voice] the subject is the seat of the process, even if that process . . . demands an object; the subject is the center as well as the agent of the process; *he achieves something which is being achieved in him*) (Benveniste, *Problèmes,* p. 172; italics mine).

Jean Humbert, in his own analysis of the Indo-European roots of the middle voice, makes a similar observation, pulling this form even closer to Rousseau's posture in the *Reveries:* "Les grammariens indiens avaient imaginé, pour désigner l'actif et le moyen, deux dénominations heureuses: *parasmaipadam* 'mot pour un autre,' et *atmanepadam* 'mot pour soi-même'" (Indian grammarians imagined, as a way of designating the active and the middle, two particularly felicitous terms: *parasmaipadam* "a word for the other," and *atmanepadam* "a word for the self").[13]

An axial episode, initiating Rousseau's discovery of an almost posthumous sense of self, dramatizes his restriction of the normally active voice of autobiography (a genre founded on the author's paramount concern with providing an adequate representation of self to the other for whom he writes) to a self-enclosed and self-directed discourse whose implications seemingly concern only the writing subject. On the afternoon of October 24, 1776, particularly satisfied at having found no fewer than three rare plants during his walk through the heights of Menilmontant, Rousseau suffered an accident. Knocked head over heels by a Great Dane coursing in front of a speeding carriage, he fell unconscious in the roadway. Rousseau describes this brush with death not only as a moment of intense joy but as a second birth—a birth not to the world of man, but to a union with the whole of nature: "Je naissois dans cet instant à la vie, et il me sembloit que je remplissois de ma legere existence tous les objets que j'appercevois" (I was born into life at that instant, and it seemed to me that I filled all the objects I perceived with my frail existence) (*Rêveries*, 1 : 1005). After describing this momentary ecstasy at the brink of death, Rousseau goes on, during the days that follow, to draw from this event a lasting lesson. Rumor and exaggeration having played their part, Rousseau finds himself afforded the luxury of a glimpse at what his enemies had planned for the period following his final exit: a carefully organized subscription fund has been set up to pay for printing the manuscripts found in his lodgings after his death. For Rousseau this news could only mean that his enemies held ready a whole set of spurious writings to publish under his name as soon as he was no longer there to disavow them.

The whole project of writing the truth, at least as Rousseau has so assiduously practiced it, is once and for all stamped with the seal of futility. His writings, the one possible form in which his truth might have addressed the living from beyond death, have been poisoned at their source. Rousseau concludes from this discovery, however, neither that he should despair nor that he should be silent: "Cette idée, loin de m'être cruelle et déchirante me console, me tranquillise, et m'aide à me résigner" (This idea, far from being cruel and rending to me, consoles me, calms me, and helps me to resign myself) (*Rêveries*, 1 : 1010). Rousseau decides during the time left him to speak and write as a voice beyond death, a resolutely posthumous voice renouncing all contact and communication with any consciousness other than his own. Throughout the *Reveries*, Rousseau defines the days remaining to him as a period during which he is, as far as all others are concerned, already dead, already abstracted from any dialectics of self and other.

Writing in a voice totally unlike that of the *Dialogues*, where every tentative conclusion is hammered out through the interplay of an *I* and a *you* probing and testing each other, Rousseau achieves in the *Reveries* a discourse emanating from one self-sufficient *I*, a first person defined by its radical isolation from any conceivable *you*. All others, now relegated to the distant anonymity of the collective *they*, relinquish their relevance to the writing self: "*Me* voici donc seul sur la terre, n'ayant plus de frere, de prochain, d'ami, de société que *moi-même*. Le plus sociable et le plus aimant des humains en a été proscrit par un accord unanime. *Ils* ont cherché dans les rafinemens de *leur* haine quel tourment pouvoit être le plus cruel. . . ."(*I* am now alone on earth, no longer having any brother, neighbor, friend, or society other than *myself.* The most sociable and the most loving of humans has been proscribed from society by a unanimous agreement. In the refinements of *their* hatred *they* have sought whatever torture might be the cruelest. . . .) (*Rêveries,* 1 : 995; italics mine).

Rousseau's relation to others, if relation there must be, is defined in this work not only as one beyond reciprocity (he refuses the temptation to render evil for the evil done him) but as a total and studied abstention from all engagement: "Hors d'état de bien faire et pour moi-même et pour autrui, je m'abstiens d'agir; et cet état qui n'est innocent que parce qu'il est forcé, me fait trouver une sorte de douceur à me livrer pleinement sans reproche à mon penchant naturel" (Unable to do good for myself or for others, I abstain from acting; and that condition, which is innocent only because it is compulsory, makes me find a sort of delight in yielding fully and without reproach to my natural inclination) (*Rêveries,* 1 : 1056). Behind this abstraction of self from the active mode is Rousseau's conviction that his very consciousness of others, any knowledge he might have of them, is cut off from any true knowledge of their motivations: "Certain qu'on ne me laisse pas voir les choses comme elles sont, je m'abstiens de juger sur les apparences qu'on leur donne, et de quelque leurre qu'on couvre les motifs d'agir, il suffit que ces motifs soient laissés à ma portée pour que je sois sûr qu'ils sont trompeurs" (Certain that I am not allowed to see things as they are, I abstain from judging events according to their given appearances; and with whatever lure the motives for acting are covered, it is enough that these motives be left within my view for me to be sure they are deceitful) (*Rêveries,* 1 : 1056). Rather than as a source of anguish or despair, however, Rousseau embraces this scission as a salutary independence, the foundation of a claim to nothing less than an almost godlike impassivity: "Il ne me reste plus rien à esperer ni à craindre en ce monde, et m'y voila tranquille au fond de l'abyme, pauvre mortel infortuné, mais impassible comme Dieu même" (I have nothing more to hope for or to fear in this world; and here I am, tranquil at the bottom of the abyss, a poor unfortunate mortal, but unperturbed like God himself) (*Rêveries,* 1 : 999).

Again and again the solitary writing and reading self points to its own intrasubjective tensions not only as, in Benveniste's words, the agent initiating this text but also as the single and self-sufficient center from which every movement of consciousness must originate and toward which it is directed: "Seul pour le reste de ma vie, puisque je ne trouve qu'en moi la consolation, l'espérance et la paix je ne dois ni ne veux plus m'occuper que de moi" (Alone for the rest of my life—since I find consolation, hope, and peace only in myself—I no longer ought nor want to concern myself with anything but myself) (*Rêveries*, 1 : 999). Likewise, the practice of botany, the activity constantly developed as a metaphoric equivalent to writing, has as its goal not identifying and collecting specimens (to make them a "text" directed toward and readable by the other) but the self-contained and self-directed solicitation of memories available to the botanist alone as he reflects back on the experience of his loss and rediscovery of self in the whole of nature: "Je quittai peu à peu ces menues observations [of individual plants] pour me livrer à l'impression non moins agréable mais plus touchante que faisoit sur moi l'ensemble de tout cela" (I gradually turned away from these minute observations [of individual plants] so as to give myself up to the no less charming but more moving impression which the whole made upon me) (*Rêveries*, 1 : 1004).

As a text, the *Reveries* expresses a decision to write that is inflected everywhere by a desire strikingly similar to what Benveniste has described as the crucial criterion of the middle voice: to write only for the self is to bring to completion a process both immanent in and achieved entirely within the writing subject. To write the self for the self is to enclose consciousness in the memory and resurrection of a past so complete and so fulfilling that every present moment spent plumbing that past promises only more extended and complete experiences of the same blissful self-sufficiency in the future. This eugenics of self-containment, so long as it is held safe from the alienating temporality of the other, initiates a movement that resolves the crisis of knowledge in which the enterprise began. Instead of allowing a futile hemorrhaging of consciousness toward the unknowable other, the writing self, scrutinizing only itself, can assuredly accomplish the single epistemological project truly accessible to the writer—a knowledge of the self generated by and intended only for that self.

If we consider the scope of Rousseau's departure not only from the normative self-representational discourse of his period but from his own earlier textual practice in the *Confessions* and *Dialogues*, it is difficult to imagine a literary work placing itself more resolutely than the *Reveries* in what Humbert has designated the middle-voiced register of the "word for the self" as opposed to the "word for the other."

The entire fourth promenade, returning once again to the still painful memory of the lie told after the theft of the pink and silver ribbon, moves in precisely this direction as it redefines truth. Rousseau's argument, in which he carefully distinguishes between evil "lies" (a deceptive and self-serving departure from what actually happened that is carried out at the expense of some innocent party) and potentially truth-serving "fables" (an equal departure from fact but one that harms no one while ensuring the perception of a greater truth), is intended to redefine what he sees as a too-constrictive understanding of the notion of truth. Instead of objectively representing reality as independent of the persons perceiving it, truth must use "fables" so that as *words for the other* they in no way betray their more important function as *words for the self:* "La profession de veracité que je me suis faite a plus son fondement sur des sentimens de droiture et d'équité que sur la réalité des choses et . . . j'ai plus suivi dans la pratique les directions morales de ma conscience que les notions abstraites du vrai et du faux. J'ai souvent débité bien des fables, mais j'ai trés rarement menti" (My commitment to truth is founded more on feelings of uprightness and equity than on the reality of things, and . . . in practice I have more readily followed the moral dictates of my conscience than abstract notions of true and false. I have frequently concocted fables, but very rarely lied) (*Rêveries,* 1 : 1038).

Humbert, trying to define the semiotic premium of the middle voice, the specific effect of meaning made possible by its diacritical opposition to the active, concluded that this voice allows for a far more nuanced designation of the subject's *involvement,* his *personal stake,* in the events being recounted: "En face de l'actif correspondant, le moyen exprime que l'action accomplie possède aux yeux du sujet une *signification personnelle.* On entend par là que l'action est rapportée, soit au *sujet lui-même,* soit à ce qui constitue *sa sphère propre*" (As opposed to the corresponding active form, the middle voice expresses the fact that the action being carried out has, in the eyes of the subject, a *personal signification.* By that it must be understood that the action is referred either to *the subject himself* or to what makes up his *own sphere*) (Humbert, *Syntaxe,* p. 103; Humbert's italics). This premium, Humbert continues, makes the middle voice the preeminent mode for the expression of both "success" and "failure" as the personalized implications of whatever action the subject happens to be engaged in: "Il en resulte que le moyen pourra rendre, non seulement le *succès* de la volonté qui s'impose, mais encore les *défaites* subies quand elle s'incline devant une volonté plus forte" (It follows from this that the middle can express not only the *success* of a will that imposes itself but also the *defeats* suffered when that will must defer to a stronger one) (Humbert, *Syntaxe*, p. 103).

I have presented those aspects of the *Reveries* that justify analyzing it through the semiotic model of the middle voice as though, to use Humbert's term, they were a series of inevitable "successes," of positions taken immediately as they are enunciated. Even the most casual reading of the *Reveries* reveals, however, that the moments I have cited are marked by a constant tension between a loudly proclaimed success and an abiding suspicion of defeat. Rousseau's declarations of victory and his denegations of defeat form a continuum that sustains his treatment of every subject he approaches. Yet according to what might be seen as a final involution of the middle voice back upon itself, this oscillation between victory and defeat, the ambiguous and self-problematizing status of everything Rousseau says, becomes the foundation of a textual practice in which only defeat can insure success. Only so long as these defeats remain palpable might they continue to prod an ongoing act of writing in which the author's ultimate victory comes only as a middle-voiced and self-sufficing sustenance of the self by the self: "Réduit à moi seul, je me nourris il est vrai de ma propre substance mais elle ne s'épuise pas et je me suffis à moi-même quoique je rumine pour ainsi dire à vuide" (Left only to myself, I feed, it is true, on my own substance; but it is not depleted. And I am sufficient unto myself, even though I ruminate on an empty stomach) (*Rêveries*, 1 : 1075). As a textual practice, this declaration of self-sufficiency can continue to elaborate itself only so long as it remains aware of its failure, its inability to approach the very place it so adamantly points to itself as having already occupied. Rousseau's middle-voiced consolidation of his position as a lone, distant, yet superbly indifferent consciousness becomes an exercise in denegation, a declarative isometrics drawing its strength far more from what it must oppose than from what it would affirm. The simple and immediate joy of being himself remained palpable only so long as that imaginary self-containment was sustained by what he was convinced remained his universal persecution by the other. Only to the extent that Rousseau remained the scapegoat of a unanimous and unjustified plot could he preserve his contact with the saving ideal of self-containment. Rousseau arrived at a position, an apparently inexpungable position, in which he could, as scapegoat, solicit, imitate, and luxuriate in an act of writing that designated him as he who must be exalted precisely because he was expulsed from the community of violence surrounding him.

The decision to write for the self alone reveals a desire that can be fulfilled only so long as it is motivated by, and acting against, what the writer remains convinced is his intense hatred by all others. Rousseau's ultimate desire was to maintain his conviction that, as a universal scapegoat, he was superior to his persecutors precisely *because* he had chosen silence and precisely *because* he refused to defend his innocence before the debased tribunal of an other by whom he knew himself to be already condemned.

□   □   □

The *Reveries* constitutes a unique anthology of desire. It is a work founded on both a profound understanding and a passionate embracing of the victimage implicit in every act of desire. "Le sujet désirant," Girard points out, "se voit toujours en position d'expulsé; c'est lui qui occupe le lieu de la victime . . . *parce qu'il la désire*" (The desiring subject always sees himself in the position of the person expulsed; he occupies the place of the victim . . . *because he desires it*).[14] Rousseau's final work willingly inscribes itself in the double bind of desire: to write as the scapegoat is to write *before,* rather than *for,* an audience whose unanimous participation in his persecution renders them by definition incapable of understanding the very truth that he, as scapegoat, must enunciate. Yet at the same time, his status as scapegoat would be inconceivable without the universal incomprehension solicited by his decision to write the truth. The intelligibility of Rousseau's text as an expression of self depends on its unintelligibility for all those by whom it might one day be read. The scapegoat, and the scapegoat alone, can understand the scapegoat. Rousseau, and Rousseau alone, can read the text he is writing. Even the slightest vacillation in that persecution, even the slightest movement toward understanding on the part of the reader, would jeopardize the singularity of Rousseau's position as a victim innocent of every evil imputed to him.

Inscribed in this double bind, the *Reveries* is a text written against the loss, the falling away, and the forgetting that everywhere threaten Rousseau's truth as he draws nearer and nearer to the final darkness of silence and death. What risks being lost and forgotten is a truth accessible to the victim alone as he finds solace in the solitary understanding of his victimage. The desire that guides the composition of this work, informing each of the discrete topics taken up in the course of its ten promenades, is to dwell on, to capture, and to represent in writing a self recovered in the ecstasy of its self-comprehension and its self-justification through an awareness of the victim's truth available only to that victim. This work exercises a profound seduction because of its power to inscribe in language, the ultimate register of the symbolic, an enunciation everywhere directed toward the imaginary ecstasy of a self transfixed, held safe, and exalted in the contemplation of the text as double, the text as a document rich in a truth that can be grasped only by the self as it contemplates itself in the mirror of its writing.

All hope of justice forsaken and the incomprehension of the other accepted as a precondition of writing, Rousseau chose the solitude of a consciousness hypnotized by, yet struggling to preserve and extend, a textualized representation of self as the perfect, yet perfectly imaginary, doubling back upon itself of a truth that can be glimpsed only as it loses itself in the mirror of its enunciation. Turned back upon himself, contemplating in the present only what is left of his past, Rousseau set out to achieve a congruence of self with representation conceivable only in the unreadable text. The solace of the other, once so ardently desired, having revealed itself as a universal play of violence and persecution, this redirection of language toward a project situated entirely in the imaginary signals a collective *Männerdammerung,* a saddened resignation to the inability of the other even to read.

Conclusion

Ce qui, du point de vue de la conscience ou de l'existence immédiatement vécue, caractérise le cheminement
discursif de la pensée, consiste précisément dans le fait
que les lumières de la fin éclairent les ténèbres du com-
mencement. La fin est le principe en vue de quoi tout le
reste se comprend et en qui les étapes intermédiaires
trouvent leur justification ou éventuellement leur
condamnation.

Edmond Ortigues, *Le Discours et le symbole*

The development of Rousseau's work, as each chapter of this study
has tried to argue, follows a profoundly ambiguous and paradoxical
trajectory. Whereas the *Discourse on the Origin of Inequality,* one
of Rousseau's earlier works, presents itself as a carefully articulated,
almost syllogistic argument for an all-inclusive historical anthropology of mankind's progressive enslavement, the *Essay on the Origin of Languages,* in many ways a metacritical reflection on the failure of that earlier work, establishes itself instead as a meditation on
the intrinsic limits of human language. In so doing, it presupposes
a different ideal of language and communication. This later text
proposes, as we have seen, a "transitive solipsism" whose essential
function is to hold the speaker safe from all the deceptions and dis-
appointments that accompany any attempt to address the other. In
a work like the *Levite of Ephraim,* the expression of this ideal leads
not to any attempt to convince or logically persuade the reader but
to the glorification of that wronged innocent who when once the
truth of his victimage has been made manifest becomes the agent of
a salvation that extends to the entire community.

This shift from an ideal of language that aims at the reasoned
persuasion of the reader to a second, purely reflexive, ideal of a language that ensures the perfect self-representation of the speaker
both reflects and explains Rousseau's fundamental relation to his
age, to the historical reality of what we call the Enlightenment. A
work like the *Second Discourse,* because of the way it was written
and its negative critique of all existing political orders, could easily
be misread as participating in the "progressive," programmatic
agenda of the *philosophes.* Revealing the moral and political du-

plicity of the existing political order could easily be taken as clearing the way, sweeping aside the past, so that the universal city of light and reason cherished by those *philosophes* might one day take its place. There is a deceptive coincidence between the intent of that early work and the whole array of different impulses that consolidate themselves a century later into the dominant Western imperialisms of Reason and Progress that the eighteenth century left as its legacy. Was not Rousseau, after all, a collaborator during this same period of his life in the work of the *Encyclopédie*, that equally aggressive encircling and setting forth of all man's knowledge so that science, and the successive generations of its generals, might in turn encircle, identify, and eliminate the reactionary forces of superstition, unreason, and idiosyncracy?

It would soon become apparent, however, that Rousseau's contribution to the imperialism of reason was the fruit of a colossal mutual misunderstanding. Each of his later works—*Julie, Emile,* the *Confessions,* the *Dialogues*—reveals with ever greater clarity that Rousseau was, first and foremost, the spokesman of subjectivity. Rousseau's is the voice of a consciousness defined more than anything else by its singularity, by what distinguishes it and sets it apart. Rather than a collaborator, Rousseau is the paraclete: the voice speaking from the side and warning always of the dangers that lie ahead in the proud advance of a universalizing and standardizing reason. As the mistaken alliances of the past fell away, Rousseau found himself alone. As he wrote his major works, in which he progressively and more devastatingly plumbed that solitude and subjectivity, his voice, through a final movement of infinite paradox, perfectly expressed the abiding dilemma of the individual who sets out to salvage some sense of his singularity in the ever more integrated and pervasive communities of our modernity. Rousseau is so eloquent a spokesman of his and of our own age because, faced with the first and in many ways the most ambitious coalition of a knowledge and a power aimed at imposing itself equally on all, he chose to speak instead of that dimension of our experience and our existence that remains forever recalcitrant to the dictates of consensus. His works inscribe a refusal to align individual desire with an authority that can point only to its numbers for its legitimacy. Forced to write, against his will and in contradiction to his most cherished project, of how and why subjectivity, the self-reflexive awareness of the individual, can never adequately answer the questions of its purpose and its position in a simple congruence with the aims and programs of the collectivity, Rousseau became the spokesman of our age.

Rather than as a crypto-totalitarian who deserves little more than our horrified reprobation, Rousseau might more equitably be seen as an axial figure in the formation of our modernity, in the coalescence of what has become our vision of ourselves as individuals in the community of the other. In his penetrating study of the symbolic as the inevitable dimension of every relation of self to other, Edmond Ortigues argues that what most distinguishes our contemporary sense of self from that of other periods is a loss of faith that any discourse can represent a universal order of which man himself is an integrated part. Ours, Ortigues contends, is a consciousness redefined by the disintegration of any such order: "A la suite de cette crise, l'individu s'est trouvé progressivement dépouillé de tous les intermédiaires qui le reliaient aux autres sous la forme d'une hiérarchie immuable des êtres dans la nature et dans la société civile ou religieuse; ainsi peu à peu s'effectuait cette jonction immédiate de l'individu avec l'universel qu'annonçaient la philosophie cartésienne et la réforme religieuse" (As a result of this crisis, the individual has found himself progressively cut off from all intermediaries that link him to others in what would be an immutable hierarchy of beings encompassing not only the whole of nature but both civil and religious society. Little by little, that immediate conjunction of the individual and the universal announced both by Descartes and by the Reformation took its place.[1]

Few descriptions capture more provocatively the shape of the dilemma Rousseau inscribes in his works. Outside all reassuring hierarchies, Rousseau, as the emblem of modern man, responds to his isolation with the demand for a direct, unmediated relation to a transcendent instance of authority and judgment. In expressing this desire, he finds himself cut off from any objectifying symbolism that might assure his untroubled communication with his fellows. As he attempts to write his truth, he is limited to an objectively powerless and only self-sustaining act of speech, a uniquely singular *parole*, an expression of consciousness that recognizes itself as part of a history over which it can never hope to reign as master. Following his enterprise to its inevitable conclusion, Rousseau finds himself unable to express his truth in a language, a *langue*, whose comprehension by the other comes only as he alienates himself from his speech as the product of a history so singular that it can never be adequately expressed for the other.

Rousseau's contribution to the sense of self characterizing our modernity, the status of his literary, political, and philosophical works as radically innovative reflections on the relation of the individual to the community, derives from their eminently tragic sense of the individual consciousness. Confronted with an infinity of others whose understanding can be little more than a fleeting moment in the endless temporality of incomprehension, knowing that death will wrest from him all hope of imposing any lasting determination on the sense of his existence, Rousseau, under the guise of his insurgencies, solicits in his writings some contact with a symbolic order, an authoritative agency of law and meaning, capable of overcoming the agony of his solitude, his fragility, and the inevitable contravention of his truth by death.

Rousseau's appeal is finally to the act of writing as the expression of consciousness and to the statement of its truth as a force that restores to the individual a sense of community founded on an awareness of the victimage and sacrifice at the core of every existence. As he makes this appeal, his writings take their place among those works that approach the symbolic, authority, and the community not as laws that might once and forever be imposed on our world but as ongoing, interminable expressions of desire as a consciousness of self precariously poised between what once was and what will soon no longer be.

Notes

1 Wolmar's Game

1. Jean-Jacques Rousseau, *Confessions, Oeuvres complètes*, ed. Bernard Gagnebin and Marcel Raymond (Paris: Gallimard, Bibliothèque de la Pléiade, 1959–1969), 1:5. Subsequent quotations from this work will be cited parenthetically in the text. All translations of the *Confessions* are taken from J. M. Cohen, *The Confessions* (London: Penguin Books, 1953).

2. For a discussion of this concept in relation to Rousseau's work, see Jacques Derrida, *De la grammatologie* (Paris: Editions de Minuit, 1967), pp. 203–34.

3. For Freud's usage of this term, see "Family Romances," in *The Standard Edition of the Complete Psychological Works* (London: Hogarth Press) 9:240–41. Serge Leclaire has made frequent use of this concept in the analyses of case histories he presents in *Psychanalyser* (Paris: Seuil, 1968).

4. Jacques Lacan, "Fonction et champ de la parole," in *Ecrits* (Paris: Seuil, 1966), p. 279. The translation is my own.

5. In an astute analysis of this dilemma, Alain Grosrichard points out the contradictory nature of the two roles to which Rousseau is summoned by his father's grief. See "Où suis-je? Que suis-je: Réflexions sur la question de la *place* dans l'oeuvre de Jean-Jacques Rousseau à partir d'un texte des *Rêveries*," in *Rousseau et Voltaire en 1978. Actes du colloque international de Nice* (Geneva: Slatkine, 1981), p. 357.

6. As a somewhat startling elaboration of this passage, René Laforgue states: "Le voilà donc formulé pour la première fois, ce reproche par lequel Jean-Jacques se sentait persécuté. C'est comme si son père, partant son super-ego paternel, lui disait: "Tu as tué ta mère, rends-la moi, remplace-la en abandonnant ta virilité." Par la suite, au lieu de montrer "l'objet obscène," c'est-à-dire le pénis, qualifié par lui d'obscène, il montre l'anus, que les pédérastes substituent à l'organe féminin. Bien plus, il semble avoir passé des nuits entières avec son père, développant une sentimentalité qui, de toute évidence, n'avaient rien de commun avec celle d'un garçon normalement turbulent et agressif" ("Jean-Jacques Rousseau" in *Psychopathologie de l'échec* [Geneva: Editions du Mont Blanc, 1963], 127–28).

(Here we see formulated for the first time the reproach by which Jean-Jacques felt himself persecuted. It is as though his father, and thus his paternal superego, were saying to him: "You killed your mother, give her back to me, replace her in abandoning your virility." Thereafter, instead of exposing "the obscene object," that is to say, the penis, which Rousseau qualifies as obscene, he will expose the anus that pederasts substitute for the female organ. Moreover, it seems he spent whole nights with his father developing a sentimentality that, as seems obvious, had nothing in common with that of a normally turbulent and aggressive young boy.) (The translation is my own.)

7. Emile Benveniste, "Remarques sur la fonction du langage dans la découverte freudienne," in *Problèmes de linguistique générale* (Paris: Gallimard, 1966), pp. 75–87. My translations of Benveniste are from Mary Elizabeth Meek, *Problems in General Linguistics*, Miami Linguistic Series no. 8 (Coral Gables, Florida: University of Miami Press, 1971).

8. Rousseau's rationale for not visiting Madame de Larnage during his return trip to Chambéry likewise confirms this refusal to occupy, or even vie for, a position he perceives as associated with that of the parent. In justifying his refusal, Rousseau suddenly, and with no previous motivation, imagines himself, since he would be the mother's lover, as a potential seducer of her daughter, until then hardly mentioned: "Sa fille à laquelle malgré moi je pensois plus qu'il n'eut fallu m'inquiettoit encore. Je tremblois d'en devenir amoureux et cette peur faisoit déja la moitié de l'ouvrage. Allois-je donc pour prix des bontés de la mere chercher à corrompre sa fille, à lier le plus détestable commerce, à mettre la dissention, le deshonneur, le scandale et l'enfer dans sa maison? Cette idée me fit horreur. . . . Quel misérable état de vivre avec la mére dont je serois rassasié, et de bruler pour la fille sans oser lui montrer mon coeur" (Her daughter, about whom involuntarily I thought more than I should have done, worried me still more. I trembled at the idea of falling in love with her, and that fear half concluded the matter. Was I, then, to repay the mother's kindness by corrupting the daughter, by starting a most detestable intrigue, by introducing dissension, dishonor, scandal, and hell itself into that house? The very idea horrified me. . . . What a wretched state of things to live with the mother, of whom I should be tired, and to be on fire for the daughter without daring to declare my feelings) (*Confessions*, 1:259).

9. Using a different argument, Derrida arrives at the same conclusion about the brother-sister rather than parent-child sense of the word *incest* as used here by Rousseau. See *De la grammatologie*, pp. 372–74.

10. Ernest Seillière, *Jean-Jacques Rousseau* (Paris: Garnier, 1921), pp. 361–70.

11. Jean-Jacques Rousseau, *Julie, Oeuvres complètes*, ed. Bernard Gagnebin and Marcel Raymond (Paris: Gallimard, Bibliothèque de la Pléiade, 1959–1969), 2:611. Subsequent quotations from this work will be cited

parenthetically in the text. The translations of *Julie* are my own.

12. Jean Starobinski, *Jean-Jacques Rousseau: La Transparence et l'obstacle*, rev. ed. (Paris: Gallimard, 1971), p. 123. The translation is my own.

13. For an extensive discussion of the pastoral elements in Rousseau's description of Clarens, see Christie McDonald Vance, *The Extravagant Shepherd: A Study of Pastoral in Rousseau's "Nouvelle Héloïse,"* Studies on Voltaire and the Eighteenth Century, vol. 105 (Banbury, England: The Voltaire Foundation, 1973), pp. 121–56.

2 Writing from Afar

1. Jean-Jacques Rousseau, *Correspondance complète,* ed. R. A. Leigh (Geneva: Institut et Musée Voltaire; Oxford: The Voltaire Foundation, 1965–), 9:355. All subsequent quotations from this work will be cited parenthetically in the text. The translations of these letters are my own.

2. Jean-Jacques Rousseau, "Lettres à Malesherbes," *Oeuvres complètes,* ed. Bernard Gagnebin and Marcel Raymond (Paris: Gallimard, Bibliothèque de la Pléiade, 1959–1969), 1:1147. Because it is more easily accessible, the Pléiade edition will be used for these four letters. Subsequent citations from these letters will be given parenthetically in the text. The translations are my own.

3. Jean-Jacques Rousseau, *Dialogues, Oeuvres complètes,* ed. Bernard Gagnebin and Marcel Raymond (Paris: Gallimard, Bibliothèque de la Pléiade, 1959–1969), 1:984. The translation is my own.

4. For an excellent analysis of this influence, see Georges Pire, "Du bon Plutarque au Citoyen de Genève," *Revue de littérature comparée* 32, no. 4 (October–December 1958): 510–47.

5. Jean-Jacques Rousseau, *Confessions, Oeuvres complètes,* ed. Bernard Gagnebin and Marcel Raymond (Paris: Gallimard, Bibliothèque de la Pléiade, 1959–1969), 1:9. Subsequent quotations from this work will be cited parenthetically in the text. My translations follow J. M. Cohen, *The Confessions* (London: Penguin Books, 1953).

6. Alain Grosrichard, "Où suis-je? Que suis-je: Réflexions sur la question de la *place* dans l'oeuvre de Jean-Jacques Rousseau à partir d'un texte des *Rêveries,*" in *Rousseau et Voltaire en 1978. Actes du colloque international de Nice* (Geneva: Slatkine, 1981), p. 356. The translation is my own.

7. Rousseau gives the main description of this first performance of the *Devin du village* at Fontainebleau in book 8 of the *Confessions* (1:375–80). See also his further discussion of this work and the charge of plagiarism leveled against him in the second of the *Dialogues* (1:866–75).

8. Cited by Jean Guéhenno, *Jean-Jacques: Histoire d'une conscience,* 2 vols., rev. ed. (Paris: Gallimard, 1962), 1:264. The translation is my own.

9. Jean-Jacques Rousseau, "Fragments autobiographiques," *Oeuvres complètes*, ed. Bernard Gagnebin and Marcel Raymond (Paris: Gallimard, Bibliothèque de la Pléiade, 1959–1969), 1:1113. Subsequent citations from this work will be given parenthetically in the text. The translations are my own.

10. Jean-Jacques Rousseau, *Julie, Oeuvres complètes*, ed. Bernard Gagnebin and Marcel Raymond (Paris: Gallimard, Bibliothèque de la Pléiade, 1959–1969), 2:14. Subsequent citations from this work will be given parenthetically in the text. All translations of *Julie* are my own.

3 Speech Beyond Language

1. Jean-Jacques Rousseau, *Essai sur l'origine des langues* (1817; reprint, Paris: Bibliothèque du Graphe, supplement to no. 8 of *Cahiers pour l'analyse*, 1970), p. 532. Italics mine. All subsequent quotations from this work will be cited parenthetically in the text. My translations are drawn from *On The Origin of Language*, ed. and trans. John H. Moran and Alexander Gode (New York: Unger, 1966).

2. Emile Benveniste, "De la subjectivité dans le langage," in *Problèmes de linguistique générale* (Paris: Gallimard, 1966), pp. 258–66. All subsequent quotations from this work will be cited parenthetically in the text. The translations of Benveniste are from Mary Elizabeth Meek, *Problems in General Linguistics*, Miami Linguistic Series no. 8 (Coral Gables, Florida: University of Miami Press, 1971).

3. See Denis Diderot, "Figure," in *Encyclopédie* (Geneva: Pellet, 1778), 14:458. The translation is my own.

4. For two excellent and in many ways complementary discussions of this third chapter of Rousseau's *Essay on the Origin of Languages*, see Jacques Derrida, *De la grammatologie* (Paris: Editions de Minuit, 1967), pp. 388–94, and Paul de Man, *Allegories of Reading: Figural Language in Rousseau, Nietzsche, Rilke, and Proust* (New Haven, Connecticut: Yale University Press, 1979), pp. 149–55.

5. Jean-Jacques Rousseau, *Correspondance complète*, ed. R. A. Leigh (Geneva: Institut et Musée Voltaire; Oxford: The Voltaire Foundation, 1965–), 4:957. The translation of this letter is my own.

6. See Georges Dumezil, *Mythe et épopée I: L'Idéologie des trois fonctions dans les épopées des peuples indo-européens* (Paris: Gallimard, 1968).

7. Georg Simmel, while never using the terms *solipsism* or *transitive solipsism*, nicely captures, even in his rather cursory remarks on Rousseau, the implicit meaning of this linguistic ideal. Speaking of the "sustained strength" of the natural man who for Rousseau "really is himself," Simmel states: "He can make it (his strength) flow over to others, as it were; it is sufficient to absorb them in himself and to identify himself with them"

(*The Sociology of Georg Simmel,* ed. Kurt H. Wolff [Glencoe, Illinois: The Free Press, 1950], p. 70).

4 The Freedom of Servitude

1. Jean-Jacques Rousseau, *Emile, Oeuvres complètes,* ed. Bernard Gagnebin and Marcel Raymond (Paris: Gallimard, Bibliothèque de la Pléiade, 1959–1969), 4:868. All subsequent quotations from this work will be cited parenthetically in the text. My translations follow Allan Bloom's *Emile* (New York: Basic Books, 1979).

2. Jean-Jacques Rousseau, *Correspondance complète,* ed. R. A. Leigh (Geneva: Institut et Musée Voltaire; Oxford: The Voltaire Foundation, 1965–), 10:281.

3. Otto Vossler, *Rousseaus Freiheitslehre* (Gottingen: Vandenhoeck und Ruprecht, 1963), p. 208.

4. Rousseau's actual manuscript ends with Emile as a kind of slave-counselor to the Dey of Algiers—a situation resulting from his capture by Barbary pirates during the travels following his discovery of Sophie's infidelity. We have three different versions of where things were to go from there. Moultou and Du Peyrou, when they first published this text in 1781, prefaced it with an apology lamenting this vision of "Emile désespéré, Sophie avilie" and assuring the reader that had Rousseau finished the story, a happier ending would surely have been inevitable. Pierre Prévost, a Swiss friend of Rousseau's, published in 1804 a kind of memoire-letter on Rousseau that offers a different version of Rousseau's intended ending for this work: Emile and Sophie would be happily reunited on a desert island off the coast of Africa. It is clear, however, that Prévost's version represents little more than his own rather sketchy and distorted recollections of Rousseau's random remarks on this subject. The most complete and convincing summary of the story's projected development appears in Bernardin de Saint-Pierre, *La Vie et les ouvrages de Jean-Jacques Rousseau,* ed. Maurice Souriau (Paris: Société des textes français modernes, 1907). Essentially, Bernardin's work is a transcription of his many conversations with Rousseau shortly before his death. This version takes Emile and Sophie to the same deserted island, but with Emile now adopting a patriarchal pose as husband to both Sophie and the daughter of the Spanish sailor he had earlier discovered living on the island. Aside from its internal coherence, this version is the most convincing of the three both because of its greater detail and because Bernardin offers a convincing explanation of his familiarity with Rousseau's intentions: Rousseau wanted him to rewrite the entire sequel. "Il voulut m'engager à traiter ce sujet, en me donnant et le plan et ce qu'il en avait fait" (He wanted me to promise to finish that project and he gave me both his outline and what he had already written) (p. 173). He did

not follow through on Rousseau's suggestion, finally, because, "toutes les continuations dans tous les genres sont manquées. Je n'ai point votre style: ce serait de deux couleurs" (in whatever genre, continuations by another hand are failures. I do not have your style and the whole thing would be of two colors) (p. 173). The translations are my own.

5. For what are probably the two most extensive considerations of this text, see Charles Wirz, "Notes sur 'Emile et Sophie ou les solitaires,'" *Annales Jean-Jacques Rousseau* 36 (1963–1965): 291–303, and Guy Turbet-Delof, "A propos d' 'Emile et Sophie,'" *Revue d'histoire littéraire de la France* 64 (1964): 44–59.

6. Quoted by Pierre Burgelin in his notes to the Pléiade edition of this text, 4 : clxi. The translation is my own.

7. Jean-Jacques Rousseau, *Les Solitaires, Oeuvres complètes,* ed. Bernard Gagnebin and Marcel Raymond (Paris: Gallimard, Bibliothèque de la Pléiade, 1959–1969), 4 : 909. All subsequent quotations will be cited parenthetically in the text. The translations of *Les Solitaires* are my own.

8. Jean-Jacques Rousseau, *Confessions, Oeuvres complètes,* ed. Bernard Gagnebin and Marcel Raymond (Paris: Gallimard, Bibliothèque de la Pléiade, 1959–1969), 1 : 656. All subsequent quotations will be cited parenthetically in the text. My translations follow J. M. Cohen, *The Confessions* (London: Penguin Books, 1953).

9. Rousseau's eugenics of the sexual imaginary also has its negative variant. It was the retired soldier known for his lifelong chastity who first explained to the tutor how his wise father had cured him of a natural proclivity to sensuality: "Il [his father] s'avisa de le mener dans un hôpital de verolés, et sans le prévenir de rien, le fit entrer dans une salle, où une troupe de ces malheureux expioient par un traitement effroyable le désordre qui les y avoit exposés. A ce hideux aspect, qui révoltoit à la fois tous les sens, le jeune homme faillit à se trouver mal" (His father decided to take him to a hospital for syphilitics and, without giving him any warning, made him enter a room where a troop of these unfortunates expiated by a horrible treatment the dissoluteness which had exposed them to it. At this hideous sight, which revolted all the senses at once, the young man almost became sick) (*Emile*, 4 : 518).

10. The "real" Sophie has undergone a similar programming: the reading of *Télémaque* suggested by her father. When the right moment comes, her father, no less wise an educator than Emile's tutor, presses all the right buttons with his frequent allusions to her own master text.

11. Rousseau offers relative definitions of the tyrant and the despot in the *Social Contract* book 3, chapter 10 (De contrat social, *Oeuvres complètes,* ed. Bernard Gagnebin and Marcel Raymond [Paris: Gallimard, Bibliothèque de la Pléiade, 1959–1969], 3 : 423): "Pour donner différens noms à différentes choses, j'appelle *Tyran* l'usurpateur de l'autorité royale,

et *Despote* l'usurpateur du pouvoir Souverain. Le Tyran est celui qui s'in-gere contre les lois à gouverner selon les loix; le Despote est celui qui se met au dessus des loix-mêmes. Ainsi le Tyran peut n'être pas Despote, mais le Despote est toujours Tyran" (In order to give different names to different things, I call the usurper of royal authority a *tyrant,* and the usurper of sovereign power a *despot.* The Tyrant is one who takes over against the law in order to govern according to the laws; the Despot is one who places himself above the laws themselves. Thus a tyrant need not be a despot, but a despot is always a tyrant). Rousseau's whole presentation of the Dey's rule establishes him not as a despot who might rule by fiat but as someone who remains acutely aware of the limited nature of his authority and of the need to satisfy the various vectors of demand defining the society over which he presides. My translation follows Roger D. Masters and Judith R. Masters, *On the Social Contract* (New York: St. Martin's Press, 1978).

5 The Victim's Sacrifice

1. The *Levite of Ephraim* was first published in 1781, three years after Rousseau's death, in the first volume of the Geneva edition of the *Oeuvres posthumes.* Only two critical studies have given more than passing consideration to this text: Francois Van Laere, *Jean-Jacques Rousseau, du phantasme à l'écriture* (Paris: Minard, 1967), which presents this work as a transposition of Rousseau's relation to Thérèse; and Madeleine Anjubault Simons, *Amitié et passion: Rousseau et Sauttersheim* (Geneva: Droz, 1972), which devotes part of one chapter to the *Levite* as a text that allows her to organize a number of reflections on what she sees as Rousseau's repressed homosexuality, his ambiguous attitudes toward women and sexuality, and the appearance of these same themes in his other works. *Le Lévite d'Ephraïm* is in *Oeuvres complètes,* ed. Bernard Gagnebin and Marcel Raymond (Paris: Gallimard, Bibliothèque de la Pléiade, 1959–1969). Quotations from this work will be cited parenthetically in the text. The translations of this work and its prefaces are my own.

2. Jean-Jacques Rousseau, *Les Confessions, Oeuvres complètes,* ed. Bernard Gagnebin and Marcel Raymond (Paris: Gallimard, Bibliothèque de la Pléiade, 1959–1969), 1:586. All subsequent quotations will be cited parenthetically in the text. My translations follow J. M. Cohen, *The Confessions* (London: Penguin Books, 1953).

3. In fact, Gessner's *Idylles* probably had less to do with the style of the *Levite* than with Rousseau's choice of subject. The first of Gessner's works with which Rousseau was familiar (it was translated into French by Michel Huber) was entitled *La Mort d'Abel.* Like the *Levite,* it is the adaptation of a biblical story meant to support the thesis that the Old Testament was particularly suitable for pastoral treatment because it depicted rural, agrarian

society. In his translator's preface to the *Idylles*, Huber, referring to that earlier work, speaks of "l'analogie de la vie pastorale et celles des anciens patriarches" (the analogy of pastoral life and that of the ancient patriarchs). See Salomon Gessner, *Idylles et poèmes champêtres*, trans. Michel Huber (Lyon: Librairie Bruystet, 1762), p. xxiii. It should also be noted that Huber's preface makes explicit the particular significance of pastoral composition on which Rousseau insisted. While providing an alternative to our far less satisfying present, it simultaneously proves the spiritual superiority of writers who find themselves drawn to such subjects: "Quelle situation plus agréable en effet que celle de notre âme lorsque dans le calme des passions, l'imagination nous tire du milieu de nos moeurs pour nous transporter dans les temps fortunés de l'âge d'or? Tout ce qui peint un repos tranquille, un bonheur doux et sans trouble doit plaire aux coeurs bien faits" (What situation could be more agreeable than that of the soul when, with all passions calmed, imagination draws us away from our own customs and carries us off to those fortunate times of the golden age? Everything that portrays so peaceful a rest, so sweet and untroubled a happiness, must appeal to honest hearts) (p. xxix). The translation here is my own.

4. Pierre-Paul Clément in his *Jean-Jacques Rousseau, de l'éros coupable à l'éros glorieux,* argues for another parallel between the Levite's story and the circumstances of Rousseau's life at the time he wrote this text. The Levite's inability to protect his concubine from the men of Gibeah is, he claims, similar to Rousseau's leaving Thérèse behind at Montmorency.

5. Jean-Jacques Rousseau, *Essai sur l'origine des langues* (1817; reprint, Paris: Bibliothèque du Graphe, supplement to no. 8 of *Cahiers pour l'analyse,* 1970), pp. 502–3. All subsequent quotations from this work will be cited parenthetically in the text. My translation follows *On the Origin of Language,* ed. and trans. John H. Moran and Alexander Gode (New York: Unger, 1966).

6. This problem is, of course, further complicated by the distinct differences between the Reformed and Catholic versions of this passage. Whereas the Reformed version, basing itself on the Masoretic text, translates from the Hebrew *wtznh 'lyw* to arrive at the sense of "played the harlot," the Catholic version used the Codex Alexandrinus, whose Greek *orgisthe auto* translates as "became angry." In any case, Rousseau's decision to have nostalgia motivate the concubine's return represents a departure from both versions. The English translations throughout this text are from *The Anchor Bible: Judges,* ed. Robert G. Boling (Garden City, New York: Doubleday and Company, 1975). The Chouraqui translation is from André Chouraqui, ed., *La Bible: Josué et Juges* (Paris: Desclée de Brouwer, 1974), p. 188.

7. Jean-Jacques Rousseau, *Du contrat social, Oeuvres complètes,* ed. Bernard Gagnebin and Marcel Raymond (Paris: Gallimard, Bibliothèque de la Pléiade, 1959–1969), 3:381. All subsequent quotations from this work

will be cited parenthetically in the text. My translations follow Roger D. Masters and Judith R. Masters, *On the Social Contract* (New York: St. Martin's Press, 1978).

8. In a curious footnote at the end of the *Lettre à Monsieur d'Alembert sur les spectacles,* ed. M. Fuchs (Paris: Droz, 1948), Rousseau presents what might be seen as his personal version of a similar allegiance to communal and paternal authority as sanctified by the voice of the father addressing the son. Recalling his boyhood joy during the annual festivities following the day of military maneuvers by the Saint-Gervais regiment, Rousseau emphasizes the martial and communally unifying nature of this event: "L'accord de cinq ou six cens hommes en uniforme, se tenant tous par la main, et formant une longue bande qui serpentoit en cadence et sans confusion, avec mille tours et retours, mille espèces d'évolutions figurées, le choix des airs qui les animoient, le bruit des tambours, l'éclat des flambeaux, un certain appareil militaire au sein du plaisir, tout cela formoit une sensation très vive qu'on ne pouvoit supporter de sang-froid" (The harmony of five or six hundred men in uniform, holding one another by the hand and forming a long ribbon which wound around serpent-like, in cadence and without confusion, with countless turns and returns, countless sorts of figured evolutions, the excellence of the tunes which animated them, the sound of the drums, the glow of the torches, a certain military pomp in the midst of such pleasure, all this created a very lively sensation that could not be experienced coldly) (p. 181). As part of this scene, Rousseau offers his verbatim rendition of the all-important lesson his father drew from this experience. The father's statement, like that made by the Old Man of Lebona to Elmacin, contains both a summons to filial respect for the community and, with its puzzling reference to apparently inevitable voyages, an implicit expulsion of the son from that same community: "Mon père, en m'embrassant, fut saisi d'un tresaillement que je crois sentir et partager encore. 'Jean-Jacques, me disoit-il, aime ton pays. Vois-tu ces bons Genevois; ils sont tous amis, ils sont tous frères: la joie et la concorde règnent au milieu d'eux. Tu es Genevois: *tu verras un jour d'autres peuples; mais, quand tu voyagerois autant que ton père, tu ne trouveras jamais leur pareil*'" (My father, embracing me, was seized with a trembling which I think I still feel and share. "Jean-Jacques," he said to me, "love your country. Do you see these good Genevans? They are all friends, they are all brothers, joy and concord reign in their midst. You are a Genevan; *one day you will see other peoples; but even when you will have traveled as much as your father, you will not find their like*") (p. 182; italics mine). As though completing this cluster of themes so similar to those at work in *The Levite,* Rousseau cites the lingering memory of this lost paradise as a proof of his superiority to all those who would have remained insensitive to such a scene: "Je sens bien que ce spectacle dont je fus si touché, seroit sans attrait

pour mille autres: il faut des yeux faits pour le voir, et un coeur fait pour le sentir" (I am well aware that this entertainment, which moved me so, would be without appeal for countless others; one must have eyes made for seeing it and a heart made for feeling it) (p. 182). The translations are from Allan Bloom, *Politics and the Arts* (Glencoe, Illinois: The Free Press, 1960).

6 The Lawgiver's Paraclete

1. Eric Weil, "Jean-Jacques Rousseau et sa politique," *Critique* 56 (January 1952): 8. All subsequent quotations from this article will be cited parenthetically in the text. The translations are my own.

2. Jean-Jacques Rousseau, *Discours sur les sciences et les arts* and *Discours sur l'origine de l'inégalité, Oeuvres complètes,* ed. Bernard Gagnebin and Marcel Raymond (Paris: Gallimard, Bibliothèque de la Pléiade, 1959–1969), 3:17. All subsequent quotations from these works will be cited parenthetically in the text. For the two *Discourses* my translations follow Roger D. Masters and Judith R. Masters, *The First and Second Discourses* (New York: St. Martin's Press, 1964).

3. Jean-Jacques Rousseau, *Du contrat social, Oeuvres complètes,* ed. Bernard Gagnebin and Marcel Raymond (Paris: Gallimard, Bibliothèque de la Pléiade, 1959–1969), 3:385. All subsequent quotations from this work will be cited parenthetically in the text. My translations follow Roger D. Masters and Judith R. Masters, *On the Social Contract* (New York: St. Martin's Press, 1978).

4. Jean-Jacques Rousseau, *Dialogues, Oeuvres complètes,* ed. Bernard Gagnebin and Marcel Raymond (Paris: Gallimard, Bibliothèque de la Pléiade, 1959–1969), 1:935. The translation is my own.

5. J. L. Talmon, *The Rise of Totalitarian Democracy* (London: Secker and Warburg, 1952), and the second volume of Lester Crocker's biography, *Jean Jacques Rousseau: The Prophetic Voice (1758–1778)* (New York: Macmillan, 1973).

6. Denis Diderot, *Le Fils naturel, Oeuvres complètes* (Paris: Hermann, 1980), 10:60–61. All subsequent quotations from this work will be cited parenthetically in the text. The translations are my own.

7. Jean-Jacques Rousseau, *Confessions, Oeuvres complètes,* ed. Bernard Gagnebin and Marcel Raymond (Paris: Gallimard, Bibliothèque de la Pléiade, 1959–1969), 1:455. All subsequent quotations are cited parenthetically in the text. My translation follows J. M. Cohen, *The Confessions* (London: Penguin Books, 1953).

8. Jean-Jacques Rousseau, *Correspondance complète,* ed. R. A. Leigh (Geneva: Institut et Musée Voltaire; Oxford: The Voltaire Foundation, 1965–), 4:169. The translation is my own.

9. *Lettre à Monsieur d'Alembert sur les spectacles,* ed. M. Fuchs (Paris:

Droz, 1948), p. 158. All subsequent quotations from this letter will be cited parenthetically in the text. The translations are from Allan Bloom, *Politics and the Arts* (Glencoe, Illinois: The Free Press, 1960).

10. One of the most provocative studies of the role of paradox in Rousseau's treatment of political liberty can be found in Felicity Baker, "La Route contraire," in *Reappraisals of Rousseau: Studies in Honor of R. A. Leigh,* ed. S. Harvey, M. Dobson, D. Kelley, and Samuel S. B. Taylor (Totowa, New Jersey: Barnes and Noble, 1980), pp. 132–62. For another important discussion of the relation between liberty and authority in the political writings, see R. A. Leigh's comparison of the general will with the theological concept of grace and its operation in relation to free will: "Liberté et autorité dans le *Contrat social,*" in *Jean-Jacques Rousseau et son oeuvre: problèmes et recherches* (Paris: Klincksieck, 1964), pp. 249–64.

11. Adrien Rechastelet, "Introduction," cited by Pierre Clastres and Claude Lefort in their edition of Etienne de La Boëtie, *Le Discours de la servitude volontaire,* (Paris: Payot, 1976), p. 171.

12. Leo Strauss, *Persecution and the Art of Writing* (Glencoe, Illinois: The Free Press, 1952), p. 25.

13. Michel Serres, *Le Parasite* (Paris: Grasset, 1980), p. 159. The translation is my own.

7 Anthologies of Desire

1. Jean-Jacques Rousseau, *Rêveries du promeneur solitaire, Oeuvres complètes,* ed. Bernard Gagnebin and Marcel Raymond (Paris: Gallimard, Bibliothèque de la Pléiade, 1959–1969), 1:995. Subsequent quotations from this work will be cited parenthetically in the text. My translations follow Charles E. Butterworth, *The Reveries of the Solitary Walker* (New York: New York University Press, 1979).

2. Jean Guéhenno, *Jean-Jacques Rousseau: Histoire d'une conscience,* rev. ed. (Paris: Gallimard, 1962), 2:257–70.

3. Lester Crocker, *Jean-Jacques Rousseau: The Prophetic Voice (1758–1778)* (New York: Macmillan, 1973), pp. 265–323.

4. For a discussion of the various hypotheses on Rousseau's mental or physical illnesses, as well as a lucid statement on the limits of such hypothesizing, see Jean Starobinski, "Sur la maladie de Rousseau," in *Jean-Jacques Rousseau: La Transparence et l'obstacle,* rev. ed. (Paris: Gallimard, 1971), pp. 430–44.

5. Jean-Jacques Rousseau, *Confessions, Oeuvre complètes,* ed. Bernard Gagnebin and Marcel Raymond (Paris: Gallimard, Bibliothèque de la Pléiade, 1959–1969), 1:180. All subsequent quotations from this work will be cited parenthetically in the text. My translations are taken from J. M. Cohen, *The Confessions* (London: Penguin Books, 1953).

6. Plutarch, "De l'utilité à tirer de ses ennemis," in *Oeuvres morales de Plutarch*, ed. E. Clavier and trans. Jacques Amyot (Paris: Cussac, 1802), 2:184–85. All subsequent quotations from this work will be cited parenthetically in the text. The translations from Amyot's French are my own.

7. Marcel Raymond, "Introduction aux *Rêveries*," in *Oeuvres complètes*, 1:lxxvi.

8. These eight letters, written between August 1771 and April 1773, have been published together under the title "Lettres sur la botanique" in the fourth volume of the Pléiade *Oeuvres complètes*. The term "mémoratif" occurs in the letter of April 11, 1773 (4:1191). The translations are my own.

9. For a discussion of this subject, see A. Jansen, *Jean-Jacques Rousseau als Botaniker* (Berlin, 1885), pp. 232–33, and A. Matthey-Jeantet, *L'Ecriture de Jean-Jacques Rousseau: Sa pasigraphie et les abréviations* (Le Locle, Switzerland: 1912), as well as Roger Vilmorin's notes to the fourth volume of the Pléiade edition of the *Oeuvres complètes*.

10. Jean-Jacques Rousseau, *Dialogues, Oeuvres complètes*, ed. Bernard Gagnebin and Marcel Raymond (Paris: Gallimard, Bibliothèque de la Pléiade, 1959–1969), 1:834. All subsequent quotations from this work will be cited parenthetically in the text. The translations are my own.

11. Jean-Jacques Rousseau, *Correspondance complète*, ed. R. A. Leigh (Geneva: Institut et Musée Voltaire; Oxford: The Voltaire Foundation, 1965–), 34:184–85. The translation is my own.

12. Emile Benveniste, *Problèmes de linguistique générale* (Paris: Gallimard, 1966), p. 168. All subsequent quotations from this article are cited parenthetically in the text. Again, my translations are taken from Mary Elizabeth Meek, *Problems in General Linguistics*, Miami Linguistic Series no. 8 (Coral Gables, Florida: University of Miami Press, 1971).

13. Jean Humbert, *La Syntaxe grecque*, rev. ed. (Paris: Klincksieck, 1954), p. 103. All subsequent quotations from this work are cited parenthetically in the text. The translations are my own.

14. René Girard, *Des choses cachées depuis la fondation du monde* (Paris: Grasset, 1978), p. 408; italics his. The translation is my own.

Conclusion

1. Edmond Ortigues, *Le Discours et le symbole* (Paris: Aubier, 1962), p. 9. The translation is my own.

Bibliography

Works by Rousseau

Oeuvres complètes, Vols. 1–4. Edited by Bernard Gagnebin and Marcel Raymond. Paris: Gallimard, Bibliothèque de la Pléiade, 1959–1969.

Essai sur l'origine des langues. 1817. Reprint. Supplement to no. 8 of *Cahiers pour l'analyse.* Paris: Bibliothèque du Graphe, 1970.

Lettre à Monsieur d'Alembert sur les spectacles. Edited by M. Fuchs. Paris: Droz, 1948.

Correspondance complète. Edited by R. A. Leigh. Geneva: Institut et Musée Voltaire; Oxford: The Voltaire Foundation, 1965–.

Critical Works

Ansart-Dourlen, Michèle. *Dénaturation et violence dans la pensée de Jean-Jacques Rousseau.* Paris: Klincksieck, 1975.

Baczko, Bronislaw. *Rousseau: Solitude et communauté.* Paris: Mouton, 1974.

Baker, Felicity. "La Route contraire." In *Reappraisals of Rousseau: Studies in Honor of R. A. Leigh,* edited by S. Harvey, M. Dobson, D. Kelley, and Samuel S. B. Taylor. Totowa, New Jersey: Barnes and Noble, 1980, pp. 132–62.

Beaujour, Michel. *Miroirs d'encre.* Paris: Seuil, 1980.

Bensoussan, D. *La Maladie de Rousseau.* Paris: Klincksieck, 1974.

Benveniste, Emile. *Problèmes de linguistique générale.* Paris: Gallimard, 1966.

Bernardin de Saint-Pierre, Jacques-Henri. *La Vie et les ouvrages de Jean-Jacques Rousseau.* Edited by Maurice Souriau. Paris: Société des textes français modernes, 1907.

Blanchard, William. *Rousseau and the Spirit of Revolt.* Ann Arbor: University of Michigan Press, 1967.

Borel, Jacques. *Génie et folie de Jean-Jacques Rousseau.* Paris: Corti, 1966.

Burgelin, Pierre. *La Philosophie de l'existence de Jean-Jacques Rousseau.* Paris: Presses universitaires de France, 1952.

Chapman, John. *Rousseau: Totalitarian or Liberal?* New York: Columbia University Press, 1956.

Chouraqui, André, ed. *La Bible: Josué et Juges.* Paris: Desclée de Brouwer, 1974.

Clément, Pierre-Paul. *Jean-Jacques Rousseau, de l'éros coupable à l'éros glorieux.* Neuchâtel, Switzerland: La Baconnière, 1976.

Cranston, Maurice. *Jean-Jacques: The Early Life and Works of Jean-Jacques Rousseau, 1712–1754.* London: Allen Lane, 1983.

Crocker, Lester. *Jean-Jacques Rousseau: The Quest (1712–1758).* New York: Macmillan, 1968.

————. *Jean-Jacques Rousseau: The Prophetic Voice (1758–1778).* New York: Macmillan, 1973.

de Jouvenel, Bertrand. Introduction to *Du contrat social,* by Jean-Jacques Rousseau. Geneva: Bourquin, 1947.

de Man, Paul. *Allegories of Reading: Figural Language in Rousseau, Nietzsche, Rilke, and Proust.* New Haven, Connecticut: Yale University Press, 1979.

Derrida, Jacques. *De la grammatologie.* Paris: Editions de Minuit, 1967.

Diderot, Denis. *Le Fils naturel.* In *Oeuvres complètes,* vol. 10. Paris: Hermann, 1980.

Dumezil, Georges. *Mythe et épopée I: L'Idéologie des trois fonctions dans les épopées des peuples indo-européens.* Paris: Gallimard, 1968.

Eigeldinger, Marc. *Jean-Jacques Rousseau, univers mythique et cohérence.* Neuchâtel, Switzerland: La Baconnière, 1977.

Ellensberg, Stephen. *Rousseau's Political Philosophy.* Ithaca, New York: Cornell University Press, 1976.

Ellrich, Robert J. *Rousseau and His Reader: The Rhetorical Situation of the Major Works.* Chapel Hill: University of North Carolina Press, 1969.

Foucault, Michel. Introduction to *Dialogues,* by Jean-Jacques Rousseau. Paris: Armand Colin, 1962.

Fralin, Richard. *Rousseau and Representation: A Study of the Development of his Concept of Political Institutions.* New York: Columbia University Press, 1978.

Freud, Sigmund. "Family Romances." In *The Standard Edition of the Complete Psychological Works.* London: Hogarth Press, 1959, 9:240–41.

————. "Negation." In *The Standard Edition of the Complete Psychological Works.* London: Hogarth Press, 1961, 19:234–36.

Gagnebin, Bernard. "Le Rôle du législateur dans les conceptions politiques de Rousseau." In *Etudes sur le Contrat social de Jean-Jacques Rousseau.* Paris: Belles-Lettres, 1964, pp. 277–90.

Gay, Peter. *The Party of Humanity.* New York: Knopf, 1964.

Gessner, Salomon. *Idylles et poèmes champêtres.* Translated by Michel Huber. Lyon: Librairie Bruystet, 1762.

Gildin, Hilail. *Rousseau's Social Contract: The Design of the Argument.* Chicago: University of Chicago Press, 1983.

Gilliard, Edmond. *De Rousseau à Jean-Jacques.* Lausanne: Mermod, 1950.

Girard, René. *La Violence et le sacré.* Paris: Grasset, 1972.

————. *Des choses cachées depuis la fondation du monde.* Paris: Grasset, 1978.

Goldschmidt, Victor. *Anthropologie et politique: Les Principes du système de Rousseau.* Paris: Vrin, 1974.

Grimsley, Ronald. *Jean-Jacques Rousseau: A Study in Self-Awareness.* Cardiff: University of Wales Press, 1961.

Grosrichard, Alain, "Où suis-je? Que suis-je: Réflexions sur la question de la *place* dans l'oeuvre de Jean-Jacques Rousseau." In *Rousseau et Voltaire en 1978. Actes du colloque international de Nice.* Geneva: Slatkine, 1981.

Guéhenno, Jean. *Jean-Jacques: Histoire d'une conscience.* Rev. ed. 2 vols. Paris: Gallimard, 1962.

Guillemin, Henri. *Un homme, deux ombres.* Geneva: Editions du Milieu du Monde, 1943.

Huizinga, J. H. *The Making of a Saint: The Tragi-comedy of Rousseau.* London: Hamilton, 1975.

Humbert, Jean. *La Syntaxe grecque.* Rev. ed. Paris: Klincksieck, 1954.

Jansen, A. *Jean-Jacques Rousseau als Botaniker.* Berlin, 1885.

Kress-Rosen, Nicole. "Réalité du souvenir et vérité du discours, étude de l'énonciation dans un texte des *Confessions.*" *Littérature* 10 (May 1983): 20–30.

Lacan, Jacques. *Ecrits.* Paris: Seuil, 1966.

————. *Le Séminaire II: Le Moi dans la théorie de Freud et dans la technique de la psychanalyse.* Paris: Seuil, 1978.

————. *Le Séminaire III: Les Psychoses.* Paris: Seuil, 1982.

Laforgue, René. *Psychopathologie de l'échec.* Rev. ed. Geneva: Editions du Mont Blanc, 1963.

Lange-Eichbaum, Wilhelm. *Genie, Irrsinn, und Ruhm.* Munich: Verlag Ernst Reinhardt, 1942.

Launay, Michel. *J.-J. Rousseau écrivain politique.* Cannes: Coopérative de l'enseignement laïc-Association pour une coopérative d'édition et de recherche, 1972.

Leclaire, Serge. *Psychanalyser.* Paris: Seuil, 1968.

Lecointre, S., and J. Le Galliot. "Essai sur la structure d'un mythe personnel dans les *Rêveries.*" *Semiotica* 4 (1971): 334–64.

Leigh, R. A. "Liberté et autorité dans le *Contrat social.*" In *Jean-Jacques Rousseau et son oeuvre: Problèmes et recherches.* Paris: Klincksieck, 1964.

Lejeune, Philippe. *L'Autobiographie en France.* Paris: Armand Colin, 1971.

————. *Le Pacte autobiographique.* Paris: Seuil, 1975.

McDonald, Christie V. *The Dialogue of Writing.* Waterloo, Ontario: Wilfred Laurier University Press, 1984.

Masson, Pierre-Maurice. *La Religion de Jean-Jacques Rousseau.* 3 vols. Paris: Hachette, 1916.

Masters, Roger D. *The Political Philosophy of Rousseau.* Princeton, New Jersey: Princeton University Press, 1968.

May, Georges. *Rousseau par lui-même.* Paris: Seuil, 1961.

Miller, Jim. *Rousseau, Dreamer of Democracy.* New Haven, Connecticut: Yale University Press, 1984.

Mornet, Daniel. *Rousseau, l'homme et l'oeuvre.* Paris: Hatier-Boivin, 1950.

Munteano, Basil. *Solitude et contradiction de Jean-Jacques Rousseau.* Paris: Nizet, 1975.

Ortigues, Edmond. *Le Discours et le symbole.* Paris: Aubier, 1962.

Perkins, Merle L. *Jean-Jacques Rousseau: On the Individual and Society.* Lexington: University of Kentucky Press, 1974.

Pire, Georges. "Du bon Plutarque au Citoyen de Genève." *Revue de littérature comparée* 32, no. 4 (October–December 1958): 510–47.

Plutarch. "De l'utilité à tirer de ses ennemis." In *Oeuvres morales de Plutarque,* edited by E. Clavier and translated by Jacques Amyot. Paris: Cussac, 1802, 2:181–209.

Raymond, Marcel. *Jean-Jacques Rousseau, la quête de soi et la rêverie.* Paris: Corti, 1962.

Roustang, Francois. "L'Interlocuteur du solitaire." In *Individualisme et autobiographie en Occident,* edited by Claudette Delhez-Sarlet and Maurizio Catani, Brussels: Editions de l'Université de Bruxelles, 1983, pp. 163–76.

Schwartz, Joel. *The Sexual Politics of Jean-Jacques Rousseau.* Chicago: University of Chicago Press, 1984.

Seillière, Ernest. *Jean-Jacques Rousseau.* Paris: Garnier, 1921.

Serres, Michel. *Le Parasite.* Paris: Grasset, 1980.

Shklar, Judith N. *Men and Citizens: A Study of Rousseau's Social Theory.* Cambridge: Cambridge University Press, 1969.

Simmel, Georg. *The Sociology of Georg Simmel.* Edited by Kurt H. Wolff. Glencoe, Illinois: The Free Press, 1950.

Simons, Madeleine. *Amitié et passion: Rousseau et Sauttersheim.* Geneva: Droz, 1972.

Spink, John. *Rousseau et Genève.* Paris: Boivin, 1934.

Starobinski, Jean. *L'Invention de la liberté.* Geneva: Skira, 1964.

————. *La Relation critique.* Paris: Gallimard, 1970.

————. *Jean-Jacques Rousseau: La Transparence et l'obstacle.* Rev. ed. Paris: Gallimard, 1971.

Strauss, Leo. *Persecution and the Art of Writing.* Glencoe, Illinois: The Free Press, 1952.
———. *Natural Right and History.* Chicago: University of Chicago Press, 1953.
Talmon, J. L. *The Rise of Totalitarian Democracy.* London: Secker and Warburg, 1952.
Tripet, Arnaud. *La Rêverie littéraire.* Geneva: Droz, 1979.
Trousson, Raymond. "Quinze années d'études rousseauistes." *Dix-huitième siècle* 9 (1977): 243–386.
Turbet-Delof, Guy. "A propos d' 'Emile et Sophie.'" *Revue d'histoire littéraire de la France* 64 (1964): 44–59.
Vance, Christie McDonald. *The Extravagant Shepherd: A Study of Pastoral in Rousseau's "Nouvelle Héloïse."* Studies on Voltaire and the Eighteenth Century, vol. 105. Banbury, England: The Voltaire Foundation, 1973.
Van Laere, François. *Jean-Jacques Rousseau, du phantasme à l'écriture.* Paris: Minard, 1967.
Vossler, Otto. *Rousseaus Freiheitslehre.* Gottingen: Vandenhoeck und Ruprecht, 1963.
Wahl, Jean. "La Bipolarité de Rousseau." *Annales Jean-Jacques Rousseau* 23 (1955): 49–55.
Weil, Eric. "Jean-Jacques Rousseau et sa politique." *Critique* 56 (January 1952): 2–28.
Williams, Huntington. *Rousseau and Romantic Autobiography.* Oxford: Oxford University Press, 1983.
Wirz, Charles. "Notes sur 'Emile et Sophie ou les solitaires.'" *Annales Jean-Jacques Rousseau* 36 (1963–1965): 291–303.

Collective Works

Hobbes and Rousseau. Edited by Maurice Cranston and Richard S. Peters. New York: Doubleday, 1972.
L'Impensé de Jean-Jacques Rousseau. Cahiers pour l'analyse. Vol. 8. Paris: Seuil, 1970.
Jean-Jacques Rousseau. Neuchâtel, Switzerland: La Baconnière, 1962.
Jean-Jacques Rousseau: La Crise contemporaine de la conscience. Colloque international du deuxième centenaire de la mort de Jean-Jacques Rousseau. Paris: Beauchesne, 1980.
Rousseau after Two Hundred Years: Proceedings of the Cambridge Bicentennial Colloquium. Edited by R. A. Leigh. Cambridge: Cambridge University Press, 1982.
Rousseau et Voltaire en 1978. Actes du colloque international de Nice. Geneva: Slatkine, 1981.

Index

Accusations, 2; in Diderot's *Le Fils naturel*, 147–49; on identification with Lawgiver, 153; on misanthropy, 25, 146, 151; on paternal responsibility, 148–49; on pessimism, 151; on totalitarianism, 143–45, 152–53, 157

Active voice: compared with middle voice, 186–87; defined, 181–82; distinguished from passive voice, 181; reversibility with passive voice, 42–43

Agriculture: discovery of, 132; effect of technological advances in, 133

Algebraic symbols for plant names, 170

Anet, Claude, 95; death of, 6–7, 9, 174; and love triangles, 6–10, 11; paternal authority delegated to, 7, 174; and Rousseau's happiness in filial role, 6–10, 173; and Rousseau's interest in botany, 173

Anthologies of desire, 159–89; and *Reveries*, 188

"Anthologizing," 168–69

Antirevolutionary sentiment, 142; vs. social reform, 145

Arabic language, 72, 73

Arrest ordered for Rousseau, 103, 104, 122

Arts: criticism of, 130–31, 134, 137, 146; and defense of nonpharmaceutical botany, 172

Audience: creation of, 140, 152; of *Devin du village*, 37–40; hypothetical, 152, 156–57; imaginary union with, 34; Rousseau as sole member of, 35; of Rousseau's interpretation of history, 136; of Rousseau's political texts, 129, 136, 138, 139, 140, 151–53; of *Social Contract*, 151–54, 156–57; and superiority of the author, 152–53; understanding of, 152–54, 157. *See also* Readers

Author: exchange with audience, 180; relationship with thoughtful readers, 154–55; as a scapegoat, 154; superiority of, 152–53

Authority: absence of, 111; accommodated with freedom, 90; and botany as metaphor for writing, 178, 180; and denunciation of herbal medicine, 172; and desire in education, 79, 96; dialectical and paradoxical vision of, xi, 40–41; of Lawgiver, 157–58; in love story in *Emile*, 94–96; Machiavellian, 15–16; in master-servant relationships, 15–16, 98–101; omniscient, 2; opposition to, 152; reconciled with desire, 25; redefined, 141; self-imposed, 84, 99; in social order in *Julie*, 15–16; submission to, xi, 91, 99, 157–58, 165; and the symbolic, 127

Autobiographical writings: active voice used in, 182; denial and denegation in, 24–25; initial efforts for, 23, 24; on innocence, 102 (*see also* Innocence of Rousseau); linked with political, literary, pedagogical, and philosophical writings, x, 110, 138, 157; in letters to Malesherbes, 22–50 *passim;* and Oedipal situation, 5, 7, 9, 11; parental portraits in, 2–5;

Compositor:	G & S Typsetters, Inc.
Printer:	Cushing-Malloy, Inc.
Binder:	John H. Dekker & Sons
Text:	10/12 Sabon
Display:	Sabon